P9-CKC-551

Herbert Hoover and Germany

By LOUIS P. LOCHNER

Fritz Kreisler

Always the Unexpected: A BOOK OF REMINISCENCES

Herbert Hoover and Germany

Herbert Hoover and Germany

LOUIS P. LOCHNER

The Macmillan Company *New York*
1960

First Printing

The Macmillan Company, New York
Brett-Macmillan Ltd., Galt, Ontario

Printed in the United States of America

Permission to quote from copyrighted books or magazine articles is gratefully acknowledged as follows:

Appleton-Century-Crofts, Inc.—*Herbert Hoover, the Man and His Work,* by Vernon Kellogg, copyright 1920 by D. Appleton & Company;

Collier's magazine—"Feed Hungry Europe," by Herbert Hoover, Nov. 23, 1940; "Feed the Starving Now," by Herbert Hoover and Hugh Gibson, Feb. 20, 1940; "The Life of an Ex-President," by Herbert Hoover, Mar. 24, 1951; copyright 1940 and 1951, respectively, by the Crowell-Collier Publishing Company;

Doubleday & Company, Inc.—*Fighting Starvation in Belgium,* by Vernon Kellogg, copyright 1917, 1918 by Doubleday, Page & Company; *The Life and Letters of Walter Hines Page,* by Burton J. Hendrick, copyright 1921, 1922 by Doubleday, Page & Company, reprinted by permission of Dr. Ives Hendrick; *Hoover Off the Record,* by Theodore G. Joslin, copyright 1934 by Doubleday & Company, Inc.; *The Problems of Lasting Peace,* by Herbert Hoover and Hugh Gibson, copyright 1942 by Doubleday, Doran and Company; *Hoover and His Times,* by Edwin Emerson, copyright 1932 by Edwin Emerson;

Grosset & Dunlap—*Herbert Hoover—A Reminiscent Biography,* by Will Irwin, copyright 1928 by Will Irwin and United Features Syndicate, Inc., reprinted by permission of Brandt & Brandt;

Houghton Mifflin Company—*An Encyclopedia of World History,* by William L. Langer, copyright 1940, 1948 by Houghton Mifflin Company;

The Macmillan Company—*The Memoirs of Herbert Hoover,* by Herbert Hoover, copyright 1951, 1952 by Herbert Hoover; *Always the Unexpected,* by Louis P. Lochner, copyright 1956 by Louis P. Lochner;

Charles Scribner's Sons—*America's First Crusade,* by Herbert Hoover, copyright 1941, 1942 by Herbert Hoover;

Stanford University Press—*Public Relations of the Commission for Relief in Belgium,* by George I. Gay, copyright 1929 by C. R. B. Educational Foundation, Inc.; *The Blockade of Germany After the Armistice, 1918–1919,* by Suda L. Bane and Ralph Haswell Lutz, copyright 1942 by the Board of Trustees of the Leland Stanford University.

Library of Congress catalog card number: 60-8573

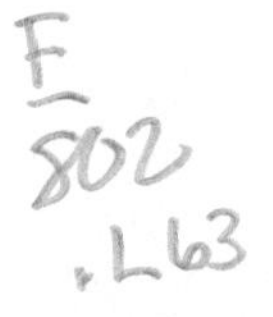

FOREWORD

Several times during one of the most turbulent periods of German history Herbert Hoover, thirty-first President of the United States, played a distinctive humanitarian role that vitally affected Germany's future. This period began with the Imperial German Government's declaration of war upon Great Britain and France and the invasion of Belgium in 1914, and has continued into our day.

Every time that Mr. Hoover felt impelled to take action, his proposals were based on his firm conviction as a dedicated American that they would contribute to peace and recovery in the Western and indeed the entire world.

The purpose of this volume is to present in chronological sequence such facts and pertinent commentary as will illuminate and clarify the exact relation of Mr. Hoover to imperial, republican, national-socialist, and postwar federal Germany and her people.

Herbert Hoover's major contacts with Germany centered around the following events:

1. During his career as an outstanding mining engineer, Mr. Hoover with the collaboration of his wife, born Lou Henry, in 1913

made available to the modern engineering world a standard work of the Medieval Ages, *De Re Metallica,* written by the Saxon savant, Georg Bauer, under his Latinized pen name of Georgius Agricola.

2. Mr. Hoover's chairmanship of the Commission for Relief in Belgium brought him into frequent contact with the German occupation authorities, whose objections to his program for feeding Belgium had to be overcome.

3. After the German capitulation in November, 1918, he insisted that the German population and especially the children must be fed by the Allied and Associated victors despite the blockade imposed upon Germany. As European Food Administrator his was the task of designing and carrying out the necessary arrangements.

4. When the young Weimar Republic faced bankruptcy in 1931, Mr. Hoover, then President of the United States, negotiated what became known as the Hoover Moratorium, whereby a stoppage of all intergovernmental debt payments during one year was effected.

5. Also during 1931, Mr. Hoover brought about a "standstill" agreement upon German private debts.

6. Early in 1938, he made a "sentimental pilgrimage" to the countries of Europe with which he had been especially associated as their food provider. In Germany he had significant encounters with Adolf Hitler and Hermann Goering.

7. In February, 1947, at the request of President Harry Truman, our Elder Statesman headed The President's Economic Mission to Germany and Austria at a time when Germany lay prostrate.

8. A German edition of the three-volume autobiography, *The Memoirs of Herbert Hoover,* appeared in 1954. German interest was thereby again focused upon him. The *Memoirs* were read avidly in translation.

9. In connection with Mr. Hoover's eightieth birthday in 1954, the German Government invited him to come to the Federal Republic as the guest of a nation eager to express its gratitude for his humane endeavors. He was honored as no other foreigner has been in our time.

These nine focal points in the relationship between Herbert Hoover and Germany are supplemented, each in their chronological place, by additional significant episodes in the course of Mr. Hoover's many contacts with the country whence his Swiss ancestors emigrated to the United States in the eighteenth century.*

This brief indication of the purpose and scope of this book would not be complete were I to fail to point out the striking similarities in the amoral principles applied and the techniques employed by both Adolf Hitler and Nikita S. Khrushchev. Also, Mr. Hoover's thinking concerning Communism is as apropos today as it was at the time his sayings and observations as herein recorded were uttered some years ago.

Concerning many events beginning with Chapter 4, I was able to write with a background of personal knowledge. For the facts presented in the first three chapters I have had to rely upon the eyewitness accounts of others and the maze of material available for research in the Hoover Institution on War, Revolution and Peace at Stanford University.

I am deeply conscious of the trust which President Hoover placed in me by permitting me to browse at will among the literally more than a million items of correspondence, statements, press releases, manuscripts, photostats, and other documentary material stored in the restricted Hoover Archives of the Institution.

My special thanks go to Messrs. Perrin C. Galpin, Tracy S. Voorhees, and Pierre J. Huss for permission to quote from their personal files, to Tracy S. Voorhees also for much valuable assistance, and to Thomas T. Thalken, archivist of the Hoover Archives, for his indispensable aid, as also to Miss Bernice Miller, private secretary to Mr. Hoover.

Louis P. Lochner

Fair Haven, N.J.

* Jonas and Anna Maria Huber, the great-great-great-great-grandparents of our President, came to Ellerstadt in the Palatinate of Germany toward the end of the seventeenth century. They had fled on a raft from Switzerland to escape the Pietistic persecution then in vogue there. Their ninth child was Herbert Hoover's great-great-great-grandfather, Andreas Huber, who according to the records of the Lutheran church of Ellerstadt was born January 29, 1723. Andreas Huber emigrated to the United States in September, 1738, when he was almost sixteen years old. He Anglicized his name, and with it that of his descendants, to read Andrew Hoover. The Hoovers professed the Quaker faith.—From Edward Emerson's *Hoover and His Times*.

CONTENTS

1

"THE BOOK THAT MADE AGRICOLA FAMOUS"

Herbert Hoover's concrete interest in Germany was aroused in a special manner when he was a young mining engineer in his late twenties. A Latin book, *De Re Metallica,* written by one Georgius Agricola, fascinated him.

Who was Agricola? Why did this book appeal so strongly to Mr. Hoover?

Two years after the discovery of America by Christopher Columbus, on March 24, 1494, Georg Bauer was born in the little German village of Glauchau in Saxony. This farmer boy was destined to become one of the outstanding scientists of his time, and to be honored by posterity with the title of Father of Mineralogy.

Trained in medicine in the University of Leipzig, he chose Joachimsthal, a prolific region of metal mining and of smelting works, as his locale for setting up a physician's practice. Here he could follow his hobby of observing how ores were treated.

In 1531 he moved to Chemnitz, the center of the German mining industry, gave up his medical practice, and made mineralogy his principal study, although he also continued to occupy himself with and produced learned works on medical, mathematical, theological, and historical subjects.

Of Georg Bauer's numerous writings, published under his Latinized name of Agricola, the most celebrated was *De Re Metallica.* It was begun in 1533, completed in 1550, but not published until 1556, four months after his death. An unusually fine series of woodcuts illustrated this first systematic treatise on mining and metallurgy.

The Memoirs of Herbert Hoover reveal how it came about that an American mining engineer and his scholarly wife became internationally famous by bringing to life the almost forgotten name of Georgius Agricola:

"For some years I had been interested in the older literature of engineering and applied science generally. I had formed quite a collection of fifteenth and sixteenth century books on early science, engineering, metallurgy, mathematics, alchemy, etc. One of these —Agricola's *De Re Metallica*—a folio published in Latin in 1556, was the first important attempt to assemble systematically in print the world-knowledge on mining, metallurgy, and industrial chemistry.

"It was the great text-book of those industries for two centuries and had dominated thought and practice all that time. In many mining regions and camps, including the Spanish South American, it was chained to the church altar and translated by the priest to miners between religious services.

"No one had ever succeeded in translating it into English, although several had tried. My own study of Latin had never gone beyond some elementary early schooling and a few intermittent attempts to penetrate further into that language and literature after I left college. Mrs. Hoover was a good Latinist after she brushed up a little, and we found we could work it out. The problem of the 'untranslatable' Agricola fascinated us both, and finally in 1907 we resolved to translate it jointly.

"There were formidable difficulties; for while Agricola's Latin was scholarly enough, he was dealing with subjects the whole nomenclature and practice of which had developed hundreds of years after the Latin language ceased to grow. He did not adopt into the text the German, Italian or English terms for the operations or substances he described, but coined and adapted Latin terms for them. It was thus obvious why Latin scholars had failed in translation into English. It had been translated after a fashion into both German and French by persons unfamiliar with the arts described. For this reason, their work had failed also.

"The job involved finding out—either from the context, from German, French, Italian, or other fragmentary literature of the times, or from study of the processes themselves—what he meant. Mrs. Hoover's ability to read German and some French helped greatly. Sometimes the task amounted more to scientific detective work than to translation. Material A might start as an unknown substance but in different parts of the book Agricola would state its varying reactions when treated or combined with known substances B or C. Thus I could often have the meaning of its terms worked out in our laboratories. Often enough, when we discovered the meaning of a term we found that there was no modern word to express it because that particular process had been long abandoned. In any event, we grappled with it sentence by sentence, during our spare time, month after month, for over five years. We lugged the manuscript all over the world for odd moments that would be available for work on it.

"The translation was completed to our satisfaction in 1912, after four complete revisions. We desired to present it to the engineering profession, and consulted our good friend Edgar Rickard, who knew everything about technical publication. Edgar knew of a commercial printer in the north of England who had a fine sense of print—a love of old books—although no practice in such work. His name was Frost. When Frost saw the manuscript and the original his eyes glistened. He exclaimed that all his life he had been a commercial printer and had always wanted to do such a book. He offered to do it at bare out-of-pocket cost. In order to make the book as like the original as possible, he found a papermaker who could produce a sixteenth-century linen paper. He had a font of type cast in exact reproduction of the original except for the ancient letter S, which is confusing to modern readers. He printed it as a folio volume with all the old prints and illustrations in astonishing fidelity to the original. . . .

"In addition to the translation, I wrote an introduction covering the times and the circumstances under which Agricola lived and worked, with a brief biography of him. We included a full statement of all the known editions. I prepared extensive footnotes describing previous processes so far as knowledge of them is preserved—including those of Roman and Greek times. The footnotes explained the processes and methods described by Agricola in relation to our modern practice. All of this involved many pleasurable hours of research."

Herbert Hoover had married Lou Henry in February of 1899 in Monterey, California, and the very next day had started with his bride for Tientsin, where he had just been appointed chief engineer of the Chinese Bureau of Mines.

Three years later the couple were on their way to Europe where, at the age of twenty-seven, Mr. Hoover had accepted a junior partnership in the mining firm of Bewick, Moreing & Company, London.

This transfer enabled Mr. Hoover for the first time to take his young wife to Germany, in 1907 or 1908, into the region about which the life of Agricola centered.

Professor Vernon Kellogg, intimate friend of the Hoovers, has described the pilgrimage in these words:

"They went to Saxony, to the home of Agricola, hoping to get clues to the difficult things in the book by seeing the region and mines which had been under his eyes while writing it, and finding traditions of the mining methods of his time. But it was as if a sponge had been passed over Agricola and his days. Fire had swept over the towns he had known and all the ancient records were gone. The towns, rebuilt, and the mines of which he had written were there, but of him and of the ancient methods he wrote about there was hardly record or even tradition. They went to Freiberg, where has long existed the greatest German school of mines, the greatest mining school in the world, indeed, until the American schools were developed. . . . There they found no more to help them than in Agricola's own towns. In fact, the Freiberg professors seemed rather irritated by the advent of these searchers for ancient mining history, for, as the savants explained, the Freiberg methods and machines were all the most modern in the world; there were no 'left-overs, no worn-out rubbish of those inefficient ages' around Germany's great school of mines.

"So the Hoovers were little rewarded by their pilgrimage to Germany for help in their attempt to resuscitate the Saxon Agricola."

When the monumental translation made its public appearance in 1913, Publisher Edgar Rickard bragged that *De Re Metallica* in English was "the book that made Agricola famous." In proof of his seemingly extravagant statement he issued a thirty-two-page, beautifully designed circular, filled with reproductions of reviews and excerpts from engineers and savants all over the world. The letters came from places as far apart as Bulawayo in Rhodesia and Washington, D.C.; London, England, and San Francisco, California; Johannesburg, South Africa, and Anaconda, Montana; Mawchi, Burma, and Glasgow, Scotland; Melbourne, Australia, and Montreal, Canada.

Among the writers of congratulatory letters were President David Starr Jordan of Stanford University ("a stunning book"), Federal Judge Learned Hand of New York ("a splendid result for odd hours of a busy life"), Professor H. S. Moore of Columbia University ("a royal gift . . . to the profession"), Mining Engineer Mark L. Requa of San Francisco ("a monument to yourself that will last forever"), Mining Expert John Ferguson of Glasgow, Scotland (the "best encyclopedia of historical metallurgy"), and many others whose encomiums are deposited in the Hoover Archives at Stanford.

Book reviewers, especially those writing for trade, professional, and scientific magazines, discussed the Herbert and Lou Hoover accomplishment widely. A few samples will suffice to indicate their attitude:

The *Mining Magazine* of London wrote in part in its February, 1913, number: "It is not only a book; it is an event. A review of a 'labor of love,' as the translators can with sincerity describe it, calls for an appreciation rather than a criticism. Indeed, the critical faculty is suffused by the glow of admiration for a task so courageously undertaken and so patiently performed."

The *Engineering and Mining Journal* of New York on February 22, 1913, observed, *inter alia:* "The appearance of Hoover's *Agricola* . . . deserves more than an ordinary book review . . . not only because of the intrinsic value of the work, but especially we think as the work crowning the professional career of a distinguished engineer, who in becoming also a successful financier has not forgotten his professional ideals and duties. . . . Amid his multifold activities he has always preserved enthusiastic attention to strictly professional studies."

The *Mining and Scientific Press* of San Francisco commented on March 8, 1913: "Mr. Hoover, with his first-hand knowledge of mining and his thorough scholarship has been able to make Agricola's terms intelligible. . . ."

To the viewpoints of trade organs is here added, in excerpt, the voice of the London *Times* for February 19, 1913: "The difficulties of translation, into any language, have been exceptionally great as the result of Agricola's selecting Latin as his medium. That language was unsuitable for his purpose, for Latin had ceased to expand a thousand years before his subject had in many particulars come into being; in consequence he was in difficulties with a large number of ideas for which there were no corresponding words in the vocabulary at his command, and instead of adopting into the text his native terms, he coined several hundred Latin expressions to answer his needs. . . . *De Re Metallica* is obviously not a text-book for modern practice, but it possesses the inestimable value of affording a means of tracing to their very source many of those methods which are familiar at the present day."

Fifteen years after the appearance of the Hoover translation and elucidation, a first-class German translation of *De Re Metallica* was brought out under the auspices of Oscar von Miller's Deutsches Museum by two distinguished German engineers, Professors Carl Matschoss, President of the Society of German Engineers, and Carl Schiffner, an internationally known mining expert. At that time Dr. Friedrich Hassler of Berlin commented in the September, 1928, issue of *Forschungen und Fortschritte:*

"Already during the years before the [first] world war the idea had often been advanced that a new translation of the original text ought to be published. Before this intention could be carried out, there appeared the excellent edition by the American mining engineer, Herbert Clark Hoover, whose great social and administrative accomplishments, most recently in the position of Secretary of Commerce of the United States, are known in the entire world.

"Together with his wife, born Lou Henry, Hoover had within five years accomplished the tremendous task of not only supplying the English-reading world with an excellent translation, but also of supplementing it with numerous historical annotations.

"In his foreword Hoover, too, refers to the inadequacy of the old German edition and expresses surprise that we had not yet made our compatriot known to a wider circle by publishing a new edition of his principal work. However, the situation which had developed, whereby the [German] engineers availed themselves of the English translation to get to know Agricola, could be remedied only after the effects of the war and inflation years had been overcome."

A copy of the new German edition, whose make-up was closely patterned upon the American, was presented to Mr. Hoover by the German Ambassador in Washington on behalf of the Deutsches Museum of Munich. In thanking the museum for the gift, the then Secretary of Commerce wrote to Dr. von Miller: "I thank you indeed for the kind thought which prompted you to send this book to me and Mrs. Hoover. We spent many happy hours in our translation of this work, and we are very glad to have this edition of it."

The four hundredth anniversary of Agricola's death on November 21, 1955, prompted the German Academy of Sciences in Berlin to publish a nine-by-twelve-inch illustrated book, *Georgius Agricola,* which in its 376 pages commemorates the contributions of the Saxon savant to the various sciences in which he was versed.

The copy sent to Mr. Hoover is dedicated in the following words (in German):

"To Former President Hoover, the pioneer researcher in the area of the history of mining, and the sponsor of remembrance of Agricola. Dedicated with highest esteem." (Signed) [Georg] Spackeler, Professor emeritus of the Freiberg Mining Academy, Chairman of the Central Agricola Committee.

2

THE BATTLE TO FEED BELGIUM

The story of the Commission for Relief in Belgium has been told and retold minutely and documented exhaustively.

Eyewitnesses and participants in this gigantic international relief undertaking, including Herbert Hoover, its chairman, Professor Vernon Kellogg and diplomat Hugh Gibson, high-ranking members of Mr. Hoover's "team," and Will Irwin, one of the "greats" of American journalism—to mention but a few—have preserved the story for posterity.

George I. Gay, also on the staff of the Commission, with the assistance of Professor H. H. Fisher, formerly of Stanford University, has supplied copious evidence in a two-volume book of documents, *Public Relations of the Commission for Relief in Belgium,* to reinforce the story.

We are here concerned only with what might be termed the "German angle" to the Belgian enterprise. For an understanding, however, of the involvement of Germany in the episode and of its corollary, Mr. Hoover's involvement in complicated negotiations with the German occupation authorities, it is necessary to recapitulate the general scope of the work of the Commission for Relief in Belgium. Also, the attitude of the Allied and Associated Powers toward the Commission and its work had an important bearing upon Mr. Hoover's negotiations with the Germans and must, therefore, at least be highlighted.

The scope of activities of the Commission for Relief in Belgium has been summarized tersely by Mr. Gay in his Preface to 1145 pages of documentation:

"An official of the British Foreign Office once described the Commission for Relief in Belgium as a piratical state organized for benevolence. This description, however extravagant in certain particulars, has the virtue of suggesting the attributes of an organization without precedent in international relations. It is a fact that the Commission performed functions and enjoyed prerogatives which usually appertain to state rather than to private institutions. It had, for example, its own flag; it made contracts and informal treaties with belligerent governments; its ships were granted privileges accorded to no other flag; its representatives in regions of military occupation enjoyed powers and immunities of great significance. The Commission itself was neutral as between the opposing lines, but in the pursuit of its duties it waged frequent controversy with both belligerents, and it received aid and essential cooperation from both. Its contacts, however, were by no means restricted to the European scene of war; they extended westward to North and South America, southward to the tip of Africa, and eastward to India and Australasia.

"By virtue of these privileges, duties, and connections, the C.R.B. was in one sense an international public body under the patronage of diplomatic officers of the neutral states of the United States,

Spain, and the Netherlands. Actually it was a private organization, without incorporation or well defined legal status, to which the governments engaged in war on the western front entrusted responsibilities which no government or public body could discharge. The chairman of the Commission, Herbert Hoover, and those associated with him in its direction, were private citizens of the United States; they looked first to their countrymen for moral and material support; they received the valued counsel and cooperation of American diplomatic representatives in belligerent states; and the American people generally looked upon the C.R.B. as an American enterprise. The American Government, however, was in no sense responsible for the acts of the Commission, nor were the Spanish and Dutch Governments, nor the Governments of Belgium and France, of Great Britain and the British Dominions, whose citizens participated in varying degrees in the Commission's work.

"Inversely the Commission was not exclusively accountable to any single government or state, but in a different measure to many of them. To the Western Allies it was accountable for the fulfillment of German guarantees respecting relief and for the protection and equitable use of imported and native supplies; to the Germans, for the exclusive employment for the benefit of Belgian and French civilians of its many special privileges. To the people of Belgium and Northern France, whom the fortunes of war had deprived of the protection of their Governments, the Commission was a volunteer champion striving with all its power and with the indispensable collaboration of the Belgian *Comité National* and the *Comité Français* to succor and defend them. To the Belgian, French, British, and later the United States Governments which furnished subventions for relief, and to the millions of individuals of all corners of the world who contributed money, goods, or services, the Commission was answerable for the honest and efficient use of the resources placed at its disposal—resources which in money and goods alone amounted to nearly a billion dollars, a sum about equivalent to the net debt of the United States in the years prior to the war.

"This brief statement of responsibilities by no means covers the entire field of the Commission's obligations, but it indicates the complexity and variety of its public relations. . . ."

The success or failure of the venture, no matter how generous the contributions to its purposes or how excellent the organization might be, depended in the last analysis on the willingness, on the one hand, of the Allied Powers to allow relief for the Belgians to pass their blockade of Germany, to land cargoes in some port from which transport into Belgium and Northern France could be readily made, and to sanction the financial operations of the Committee for Relief in Belgium. On the other hand, permission had to be obtained from the German government and especially the German occupation authorities for undertaking the operations envisaged by the Commission, and a guarantee negotiated to the effect that the relief ships would not be molested by German submarines.

The pivotal Allied country, because of its domination of the seas, was Great Britain. Its wartime Prime Minister, David Lloyd George, had to be won over. This was a difficult task.

The decisive meeting took place on January 21, 1915. The Commission had by then been in operation for three months. In other words, the British government had had ample time to observe the workings of and crystallize its thinking about Belgian relief. In a dramatic session Mr. Hoover faced an initially hostile British Prime Minister and a group of his advisers.

The debate was summarized in an illuminating memorandum which was drawn up by Mr. Hoover and is in part reproduced herewith:

"Mr. Lloyd George stated that he had put his veto upon the project, because he felt that, indirect as the matter was, it was certainly assisting the enemy, and that this assistance would take place in several ways. In the first instance, we were giving the Belgians more food resources with which to stand requisitions in food by the Germans; that we were giving them more resources generally with which to stand monetary levies; and that beyond all this, in relieving the Germans from the necessity of feeding the civil population we were directly prolonging the war, which was bound to be one of wholly economic character and that economic pressure was the principal method by which the Allies would ultimately win. He expressed the belief that the Germans would, in the last resort, provision the people of Belgium; that our action was akin to the provisioning the civil population of a besieged city and thus prolonging the resistance of the garrison; that he was wholly opposed to our operations, benevolent and humane as they were; and that therefore he could not see his way to grant our request.

"I pointed out that, first, as to the requisitioning of food, the Germans had given an undertaking that after the first of January no such requisitions would be made, and I read out to him the undertaking which had been given to the American Minister in Berlin and informed him that we were satisfied from the many agents that we had in Belgium that the Germans were carrying this out with the utmost scrupulousness. I furthermore informed him that the Germans had impressed none of our actual food. Also, I stated that I did not believe that the feeding of the civil population increased the resources which they had available for money levies; that we were introducing no new money into Belgium, but were simply giving circulation to the money already existing, and that there was no danger of the Germans taking the money which we collected for foodstuffs because that money was in the possession of the American Minister.

"On the second point, as to whether the Germans would ultimately provision the civil population, I told him that I was satisfied that they would not do so; that when we undertook this labor we undertook it with the greatest reluctance and our first move was to satisfy ourselves that this population would starve unless America intervened and converted the hitherto negative quality of neutrality into one of positive neutrality; that as proof that the Germans would not provision the civil population I thought it was desirable that he should understand the German views on this question, and I recited to him the confirmation by the German military of the current statement in Germany that there was no clause in the Hague Convention obliging the Germans to provision the civil population of Belgium; on the contrary, it incidentally provided that the civil population should support the military.

"I told him further, that the Germans contended that the Belgians were a people of great resources, that these resources would become valuable at once on a partial recovery of industry, that this recovery of industry could take place instantly they were given a port through which they could trade with the neutral world, that in taking the port of Antwerp and opening it to neutral ships they had given the Belgian civil population a means of provisioning themselves, but that this outlet had been blocked by the British Navy and the British must therefore bear the responsibility. Further, that the Belgian population, by continuing its hostility and its passive resistance was assisting the Allies by compelling the Germans to operate the public services, rendering trade useless to them, also the arsenals, and requiring from them a considerable army of occupation; and that as the Allies do all this they must take the responsibility of these people starving. Furthermore, the Germans contend that while they have ample food supplies to carry their own people through the struggle, they have not sufficient to carry on their backs the ten million people in Belgium and France inside their lines; and that as they are struggling for national existence they must feed their own people and attend to their own military exigencies first.

"I pointed out that I did not offer these arguments as my own but to illustrate the fixity of mind by which the German people justify their action in refusing to feed the Belgians, and asked him if he could conceive for one moment that with this mental attitude of conviction on their part that they were right and the Allies were wrong, they would be likely to feed the Belgians. I pointed out that starvation had actually occurred in Belgium; that some, although perhaps little, riot had occurred, but sufficient to indicate the fixity of the Germans in their intention. I further pointed out the position of the French people in the Meuse Valley, who had not had our assistance and were dying of starvation although under German occupation; and I expressed the conviction that the Germans would never feed the civil population.

"He denounced the whole of this as a monstrous attitude; to which I replied that, be that as it might, one matter stood out in my mind and that was that the English people had undertaken this war for the avowed purpose of protecting the existence of small nations, of vindicating the guaranteed neutrality by which small nations might exist, for the avowed purpose of guaranteeing to the world the continuance of democracy as against autocracy in government; and that it would be an empty victory if one of the most democratic of the world's races should be extinguished in the process and ultimate victory should be marked by an empty husk. I said that the English people were great enough to disregard the doubtful military value of advantages in favor of assurances that these people should survive, and I felt the obligation went even further than mere acquiescence in our work and extended to an opportunity to the English to add to their laurels by showing magnanimity toward these people, a magnanimity which would outlast all the bitterness of this war.

"Mr. Lloyd George stated to his colleagues abruptly: 'I am convinced. You have my permission. I would be obliged if you gentlemen would settle the details of the machinery necessary to carry it out.' Then turning to me he said that I would forgive him for running away, but that he felt the world would yet be indebted to the American people for the most magnanimous action which neutrality had yet given way to.

"(Signed) H. C. Hoover"

Professor Kellogg has referred to the Hoover interview with Lloyd George as "momentous." The expression is decidedly apropos when one considers that, once having been persuaded by Mr. Hoover that starvation in Belgium must be fought, the British Prime Minister and his government—and with it also the French government—loyally and persistently stood by the Commission and its work. Ultimately a subvention of $5,000,000 per month, contributed by the British and French governments, was passed on to the Commission via the Belgian government.

Immediately upon taking on the chairmanship of the Commission, Mr. Hoover had requested the American Ambassador in Berlin, James W. Gerard, to attempt to secure the approval of the German Foreign Office for at least one fraction of the Commission's work—that of feeding the poor of Belgium. The Wilhelmstrasse had replied on October 16, 1914, that the request "has the approval of the German Government."

Mr. Hoover followed this first consent up by a hurried personal trip to Berlin, where he negotiated with Chancellor Theobald von Bethmann-Hollweg, Minister for Foreign Affairs Gottlieb von Jagow, Minister for Finance Karl Helfferich, Under-Secretary for Foreign Affairs Arthur Zimmermann, and Banker Carl Melchior, financial adviser to the Minister of Finance.

As a result, the American Embassy was officially informed on November 14 that the German Governor-General in Belgium had been requested to aid the Commission for Relief in Belgium as far as military interests permitted. Nine days later the Imperial German government went even farther and expressed itself as "in complete sympathy with the meritorious efforts of the American Commission in Belgium to provide the population of that country with foodstuffs."

This declaration was accompanied by a guarantee of freedom from seizure to nonneutral vessels carrying supplies for the Commission to Dutch ports.

There was one condition attached to this guarantee: it would become operative only if the British government also agreed not to interfere with the movements of the Commission's ships.

New time-consuming negotiations ensued, but the British Admiralty finally agreed to guarantee the free passage of the Commission's ships.

Meanwhile Herbert Hoover, serenely confident that common sense and decency would prevail, continued to purchase and import foodstuffs into Belgium while the wrangling over special papers and passes continued. In the end everything came out in such a way that the Commission managed to do what had to be done.

One of the obstacles which the Commission had again and again to overcome was the fear of the Allies lest the foodstuffs imported from overseas and from England and France might not be supplied solely to Belgian and French civil populations in the occupied territories; in other words, lest at least some of it might be siphoned off by the Germans.

Equally grave was the fear of the Allies lest the German occupation authorities, while leaving the Commission's food shipments untouched, might drain similar native foods from Belgium and Northern France by requisitions, so that, in effect, the very Allies who had set up a blockade against their adversary would indirectly supply food to him.

As a result of further negotiations with the Berlin authorities, Under-Secretary Zimmermann in a letter to Ambassador Gerard dated December 31, 1914, stated that "the Imperial Governor-General in Belgium will issue without delay an order prohibiting all the troops under his command from requisitioning food or forage of any kind whatsoever which would require to be replaced by the American Committee for Belgian Relief. The Governor-General will, in addition, authorize the Minister of the United States and the Spanish Minister at Brussels as Honorary Chairmen of the Committee, to convince themselves in any way which may to them seem advisable that the prohibition is observed most scrupulously."

Another important concession obtained by Mr. Hoover and his staff was to the effect that the entire product of the Belgian grain harvest of 1915 could be used for baking wheat and rye bread for the Belgian population. Other concessions followed. Allied fears were allayed and the Commission could continue its humanitarian work effectively.

Professor Kellogg later testified in his *Fighting Starvation in Belgium:* "On the whole, and to that large degree which has been necessary to allow us to continue the work of relief of Belgium with clear consciences, and to allow the Allied Governments to permit and actually to support the work, the answer to the query: 'But don't the Germans get the food?' is a categorical and positive 'No!' "

When the possibility of America's active involvement in the First World War as a belligerent loomed menacingly on the horizon, Mr. Hoover and his associates succeeded in obtaining an assurance by the Imperial German government, finally transmitted via the Spanish minister in Brussels on March 12, 1917, to the effect that safe-conducts to American representatives on the Commission would be given whenever applied for, whatsoever the situation might be between the United States and Germany.

This assurance enabled the American members to remain in Belgium and Northern France even after diplomatic relations had been severed between the United States and Germany on February 3, 1917 and until the outbreak of actual hostilities on April 6.

Other major assurances and guarantees—besides innumerable relatively small but indispensable ones—exempted relief supplies other than food from requisition. These included imported pharmaceutical products unobtainable from Germany, clothing, salt, imported fodder, some 2,000 horses unsuitable for war service but urgently needed by the Commission for moving its goods, also wines, incense-wax, and sanctuary oil to fulfill needs of the Roman Catholic Church.

Precise routings and other arrangements had to be agreed upon to prevent destruction of Commission ships by German submarines. Passes had to be issued for imported relief provisions. Exemption from customs duties and canal tolls had to be secured from the occupation authorities for all relief supplies. Authorization had to be negotiated for Commission delegates to make inspection trips in the frontier zones accompanied by a German officer.

These are but a few samples of the tedious, meticulous negotiations upon which the Commission had to embark. All this took time. It took more than that: it took courage.

Vernon Kellogg gave a glimpse of the spirit which animated the members of the Commission, when he wrote in *Fighting Starvation in Belgium:* "Its members have crossed the Channel in convoyed English déspatch boats, passed through closed frontiers, scurried about in swift motors over all the occupied territory to which few other cars than military ones ever moved, visited villages at the front under shell fire, lived at the very Great Headquarters of all the German armies of the West, been trusted on their honor to do a thousand and one things and be in a thousand and one places prohibited to all other civilians, and have lived up to the trust. They have suffered from the mistakes of uninformed or stupid soldiers, and spent nights in jail; they have taken chances under bombing airmen, and been falsely but dangerously accused as spies; but despite obstacles and delays and danger they have carried the little triangular red-lettered white C.R.B. flag to every town and hamlet in the imprisoned land, and have gulped and passed on wet-eyed as the people by the roads uncovered to the little flag, with all its significance of material and spiritual encouragement. Under this flag they have been protector and protected at once."

Herbert Hoover led a charmed life during his many voyages through mine-infested waters and under skies from which bombs might drop at any time. A passage in the first volume of his *Memoirs* illustrates what situations he got into during his forty crossings of the English Channel while serving as head of the Commission:

"At the end of September (1916), on one of my perpetual North Sea crossings, I came to the Hook of Holland from Brussels to take the Dutch boat for Harwich. The requirement was as usual to be on board in the evening as the boat left at daylight. One slept comfortably at least until then.

"Late next morning I was awakened by a gruff voice telling me in German to keep still. The man wore the uniform of a German marine. As he pointed a revolver with the seeming calibre of a beer glass I had no inclination to raise a disturbance. He seemed wholly disinclined to carry on a conversation, but every little while repeated his words of little comfort. Combining feeble German with gestures, I suggested that I might ring the bell over the bunk. To this he made no ultra-violent objection. When the Dutch steward arrived, he informed me that we had been captured at daylight by the Germans and taken into Zeebrugge. So far as I was concerned it had been a most peaceable battle. With the steward as a messenger to the German officer in command I obtained the privilege of getting up and going on deck in search of breakfast. There I found that we were in Zeebrugge harbor, surrounded by four or five German destroyers. All the passengers except myself and an elderly Dutch gentleman had been crowded onto the stern deck and were being examined one by one by two German officers seated behind tables. One of the officers asked if I were Mr. Hoover. On my reply he courteously told me that we would be delayed some hours, but that when they were done with their search of the mail and passengers we would be allowed to proceed to England.

"The German officer sent for me later and explained that they were going to intern some thirty English passengers—part of whom were escaped prisoners from Germany and five civilians who had wives with them. The wives were insisting upon going with their husbands. Would I persuade them not to? They would be in separate internment camps for months or perhaps years. I did my best, but the two who had children at home were the only ones who could be persuaded. But the others were forcibly left on our boat. The parting of these women from their husbands was a scene in keeping with the universal tragedy of war.

"When the search was over and we were waiting for a signal to depart I was standing with the Dutch gentleman observing proceedings from the upper deck. Suddenly an explosion broke in our faces and my companion fell in a heap. It flashed through my mind that we were being fired upon from the shore. Then a Dutch sailor yelled 'Aeroplane!' I looked up to see a French plane circling over us, kindly dropping a bomb each time it came around. It came around five times. The first bomb had struck the bow of a barge fifty feet away, and the Dutch passenger had been slightly hurt with splinters. My neck had a crick in it for a week from the earnestness of my interest in the next four rounds from that plane. The bombs did not strike either us or the German destroyers, but the expectation that the aim would be better next time was absorbing.

"In January, 1917, on what turned out to be the last return trip I was to make from Belgium during the war, I went to the Hook of Holland to take the Dutch boat for Tilbury. The Dutch maintained only one steamer in service at one time and the price of passage and mail probably paid for a boat each trip. As each boat in rotation was sunk by mines or other accidents of war, they substituted another one. Those of the crew who survived took up their duties on the succeeding ship. In forty crossings I managed to avoid playing a role in a tragedy of the North Sea, but after several boats were lost I became less and less satisfied with the mathematical theory of chances.

"I had established a procedure of paying the steward for my cabin and meals at the end of the voyage. On boarding the boat this time I congratulated the steward on his having escaped from the sinking of the steamer *Queen,* which had gone down some days before. As I ate breakfast he continued to stand around, first on one foot and then on another. Finally he blurted out, 'You must pay cash.' I protested in pained tones that he was an old friend of mine, that he and I had been traveling together for over two years, that I had always paid generously, and that it hurt me to feel that I had lost his confidence. His encouraging reply was, 'Well, ten passengers were drowned on the *Queen,* and they owed me sixty-five guilders. I can't take any more risks.' "

This chapter would not be complete unless it gave at least an example of the sort of spirit which Herbert Hoover occasionally encountered when negotiating with the German authorities. The *Memoirs,* Volume I, describe such an incident.

After expressing his satisfaction over the manner in which the various agreements arrived at with the Allies and the Germans had worked until the summer of 1916, Mr. Hoover continues:

"Everything went smoothly in this particular until we arrived in sight of the harvest in the summer of 1916, when a storm blew up. The problem was also complicated by the fact that the Germans had planted many abandoned farms. Our men, together with our

Belgian and French committees in those areas, estimated the surplus crop. The Germans did not agree with our conclusions on the quantity that should be handed to us in compensation from Germany. The British and French Intelligence, no doubt on information of the French and Belgian Committee members, promptly reported our dispute to their home governments. In the middle of our negotiations both these governments blew off in the press as to this proposed German atrocity—which did not help.

"There was a serious difference. The German army's estimate was equal to about $40,000,000 less food than we contended for. At this point I went to Charleville to join Dr. Kellogg in the discussion. We were unable to agree with General von Sauberzweig, the Quartermaster General. Believing we could do better with the top officials in Berlin we settled with the General that we would all meet in the Esplanade Hotel in Berlin a few days later—on August 4—and thrash it out at the top. . . .

"Dr. Kellogg and I duly arrived at the Esplanade Hotel. There, on the following morning we met General von Sauberzweig, and Major von Kessler. There was no food shortage at the Esplanade although there could be a shortage of cash to pay the price of it. The officers informed us that they would take our matter up in conference with the ministers and other authorities and meet us at the hotel later. We were disappointed not to be allowed to present our case ourselves especially as we knew Minister Lewald would be there. [Dr. Theodor Lewald, the later chairman of the German Olympic Committee, was then Undersecretary of the German Ministry of the Interior.]

"At four o'clock the General and the Major returned. . . . The General seemed upset and promptly ordered a whisky and soda. The Major who spoke perfect English gave us the news of the conference. It was bad. The authorities had decided that they would make no compromise with our estimates. Worse still, they had discussed the whole question of abolishing the Commission. The Major said that it looked bad for us. He added that several of the generals had made violent speeches directed at us. Only Lewald spoke for us. Our espionage case and matter published at this time in the British newspapers had roiled them; most of them had determined that they had better throw out the Commission and blast the British for the blockade generally. They said it was no worse for Belgians and French to starve than for Germans to starve. We naturally disavowed any responsibility for the remarks of the British and French. We urged the whole case of the Belgians and Northern French over again. The General took his *n*th whisky.

"Then came one of those unforgettable episodes. After we were told that the relief was probably all over, von Kessler apologetically mentioned that the General was greatly broken up by the news he had just received that his son had been permanently blinded in a gas attack on the Western Front. I expressed sympathy for his tragedy. The General, who had still another drink, then went into a monologue about the war. He said that civilians were messing into it too much and that it was no longer a soldiers' war with manly weapons. Civilians had made these poison gases. They were engaged in many activities which they should keep out of—probably meaning us.

"He grew vehement on the starving of German women and children by the blockade 'and then, there was the case of that Cavell woman.' He seemed to want to elaborate on that. We expressed interest. He said she had organized an espionage group of a thousand Belgian women. He said he had warned them. He had punished some of them mildly. They would not stop. He was compelled as a soldier to make an example and stop it. He had her tried, she confessed, and as a soldier he was compelled to execute her to protect the German army. He had been 'painted as a monster all over the world.' He said he 'was called a murderer; a second Duke of Alva.' The neutral peoples think: 'I am the most infamous of men.'

"I had thought von Bissing, the Governor of Belgium, was responsible for the horror of Miss Cavell's execution. But I confirmed afterward that it was this General von Sauberzweig. He was temporary military Governor at that time.

"As he mumbled along I had a thought. The General obviously did not like the kind of publicity he had received in the neutral world. The Relief was apparently about to blow up. I said to Dr. Kellogg that I wanted to make a further statement to the General about the whole relief matter and asked him to translate fully. I said that the conclusion of the German authorities would mean death for millions of people, mostly children; that as he was responsible officer he would be portrayed to the world as a monster infinitely bigger and blacker than the picture they drew of him after the Cavell incident. I elaborated the theme to cover the whole German army. And as my temperature rose I emphasized this theme so strongly that Kellogg hesitated to translate my language and said so. But Major von Kessler injected that he would translate. And he did it with no reservations. It appeared that he had been fighting our battle all day and was himself in no good humor. The General made no immediate reply. Then suddenly he remarked that there might be something in what I said. Whether it was the threat, the whisky, or his grief, or the human appeal that had moved him, I do not know. He directed von Kessler to inform Minister Lewald that he thought the negotiation ought to continue. He would be obliged if the Minister would take the matter in hand and settle it.

"We broke up at once and with von Kessler went to the Ministry. Lewald seemed relieved to hear von Kessler's authorization.

"We settled in half an hour on a basis of a part reduction in our estimates to 'save face.' The Minister said that he would draft a letter and asked us to wait. When we received the draft document it was obviously written for publication, as two-thirds of it was a blast against the British and the inhumane effect of the blockade on German women and children. I suggested that he change a line in the last third so as to make clear that we were not the object of the blast. He studied the text for a few moments and said with good humor approximately this: 'Let us cut out the whole of that part anyway—we will answer the British with bullets.' Dr. Kellogg and I hurried out of Berlin within an hour for fear that our opponents in the Army might try to call the letter back and change the terms."

The problem which was the most difficult of all for Mr. Hoover and his associates to solve was that of shipping.

Will Irwin, ace correspondent, wrote in considerable detail about this phase of the Commission's many tribulations in his book *Herbert Hoover—a Reminiscent Biography.* A few paragraphs are here reproduced:

"As the war and the submarine campaign went on, ships came into unprecedented demand. Crazy vessels resurrected from the boneyard made fortunes for their owners. The demand rose until it was no longer a matter of money but of pull and diplomatic influence. And by now the Commission needed a fleet of eighty average-sized ocean freighters. The British militarist faction, especially strong in the navy, hampered Hoover's men all they could. Even when the Government in general was friendly, minor officials would throw monkey wrenches into the machinery. After the first cargoes departed for Belgium, some underling sent a circular to the war trade clubs, calling attention to the 'dangerous accumulation' of foodstuffs in Holland, warning shippers to avoid that kind of business.

"As the war rose toward its climax, as the German submarines piled up their devastation, the difficulty of getting tonnage increased. The Commission took steps to find a fleet of its own. In American harbors lay interned scores of available German ships. Hoover conceived the idea of using them for his purely humanitarian enterprise; and he opened negotiations looking toward this end. The Germans at first made violent objection; every one of their own ships in service of the Commission, they said, released just so much British or French or neutral tonnage for war work. But the fine-visioned Herr Ballin of the Hamburg-American Line intervened. When Hoover got both the Germans and the British to sign an agreement releasing these ships to the Commission, the thing seemed accomplished. But unexpectedly the French refused to sign; and other Allies raised legalistic objections. Hoover was still hammering away at these dissenters when the German declaration of unlimited submarine warfare changed every aspect of the situation. But somehow this group of super-efficient American engineers always found tonnage, and at prices rather below the current commercial rate."

Will Irwin tersely summed up the accomplishments of the Commission for Relief in Belgium in these words: "For four years it fed ten million people; brought them through without starvation or malnutrition. It maintained a stream of 350,000,000 pounds of foodstuffs a month. It gave its charges the cheapest food in Europe. It furnished them good bread, not husks or scrapings. Germany, and later France, lived toward the end on a mélange of miscellaneous cereals, husks, and potato flour. It supplied the children milk, fats, the special foods necessary to maintain their health and encourage their growth. It carried the destitute—eventually about 55 per cent of the Belgians and northern French—largely on profits from the affluent.

"At the request of the restored Belgian Government, the Commission continued its work for six months after the armistice. During this period the price of all foodstuffs was so much lower in Belgium than in other allied countries that the authorities feared international jealousy. They asked Hoover, therefore, to raise his prices!"

In concluding his version of the feeding of Belgium in his *Memoirs,* Mr. Hoover gave testimony on a question much discussed in Allied circles during and after the First World War—the question of alleged German atrocities. He commented: "There exists a vast literature upon German atrocities in Belgium and France. It is mostly the literature of propaganda. Even Lord Bryce was drawn into it—and greatly exaggerated it. He invited me to lunch one day and urged me to give him a statement for publication. Being a reasonable man, he finally agreed that to do this would make it impossible for me to do any more relief work on territory held by the Germans. However, I never found much foundation for the stories of individual outrage or cruelty. Things were done, however, by order of superior officers which to me were far worse. The wholesale execution of civilian hostages at Dinant and Tamines, and the burning of whole villages and the library and church of St. Pierre at Louvain are examples. And it can be said for the Germans that in the horrible case of Dinant the German colonel was dismissed, and a German court of inquiry delivered a scorching denunciation of the act. It can be repeated as a generalization that armies in action are not guests at afternoon receptions. Every army has a percentage of criminally minded, and the abolition of moral restraints in war is scarcely calculated to lift their souls into the realm of idealism."

One may wonder what salary or other emolument Herbert Hoover received to compensate him at least partially for the time and energy that could otherwise have been devoted to his lucrative mining operations.

I found the answer in a matter-of-fact business letter, buried in a maze of documentation concerning the Commission for Relief in Belgium in the Hoover Institution at Stanford University. It stems from a source which stood outside the whole Belgian undertaking yet was charged with careful and responsible scrutiny of its operations.

The letter was written on February 3, 1927, by the international auditing firm of Deloitte, Plender, Griffiths and Company, with offices in London, New York, and Paris. It states, *inter alia:* "Our firm acted as auditors of the Commission from the inception of its active operations until the termination thereof, some five years later. . . .

"The records are evidence of the important services rendered by the Commission's principal officials, which services were given without remuneration. In this connection, we would state that Mr. Hoover set an example by not accepting, directly or indirectly, any form of remuneration from the Commission and by refusing, throughout the period of the Commission's activities, to take from the funds of the Commission the cost of his traveling or other out-of-pocket expenses while engaged on the business of the Commission."

Further light on Mr. Hoover's financial relation to the humanitarian work which he headed is contained in Burton J. Hendrick's *The Life and Letters of Walter Hines Page,* American Ambassador to Great Britain during World War I. After stating that "Life is worth more for knowing Hoover," and recapitulating the later President's accomplishments for the relief of Belgian distress, Mr. Page revealed: "He [Hoover] came to me the other day and said, 'You must know the Commission is $600,000 in debt. But don't be uneasy. I've given my personal note for it' (he's worth more than that)."

3

POST-ARMISTICE BLOCKADE OF GERMANY

The entry of the United States into the First World War on April 6, 1917, made it inevitable for the management of the Commission for Relief in Belgium to pass out of American hands. Its work was turned over to the Dutch and Spanish in due time. Herbert Hoover was appointed United States Food Administrator.

With the signing of the Armistice on November 11, 1918, new duties devolved upon him. President Woodrow Wilson asked him to administer the economic rehabilitation on behalf of nearly thirty European countries including Germany. Some 400,000,000 people of Europe were caught in war's aftermath.

Mr. Hoover and his immediate associates, Robert A. Taft, Dr. Alonzo Taylor, Julius H. Barnes, and Lewis L. Strauss, all of whom had worked under him in the United States Food Administration, sat in daily conference as their ship, the S.S. *Olympic,* on November 16, 1918, started for England. The same idealism which prompted these conferences also animated the group of former Belgian Relief workers, both English and American, who welcomed the former chief and his associates upon their arrival in the Old World.

As Mr. Hoover put it in his *Memoirs:*

"Our discussions were mostly on the peace to come. Idealism burned brightly. We felt greater by being part of a generation which had won for the earth the end of mass murder, freedom of men, the independence and safety of nations. . . .

"We were sure that humanity, having passed through the furnace of the last four years, would be less greedy, less selfish. . . . The purification of men, the triumph of democracy would bring a new golden age."

While Mr. Hoover and his four colleagues were still on the high seas, Secretary of State Robert Lansing had sent a letter to Hans Sulzer, Minister of Switzerland in charge of German interests in the United States, setting forth the official policy of the American government with reference to feeding defeated Germany.

The communication, dated November 14, 1918, stated:

"At a joint session of the two Houses of Congress on November 11 the President of the United States announced that the representatives of the Associated Governments in the Supreme War Council at Versailles have by unanimous resolution assured the people of the Central Empires that everything that is possible in the circumstances will be done to supply them with food and relieve the distressing want that is in so many places threatening their very lives and that steps are to be taken immediately to organize these efforts at relief in the same systematic manner that they were organized in the case of Belgium. Furthermore, the President expressed the opinion that by the use of the idle tonnage of the Central Empires it ought presently to be possible to lift the fear of utter misery from their oppressed populations and set their minds and energies free for the great and hazardous tasks of political reconstruction which now face them on every hand.

"Accordingly the President now directs me to state that he is ready to consider favorably the supplying of foodstuffs to Germany and to take up the matter immediately with the Allied Governments, provided he can be assured that public order is being and will continue to be maintained in Germany, and that an equitable distribution of food can be clearly guaranteed."

This proffer of food aid to a vanquished enemy, which significantly supported a cherished ideal of the Quaker faith to which Mr. Hoover belongs, further raised the buoyant spirit of the man now charged with the economic rehabilitation of Europe's multimillioned population.

The very morning after his arrival in London, however, there came a "rude awakening" during a meeting with the Allied Ministers for a discussion of programs and organization. Wrote Mr. Hoover in his *Memoirs:*

"This morning session was at once an enlightenment in national intrigue, selfishness, nationalism, heartlessness, rivalry, and suspicion, which seemed to ooze from every pore—but with polished politeness. . . . There was here a dual mind. The Englishman, Frenchman, and Italian genuinely thought idealistically—as individuals. But when each viewed the problems of his own people, the impoverishment, the unemployment, the debt, and when he thought of national prestige and power, he was a different man. . . .

"It was something of a shock to realize that the war and all its elevation of spirit had not changed the collective minds of the British, French, or Italians. It was still Empire First—and against all comers, including the other two. . . .

"Within a few hours I found that the greatest famine since the Thirty Years' War did not seem to be of any great immediate concern. Nor was there much concern that it must be stemmed at once if Europe were to make recovery in a generation and if that social stability, out of which peace could be made, was to be maintained. Instead, I found myself projected immediately into battles of power politics on four fronts."

From London Herbert Hoover on December 10, 1918, traveled to Paris, where President Wilson was about to arrive as head of the American Peace Delegation.

The maneuverings which finally, after much wrangling, led to the signing and ratification of the Treaty of Versailles do not concern us in this specialized work *Herbert Hoover and Germany.* Discussion is here limited to events essential for an understanding of the situation in which Mr. Hoover found himself vis-à-vis Germany.

Hardly had he taken up his duties in Paris, when he began his fight for lifting the blockade of the neutral and enemy countries, now that the shooting war was over. His philosophy regarding food blockades is summed up in his *Memoirs:*

"To lower the morale of the enemy by reducing his food supply was one of the major strategies of the war. I did not myself believe in the food blockade. I did not believe that it was the effective weapon of which the Allies were so confident. I did not believe in starving women and children. And above all, I did not believe that stunted bodies and deformed minds in the next generation were secure foundations upon which to rebuild civilization.

"The facts were that soldiers, government officials, munitions workers, and farmers in enemy countries would always be fed; that the impact of blockade was upon the weak and the women and children. Moreover, because of the food blockade, Germany had no need to spend money abroad and she would have long since gone broke if she could have bought what her public would have demanded. I insisted that the war would not be won by the blockade on food for women and children, but by the blockade on military supplies and by military action. There were important Englishmen who agreed with me.

"I knew well enough that such revolutionary ideas would not prevail when we came into the war, but nevertheless I presented a plan to President Wilson by which we could give supplementary food, under proper neutral controls, to German children and weaker women through soup kitchens and school feeding, without essentially weakening our war effort. Through our control of world shipping we could see that such minor tonnage of food was carried by neutrals from the Southern Hemisphere. The President was sympathetic, but the Allies would not hear of such a thing."

Mr. Hoover found within days of his arrival that, although Article XXVI of the Armistice Agreement promised the German people food, no supplies were going to Germany.

One main reason was the blockade. As a consequence, in the opinion of experts, the suffering of the German children, women, and men, excepting only the farmers and rich hoarders, was greater even under the blockade than it had been prior to the Armistice.

When Mr. Hoover remonstrated about Allied failure to live up to their promise, he encountered a situation which he described in his *America's First Crusade* as follows: "Destructive forces sat at the Peace Table. The life and future of twenty-six jealous European races were on that table. The genes of a thousand years of inbred hate and fear were in the blood of every delegation. Revenge for past wrongs rose every hour of the day. It was not alone the delegates that were thus inspired. These emotions of hate, revenge, desire for reparations, and a righteous sense of wrong were in fever heat with their peoples at home. England had just re-elected Lloyd George on a platform of 'Hang the Kaiser' and wringing from the enemy fantastic sums in indemnities for Britain. Clemenceau had secured a vote of confidence from the French Parliament with a blood-thirsty program of rendering Germany innocuous for all time, and collecting every centime of French losses. The oppressed races were there, with their recollection of infinite wrong. Every warring nation in Europe was exhausted, economically desperate, and most of them hungry. The governments of the Allies were committed to a maze of secret treaties dividing the spoils of victory. Their officials naturally wanted every atom of advantage for their people that could be secured. Their delegations at Paris had to go home to democracies still in these fevers to get subsequent parliamentary approval of their actions. Moreover every Allied official had a high regard for his future political life.

"Their statesmen were shackled by these malign forces. None of them were free to make peace on the 'Twenty-five Points' even if they wanted to.

"Our Americans had been more detached from the war, and had the least degree of hate. Our statesmen were free to rise above it. We had no ideas of acquiring territory or reparations or profit. What we wanted was for Europe to so order itself as to end wars. . . .

"As a matter of fact, the Allies never took the 'Fourteen Points' and the 'Eleven Points' from the 'subsequent addresses' any more seriously than any other of their eulogies of American idealism and flattery of President Wilson."

Mr. Hoover's first task in his anti-blockade campaign was to win the support of President Wilson. On January 1, 1919, he sent a formal memorandum to the Hotel Murat, the temporary White House in Paris. An abridged version of the memorandum follows:

"In a broad sense, there is no longer any military or naval value attaching to the maintenance of the blockade of enemy territory. . . .

"The problem of sustaining life and maintaining order in enemy territories revolves primarily around the problem of food supplies. . . .

"The contemplation of the provision of foodstuffs in the volumes necessary entails the provision of financial resources for the payment thereof. . . . The alternative of the use of internal [enemy] resources is now entirely impracticable under the effective financial blockade. . . . The second alternative, of advances by the Associated Governments, is impossible to contemplate.

"It becomes necessary, therefore, to at once consider some modification of the present blockade measures that will establish production and exports with which to pay for food and some other imports at as early a date as possible.

"It is our belief that . . . the solution of the entire problem cannot be obtained except through some measure of relaxation on the movement of enemy shipping to be operated by the enemy itself, in particular in coastwise voyage and to the Western Hemisphere. . . .

"A relaxation of commodity, finance, shipping, and corresponding blockades is the only measure that will protect the situation against the evils that may arise from actual hunger.

"It is not proposed that these measures proceed in the abandonment of blockade prior to peace, but that certain agreed tonnage, agreed commodities for import and export, agreed avenues of credit operations, and agreed channels of trade and communication must at once be established."

After careful study of the memorandum, the President countersigned the document, "To these conclusions I entirely agree. W.W."

From now on, and for four-and-a-half frustrating months, the President and Mr. Hoover had to fight Allied, especially French and to a lesser degree British, objections to the American proposal of ending the blockade of Germany at least partially. It took two months of negotiations to get the blockade removed even from the neutral and liberated countries.

A complicated maze of committees and subcommittees added to the difficulties of this struggle. Besides the meetings of the Big Four (Woodrow Wilson, David Lloyd George, Georges Clemenceau, and Vittorio E. Orlando), innumerable sessions were scheduled of the various subcommittees of the Allied and Associated Powers, such as the Council of Foreign Ministers, the Supreme Economic Council, the Supreme War Council, the Superior Blockade Council, the Allied Maritime Transport Council, the Shipping Control, the Supreme Council of General Supply and Relief.

After six weeks of negative and fruitless discussions, Mr. Hoover was more than happy at the arrival of Vance McCormick, Chairman of the United States War Trade Board. He proved "a valiant soldier of our policies," as Mr. Hoover expressed it. In his *Memoirs* he refers to the minutes of the various deliberative bodies enumerated in the preceding paragraph as "filled with McCormick's attempts and mine to get something done. But when we had argued up and down and round again we got nowhere except to the door of some other committee. The obstruction was being directed from the top.

"We finally persuaded President Wilson to raise the whole question in a meeting of the 'Big Four' where we could be present. The meeting took place on January 13th. I sat in a small chair behind the President's right shoulder. Vance was behind him to the left. The Allied officials likewise sat in chairs behind their Prime Ministers. In order to coach our champions in the debate we had to poke our heads out from behind. This bobbing of heads conducting a synthetic debate, where our principals did not know the technology nor the vast intrigues behind plain issues, was a little difficult. The President made a strong presentation and we managed to get acceptance of the principle that the Germans were to have food and if nothing else could be done they could pay gold and export some limited quantities of commodities.

"I thought that at least a door in the blockade was open. It wasn't. The Allied Blockade Committee refused to give the necessary orders. The British Navy refused to allow ships to go into Germany. The occupation armies refused to allow us to ship supplies across the frontiers. The Allied Committee in Berlin refused to allow the Germans to send us the gold. Every day for another two months we were given the run-around from one authority to another on some pretext."

Besides the multitudinous sessions in Paris, there were also many conferences with delegates from Germany, the principal ones being the Armistice Convention at Trèves on January 17 and 18, 1919, the Spa Conference which opened February 6, and the Brussels Meeting of March 13 and 14.

At Trèves Germany agreed to place its entire merchant fleet immediately at the disposal of the victors in order to increase the world tonnage for supplying foodstuffs to Europe, including Germany.

The fact that tonnage was thus provided did not, however, mean that food now moved into Germany or that the blockade was lifted.

At Spa agreement was reached for supplying at least 30,000 metric tons of pork products and 250,000 cases of condensed milk at prices fixed in the document, with the proviso that approximately six million pounds sterling could be spent by Germany for these purchases.

Again nothing happened. No deliveries were made until after the Brussels Agreement had been concluded on March 14, more than a month later. This finally became the instrument under which all the German operations at last proceeded. Its terms follow somewhat later in this chapter.

Herbert Hoover did not meekly accept the dilatory tactics which followed the Trèves and Spa negotiations. From time to time he sent President Wilson notes or letters. On February 1, 1919, he wrote: "There is so much obstruction that I despair . . . unless some great world opinion is brought to bear. . . ." Also, in the same letter: "The French obstruct the notion of neutrals trading with Germany, although it would alleviate both the financial problem and distress. We have no justification in humanity or politics in debarring neutrals from buying all the food they wish for their own consumption now that we have ample supplies."

On February 4 this tart reminder went to the President: ". . . There is no right in the law of God or man that we should longer continue to starve people now that we have a surplus of food." The letter continued in part: "I have worked consistently since arriving in Europe on the 25th day of November to secure these objects and I have to confess that although they have been accepted in principle in first one department and one government after another, they are constantly defeated by one bureaucratic and special self-interest after another of various governments." *

The *Diaries of Vance C. McCormick*, which have been privately

* The full texts of various notes and letters on the subject, written by Mr. Hoover, are to be found in Suda Lorena Bane and Ralph Haswell Lutz's *The Blockade of Germany After the Armistice, 1918–1919,* a volume of selected documents of the Supreme Economic Council, Superior Blockade Council, American Relief Administration, and other wartime organizations, published and copyrighted in 1942 by Stanford University Press, by whose permission these excerpts, as well as those from a letter to President Wilson dated May 14, 1919, and the Brussels Agreement which follow soon, are here reprinted.

printed, fully support Mr. Hoover's evaluation of the dilatory tactics employed and the motives behind the continuation of the blockade. A few quotations from the *Diaries* follow:

"February 28, 1919. . . . French and British anxious to hold blockade in order to prevent Germans getting raw materials to compete against them in markets of the world with their manufactured articles. Allies cannot get indemnity paid unless Germany can produce. . . .

"March 1. Meeting of Supreme Council. Trying to put through financial plan for permitting Germany to buy food. French blocked every plan. England and America dread consequences, as we seem living on a volcano. Two hundred million people not producing in world and many hungry.

"March 5. . . . French still blocking food deliveries to Germany. Situation there alarming. Cables all show state of revolution. Americans in Germany being attacked. My opinion we living on top of volcano.

"March 8. . . . At 3 P.M. went to Supreme War Council. Lloyd George made great fight. . . . Appealed for settlement now to save Germany and Europe from Bolshevism. Sonnino and Crespi for Italy agreed with Great Britain and United States and finally compromise worked out in which France made great concessions."

Prime Minister Lloyd George's "great fight" had an interesting background. As the Allied representatives kept dillydallying on the question of feeding Germany, more and more reports from sources acting independently of one another reached Mr. Hoover and reinforced his insistence that a dangerous situation was developing in Europe and especially Germany.

For instance, Economic Expert Alonzo Taylor, who had gone to Germany at Mr. Hoover's request to investigate the internal, political, and economic conditions there at first hand, on February 22 presented a voluminous report which stated in a chapter on "Social Unrest":

"The bread is heavy, indigestible and unsatisfying. There is little meat. The fat ration is so low that the cooking of food must be done without fat. The beverages are all substitutes. From every point of view of a normal diet, the food is revolting. Quantitatively the diet is too low. The entire industrial population, with the exception of the wealthy classes, is much below weight; and emaciation has proceeded to the point of lassitude and apathy, against which even the willing worker is hardly able to successfully contend. Women and children suffer the most. . . .

"Crime is rampant in Germany, offenses against the person as well as against property. The government possesses neither military nor police power, as the police service was practically disbanded after the revolution. Since many inmates of jail have been released, professional crime flourishes. The demobilized soldier carries into civil life the brutalities of a lawless warfare."

Also, Captain Harding of the British Embassy Mission to Germany wrote a secret report on a visit to Berlin, a copy of which reached Mr. Hoover. The captain observed, *inter alia:*

"Internal conditions in Germany together with the hopelessness of the outlook from an economic point of view have reduced the population to a state of despair in which there are only two classes, those who are afraid of Communism-Bolshevism or those who are converted to Communism either as an inevitable evil or as a possible solution. . . .

"Germany is bankrupt financially, whether the fact is openly admitted or not. Her industry is in a state of collapse owing to the lack of raw materials. She has no credit abroad, as witness the rate of exchange. She cannot feed herself until the next harvest. German labor is exhausted and discontented. . . . The territorial changes in the East and West also involve economic losses especially as regards food and coal, which will render recovery more difficult."

Even these reports by experts did not stir the "Big Four" to quicker action. Then, however, a dramatic episode, described by Mr. Hoover in his *Memoirs*, resulted in Lloyd George's "great fight" for saving Germany and Europe from Bolshevism. Mr. Hoover informs us:

"On the 7th of March Mr. Lloyd George asked me to call. With him was General [Herbert C. O.] Plumer, Commander of the British Occupation Army in Germany. General Plumer was in a state of emotion rare for a Briton. He announced to me in tragic tones that Germany must have food. That was no news to me. What he said later on, however, was helpful. He said that the rank and file of his army was sick and discontented and wanted to go home because they just could not stand the sight of hordes of skinny and bloated children pawing over the offal from the British cantonments. His soldiers were actually depriving themselves to feed these kids. I reinforced his arguments by mentioning the Communist governments now in possession of Munich, Hamburg, and Stettin.

"After Plumer left, Lloyd George demanded to know why I did not send in food. He said I had been appointed to that job. Thereupon, I turned on a torrent of expressions as to British and French officials that he ought to remember even in his grave. I reviewed their lack of cooperation since I had arrived in Europe and their universal sabotage and attempts to ruin our farmers, and made it about as clear as words could convey it. I pointed out that the British Navy was preventing the Germans from even fishing in the Baltic, which they had used as a food source before the Armistice. I stated the ultimate effect in history and the immediate future, and I reviewed the grasping and trickster attitudes of his British minions—whom I named as well as the French officials engaged in obstruction.

"Lloyd George was an overworked but reasonable man. His tone and attitude changed entirely. He inquired if I would deliver 'parts of that speech' to the 'Big Four.' I said that I would be delighted, but that it would carry much more weight if it came from him. He took copious notes. I then suggested that he place Lord Robert Cecil in complete command of the British economic representation in Paris where Americans were concerned. We could work with Cecil. To this he agreed. I further asked that he have Lord Robert represent the British at this meeting instead of Lord Reading. To this he also agreed. This explosion had an unexpected result. Besides the later effect of opening the blockade, it sent the obstructive officials packing off to England."

Mr. Hoover came to the March 8 meeting of the "Big Four," the published minutes of which in his opinion "greatly soften most of the pungency of the language, particularly my own," with a draft of an agreement for making it possible for food to reach Germany—the so-called Brussels Agreement of March 14, 1919, to which reference has already been made. It was approved by the "Big Four" and a delegation under the chairmanship of British Admiral Sir Rosslyn Wemyss appointed (with Herbert Hoover as chief American representative) to meet a German delegation headed by Edler von Braun at Brussels.

After the German delegation had once again been made to pledge that Germany would fully carry out the terms of the Armistice, the Agreement was communicated to it. Its salient points follow:

"1. The Associated Governments reiterate their decision to deliver to Germany the food now available in Europe for which payment has been arranged as soon as Germany shows her genuine intention to carry out her obligations, by sending to sea for that purpose the ships to be selected by the Associated Governments. . . .

"2. She shall have the right to purchase and import up to 300,000 tons of breadstuffs or their equivalent in other human foodstuffs, and 70,000 tons of fat including pork products, vegetable oils, and condensed milk monthly until September 1st.

"3. She must pay for this food and may pay in any of the following ways: . . . [here follow details concerning the export of commodities, the use of credits in neutral countries, the hire of ships, the sale of cargoes of German ships now in neutral countries, and so forth].

"4. She may export commodities (except those on a black list) to any neutral or other agreed destination. The proceeds from these exports must, however, be converted into payments for foodstuffs.

"5. . . . [Unimportant details].

"6. She may purchase and import foodstuffs, within the limits above stated, from neutrals who will, when necessary, be allowed to re-import equivalent quantities."

Again there was no thought of abandoning the blockade completely. For instance, the British continued to bar Germans from fishing in the North Sea. But at least food could now move in the direction of Germany. Mr. Hoover had won an impressive victory. He proceeded at once to set up the machinery authorized under the Brussels Agreement. At the same time he continued to fight for abandonment of the entire blockade.

Hate, however, was still so deeply ingrained among the Allies and even in some parts of America that Mr. Hoover felt impelled to issue a statement to explain, clarify, and justify his actions. The title of his pronouncement, which was released over his signature on March 21, 1919, was "Why We Are Feeding Germany." The statement was, in effect, a summary of the arguments with which he had operated for four long months. Its noble concept well merits its reproduction *in toto:*

"WHY ARE WE FEEDING GERMANY

"From the point of view of my western up-bringing, I would say at once, because we do not kick a man in the stomach after we have licked him.

"From the point of view of an economist, I would say that it is because there are seventy millions of people who must either produce or die, that their production is essential to the world's future and that they cannot produce unless they are fed.

"From the point of view of a governor, I would say it is because famine breeds anarchy, anarchy is infectious, the infection of such a cess-pool will jeopardize France and Britain, will yet spread to the United States.

"From the point of view of a peace negotiator, it is because we must maintain order and stable government in Germany if we would have someone with whom to sign peace.

"From the point of view of a reconstructionist I would say that unless the German people can have food, can maintain order and stable government and get back to production, there is no hope of their paying the damages they owe to the world.

"From the point of view of a humanitarian, I would say that we have not been fighting with women and children and we are not beginning now.

"From the point of view of our Secretary of War, I would say that I wish to return the American soldiers home and that it is a good bargain to give food for passenger steamers on which our boys may arrive home four months earlier than will otherwise be the case.

"From the point of view of the American Treasurer, I would also say that this is a good bargain, because it saves the United States enormous expenditures in Europe in the support of idle men and allows these men to return to productivity in the United States.

"From the point of view of a negotiator of the Armistice, I would say that we are in honor bound to fulfill the implied terms of the Armistice that Germany shall have food.

"Let us not befog our minds with the idea that we are feeding Germany out of charity. She is paying for her food. All that we have done for Germany is to lift the blockade to a degree that allows her to import her food from any market that she wishes and in the initial state, in order to effect the above, we are allowing her to purchase emergency supplies from stocks in Europe, at full prices.

"Taking it by and large, our face is forward, not backward on history. We and our children must live with these seventy million Germans. No matter how deeply we may feel at the present moment, our vision must stretch over the next hundred years and we must write now into history such acts as will stand creditably in the minds of our grandchildren."

Food moved so fast, once Mr. Hoover had the Brussels Agreement as his authority, that several cargoes from stocks in neutral ports reached Germany before the gold had been sent to pay for them. It helped the new democratic government of President Friedrich Ebert considerably to have this evidence of American confidence in the struggling republic.

One of the French plans for truncating Germany and thus lessening—so they believed—the danger of future German aggression was that of encouraging French and German industrialists to set up a Rhenish republic. Ebert nipped that scheme in the bud.

Another plan with similar purpose was that of having Bavaria secede and form an independent state. Premier Clemenceau was especially insistent in urging this upon President Wilson. This was quashed by the President and Mr. Hoover.

On April 21, the British, alarmed by the spread of Communism in Germany, sent President Wilson a request that Mr. Hoover increase the volume of food for Germany. Mr. Wilson passed it along to Mr. Hoover. The latter "could not resist commenting to the President" as follows:

"You and all of us have proposed, fought, and plead for the last three months that the blockade on Germany should be taken off, that these people should be allowed to return to production not only to save themselves from starvation and misery but that there should be awakened in them some resolution for a continued national life. The situation in Germany today is to a large degree one of complete abandonment of hope. . . . The people are simply in a state of moral collapse and there is no resurrection from this except through the restoration of the normal processes of economic life and hope. . . .

"We feel also from an American point of view that the refusal of the Allies to accept these primary considerations during the last three months leaves them with the total responsibility for what is now impending. . . ."

The President replied "thank you warmly" and stated that Mr. Hoover's memorandum would be "very serviceable to me indeed."

One month previously the food blockade had been relaxed as far as the former enemies Bulgaria, Hungary, and Turkey were concerned. While Mr. Hoover welcomed this action as "a hole through the blockade," yet he felt that Europe could never be rehabilitated unless the enemy countries were "brought back to work, to produce and export goods to pay for food, and to pay reparations." This in his opinion could be done only by further relaxation of the blockade.

Then, suddenly, there came a break in the clouds hanging heavily over war-torn, disillusioned Europe. On April 23, nearly six months after the Armistice, Lord Robert Cecil addressed the Supreme

Economic Council and urged his colleagues to "recognize the necessity in the interest of the economic interests of the European nations as a whole of taking such steps as would publicly encourage and foster at the earliest possible date the resumption of normal trade conditions both in Germany and in other European countries."

Again the French introduced delaying tactics. They pointed to the concluding articles of the Treaty of Versailles, which provided that the blockade was to continue until the completion of the treaty ratification by all Powers concerned—a matter that might, and in fact did, take months. They insisted upon using this clause as a club for compelling Germany to sign.

Once again Herbert Hoover addressed himself to our Chief Executive—as he had so often in the interim—four and one-half months after his first appeal to Mr. Wilson. An excerpt from the letter, dated May 14, 1919, reads:

"Dear Mr. President:

"I [must] express to you my strong view that we should not be led into joining with the Allies in a food blockade against Germany as a method of forcing peace. The margins on which the German people must live from now until the next harvest are so small that any cessation of the stream of food, even for a short time, will bring the most wholesale loss of life. It might be that the imposition of a blockade would be effectual in securing the German signature to the peace. I seriously doubt when the world has recovered its moral equilibrium that it would consider a peace obtained upon such a device as the starving of women and children as being binding upon the German people. If the Germans did resist, it is my impression that it would throw Germany into complete chaos and military occupation would need to follow in order to save Europe. . . ."

Finally, on June 30, 1919, the "Big Four" initialed instructions to the Superior Blockade Council to the effect that all restrictions upon trade with Germany, including the blockade, were to be removed immediately after Germany had ratified the Treaty of Versailles, without waiting until all signatory powers had approved of the action of their delegates.

This decision was communicated to the German delegation immediately after it had affixed its signature in the Hall of Mirrors at Versailles on June 28. Germany's ratification came a week later, July 7, 1919.

Humanitarian Herbert Hoover had won out at last.

4

FROM PRIVATE CITIZEN TO SECRETARY OF COMMERCE

Herbert Hoover left Paris in September, 1919, with his official mission as European Food Administrator ended. As he paid a farewell visit to Premier Georges Clemenceau, the sagacious French statesman, in a gloomy mood, observed, "There will be another world war in your time and you will be needed back in Europe."

How prophetic these words proved to be!

The Hoover family craved but one thing: to enjoy a respite of quiet and ease in California. Their yearning was not to be satisfied for long. For, as Mr. Hoover tells us in the second volume of his *Memoirs:*

"Soon after our return to California, I made discoveries which disturbed my ideas of a blissful living. I had come out of the seething social and political movements and economic chaos of Europe. I quickly found that America was not a quiet pool either. The country was in the midst of the inevitable after-war economic headache. . . . In addition, the bitter conflict over the Treaty [of Versailles] and the League of Nations cut across all issues. . . .

"A third hindrance to escape was the imperative obligation to finance and administer the Children's Relief in Europe for another year; and a fourth was to wind up speedily the business and the accounts of the various war organizations with which I had been associated.

"All of which required that we move to New York and Washington again."

In other words, Mr. Hoover simply could not disassociate himself from the problems faced by America as an aftermath to the First World War and from the international problems, among which that of the Republic of Germany was a major one, in the solution of which he had played so prominent a part.

His status as an unofficial, that is, nongovernmental personage lasted for only a year and a half (September, 1919, to March, 1921), but was as crowded and responsible as that of any official wielding political power. By March 5, 1921, he was a Cabinet member—United States Secretary of Commerce—a post which he filled until June 14, 1928.

The American Relief Administration had expired on June 30, 1919. The need for substantial aid, however, in Germany and elsewhere continued. Mr. Hoover, therefore, with the approval of President Wilson transformed the public organization into a private one.

Under his chairmanship committees were created in each state. Supplies still in stock from the governmental organization or en route when the official agency ceased were funneled into this organization. Gifts were solicited and an ingenious instrument was devised, known as the "food draft."

To make this novel instrument viable, it was essential to secure the cooperation of the American banking world. Mr. Hoover therefore addressed the following letter to every bank in the United States in January, 1920:

"To the Bankers of America:

"Owing to the slow economic recovery of Europe, the depreciation and exhaustion of its securities, and the shortage of export commodity production, due to the lack of raw material, the only hope of large sections passing the winter without going into sheer anarchy lies in their obtaining food supplies on some basis of support from America.

"Through the whole of Central and Eastern Europe the food supply of the people falls into two classes: first, the ration issued by the government, second, illicit circulation of food available to those who have a sufficient amount of money. The government ration is necessarily meager and nowhere near sufficient to properly maintain life, and must be supplemented. Under these circumstances, the scramble for such supplementary margin has placed the price of the illicit food supplies entirely beyond the reach of the great bulk of the population. To illustrate: A single ham outside the ration system sells for as high as one hundred and fifty dollars.

"In groping for a solution of this problem we have decided to undertake a measure on the following basis, as we believe it will contribute largely to relieve the situation:

"There are three to four million families in the United States with family affiliations in Eastern and Central Europe. Many of them are desirous of giving direct personal assistance to these relatives and friends. Some are endeavoring to perform this service by preparing or purchasing packages of food for overseas shipment. In some cases the packing and extra freight involved adds 100 per cent to the cost. We are proposing to solve this difficulty by establishing warehouses to carry stocks of staple foodstuffs in European cities where distress is particularly acute. We propose to sell, in America, orders upon these warehouses in the form of FOOD DRAFTS which can be transmitted to friends or relatives in Europe. We propose to charge the buyer of the FOOD DRAFT the factory cost of the food plus a reasonable margin to cover cost of transportation and insurance. Profits, if any accrue, will be turned over to the European Children's Fund.

"The object of this plan is to add to the total stock of available food supplies in Central and Eastern European countries. Under an arrangement set up with the governments of these countries, this food will be allowed to revolve outside the rationing system, with the hope that enough food will be injected to reduce the pressure on the narrow marginal supplies. The officials of these new governments are endeavoring to impress upon the American people that it is useless to remit money to a family in Central or Eastern Europe with the hope of improving the food situation. The sum total of food now available in Central Europe is insufficient to keep the population alive, and under these circumstances money thus becomes that much paper so far as nutrition is concerned. A hungry man wants food, not money, and under the arrangements outlined above we can meet his need. I feel that you will agree that such an enterprise, organized on a thoroughly business basis, will effect a considerable amount of actual relief abroad. I am informed that the President of the American Bankers' Association states that the Association will cooperate in all possible ways in the plan as above outlined. I do not believe, under the system which we have devised, that this will entail any great effort on the part of the banks, and the plan is one of such sympathetic character that the banks can well entertain it to aid the distressed people of Europe.

"Faithfully,

"(Signed) HERBERT HOOVER"

The response of the financiers was very gratifying. Some 5,000 banks undertook to help out and to issue drafts without any charge. The "food drafts," in multiples of ten dollars, were sold on terms which ensured the delivery of food of best quality at a fair price but also yielded a profit that went into the Children's Relief, a pure charity. This profit, on drafts totaling $8,000,000, amounted to more than $600,000 which went a long way toward the feeding of the six or seven million children still on the hands of the Children's Relief.

Mr. Hoover had hoped to be able to wind up the Children's Relief operations with the completion of the 1920 harvest in Europe. By May of that year it became obvious, however, that the governments of Europe, taken as a whole, were not strong enough to assume the added responsibility of providing adequate food for the children. Mr. Hoover and his associates therefore determined to continue the work over the winter of 1921–1922.

This decision meant that new sources of income must be found. The European Relief Council was founded, with Mr. Hoover as chairman, Franklin K. Lane as treasurer, and Christian A. Herter as secretary. The Council included the American Relief Administration, the Federal Council of the Churches of Christ, the Friends Service Committee, the Jewish Joint Distribution Committee, the Knights of Columbus, the Red Cross, and the Y.M.C.A. and Y.W.C.A. It was charged not only with joint action at home but also with the prevention of overlap in the work of American organizations in Europe.

The huge task of raising some $33,000,000 to continue the various programs in Europe for another year was solved, as described by Mr. Hoover in his *Memoirs,* Volume II, in the following manner:

"In order to have full state and local cooperation between all the organizations, it was agreed that the American Relief Administration state committees should manage the coordination of local fund-raising. We arranged for the initial appeal by President Wilson on December 13, 1920, together with proclamations by the Governors of the states.

"We dramatized the drive by banquets to the 'Invisible Guest.' The visible guests entered the room to find rows of rough board tables set with tin dishes. At the center of the head table, in the place of honor, stood an empty high chair with a lighted candle before it, symbolizing the Invisible Guest. When the company sat down, Red Cross nurses or college girls served them with the same food that we gave as an extra meal to the undernourished children in Europe—but with second helpings.

"The most profitable of these dinners was in New York on December 29, 1920. We had secured a thousand guests, at $1,000 a plate. General Pershing and I, flanking the Invisible Guest, made short addresses, and leading artists filled the rest of the program. Suddenly a gentleman whose name I never learned rose and suggested that I ask for more money on the spot. 'There is a million dollars here for the asking,' he said. In our invitations, we had stated that we would solicit no contributions beyond the $1,000 charged for the 'banquet.' I recalled this to the audience, and refused as politely as I could. Whereupon the stranger rose again and himself put to the house a motion that I proceed with a collection. It was carried, unanimously and enthusiastically. This brought, as he predicted, another million dollars. Later on, John D. Rockefeller, Jr., asked me to announce that he would give another million. So this one dinner brought in $3,000,000.

"Our joint committees put on similar dinners all over the country at an admission price of $100 to $500 a plate. I spoke in several cities and wrote many press releases and magazine articles in support."

The total receipts for this drive, which was closed in March, 1921, were $29,068,504.73. Children in eighteen nations, estimated in the earliest stages of the Children's Relief at fifteen to twenty million and then tapering off gradually, were built back to strength and in addition supplied with a vast amount of secondhand clothing, new cloth, shoes, and medical supplies. The "chattering glee of health-restored children" warmed Herbert Hoover's heart.

When one considers the large percentage of Americans of German descent who were citizens of the United States, and the further fact that Jews who had relatives or friends in Germany then had no Hitler atrocities to arouse understandable hatred of everything German, it goes almost without saying that the population of the young Weimar Republic shared in the benefactions of the "food draft" and the Children's Relief operations in a large measure.

This assertion is borne out by Edward Emerson's description, in his *Hoover and His Times,* of the Society of Friends' charitable activities in Germany and Austria: "Working under the direction of Alfred G. Scattergood . . . the American Quakers [Friends] distributed food and clothing at all German and Austrian cities with populations of ten thousand or more. Altogether they gave daily meals and needful garments to more than five million school children.

"The Quakers were aided by thousands of native volunteers and medical students working under direction of the German Food Ministry, which contributed thirteen million gold marks for this work.

"After a general meeting of the German Medical Society its commission of specialists for children's diseases established a system for the treatment of starving children founded on the Rohrer Index method of examination. This system, similar to the Pelidisi method, evolved in Austria at the same time, was based on the relation of children's weights to their ages. At the same time, though, other methods of diagnosis were employed.

"In addition to the Quaker's relief came innumerable private packages of food and clothing, sent by German Americans to their relatives and friends in the Fatherland. At the same time the American Relief Administration organized its food-draft system for European relief, whereby nearly 142,000 packages of assorted foods were distributed in Germany. The staple foods for these parcels were bought in the United States. . . .

"The prompt arrival of the food saved the children of the Fatherland for a coming generation."

To illustrate the dire need of relief in Germany Mr. Emerson quotes a German pastor and author, Gustav Frenssen, as saying after a visit to Mr. Hoover:

"There are no more laughing children in Germany, only little wizened creatures with heavy eyes and twitching shoulders, who move wearily along the streets where once they played and skipped merrily.

"I am not interested in political affairs. I don't know anything about reparations or about wars and peace parleys. I am a poet, a parson. All I know of the World War is how it has weighed upon the souls of our people. Its aftermath has been terrible. There will be a vast waste where the German Republic now tries to hold her own, if the children of the Fatherland are robbed of their childhood and are kept undernourished, so that their brains and souls are shriveled."

In concluding this section of his book, Mr. Emerson wrote:

"Throughout the many months while relief was rushed to Germany by Hoover, nearly 300 million meals were given to the hungry there. At one time there were 1,026,656 mouths to be filled. The children were reached through some 35,000 feeding centers in more than a hundred cities and towns of Germany and Austria. In Berlin and Vienna four great kitchens cooked free meals for more than 100,000 persons. In Essen alone a large central kitchen cooked for 20,000 workers and their children.

"By the end of 1921, when the crops had yielded a good harvest in the Fatherland, the American Relief Administration's gradual withdrawal from child feeding in central Europe caused the Quakers to take up the whole work. They did so with the balance of Hoover's relief funds, made available by him, and with new funds of $1,500,000 raised by German-Americans. This enabled the Quakers in Germany to continue feeding some 500,000 children a day. It lasted until the fall of 1922, when the gaunt spectre of Famine in central Europe at length was laid to rest."

The drive for the European Relief Council's funds was still on, albeit nearly completed, when Herbert Hoover once again became an official, this time Secretary of Commerce in the Republican Administrations of Presidents Harding and Coolidge. For seven and a third years he headed this branch of the Executive Department of our government, years during which he had again and again to occupy himself with the German problem.

Serving as Secretary of State with Herbert Hoover in the Harding Cabinet was the later Chief Justice of the United States, Charles Evans Hughes. A solid friendship sprang up between the two statesmen. The Secretary of State frequently consulted the Secretary of Commerce on international matters.

Both men early in 1922 were appointed to the World War Foreign Debt Commission to represent the Administration and the Congress. The other three members were Secretary of the Treasury Andrew W. Mellon, Senator Reed Smoot, and Congressman Theodore E. Burton. Even then Mr. Hoover foresaw the dangers of the postwar international debt and reparations policies. In his words:

"At one stage in the Commission's work, I proposed that we cancel all the debts incurred before the Armistice and require the payment in full of loans made after the Armistice, with a rate of interest equal to that which we paid on our own bonds. This would have strengthened our moral position, as we should have been asking repayment of advances only for reconstruction and not for war. If the Allies had paid, it would have been as good for the American taxpayer as the method finally adopted; and the probabilities of payment were greater. The British followed this plan and collected more in proportion from their debtors than we did—plus German reparations.

"I further proposed that for the small nations, the liberated countries, whose debts consisted mostly of relief loans, we set up each of these amounts as an educational foundation for the exchange of students and professors, as I had done in Belgian Relief. It would have resulted in far greater benefits to the United States than even the repayment of money."

His four colleagues on the Commission, however, insisted that Congress was not in a mood to approve these suggestions. They were therefore shelved.

Another matter that bothered the Secretary of Commerce considerably was the lavish, high-interest loans which American banks were granting to foreign countries without much regard for the question of their productivity. Mr. Hoover felt that, to serve any good purpose, such loans "must be adequately secured and should increase the productivity of the country of their destination. Out of such increase alone could they be repaid. Loans used for military purposes, for balancing budgets, and for nonproductive purposes generally would be disastrous." He also had his doubts about the methods of promotion of such loans.

Accordingly, Mr. Hoover alerted President Harding to the situation, who on his part called a conference of Secretaries Hughes, Hoover, and Mellon with representatives of the bond-issuing houses and banks.

On March, 3, 1922, following this conference, a public notice was issued to the effect that it had been agreed that all proposals for new foreign loans were to be submitted to the State Department for its opinion as to the political desirability or undesirability of each loan, whereafter the Treasury was to examine it as to its financial implication, while the Department of Commerce was to probe into the promoters as well as the security and reproductive character of the contemplated loan.

It was a period when, for instance, many municipalities in Germany were borrowing money for such nonproductive projects as gigantic sports stadia.

New York bankers disliked what they regarded as meddling by the three Departments of government, although it was clearly understood that these were to serve in a purely advisory capacity. Governor Benjamin Strong of the New York Federal Reserve Bank filed a vigorous protest with the Department of State. Mr. Hughes naturally consulted his colleague, the Secretary of Commerce.

Mr. Hoover replied in a letter addressed to Secretary Hughes under date of April 29, 1922, from which the following excerpts are quoted:

"In the public category it may be stated that credits from our citizens to foreign governments or municipalities have a different complexion from either internal credit operations or even of credits to private persons abroad, in that there is no method by which failure in payment of such loans can be prosecuted, except by the diplomatic intervention of our Government. There rests upon the Federal Government, whether desired or not, an implication that it will assist our citizens in relation to such transactions. To impose such lines of conduct on defaulting governmental creditors as will recover to our citizens their due is a path which has led to infinite complexities in international relations. . . .

"A further governmental interest lies in finance which lends itself directly or indirectly to war or to the maintenance of political and economic instability. We are morally and selfishly interested in the economic and political recovery of all the world. America is practically the final reservoir of international capital. Unless this capital is to be employed for reproductive purposes there is little hope of economic recovery. The expenditure of American capital, whether represented by goods or gold, in the maintenance of unbalanced budgets or the support of armies, is destructive use of capital. It is piling up dangers for the future of the world. . . .

"In the second category, that of moral responsibilities, the problem is also much involved, and argument can be carried to extremes; but again some middle ground does exist. Our citizens have had but little experience in international investment. They are not possessed of the information with regard to the security of many of these offerings which is possessed by the Government, or such offerings would not be entertained. A serious question arises in my mind as to whether the Federal Government has the moral right to withhold this information from its citizens. . . .

"Another instance of . . . moral responsibilities lies in loans to countries already indebted to the United States Government in large sums, who from every apparent prospect will not be able to meet these obligations. . . . Our Federal authorities must have some responsibility to inform our citizens (or the promoters of them) that these nations will probably have to confess inability to meet their creditors."

A letter written by Mr. Hoover on October 30, 1923, indicates that already at that early date he clearly foresaw economic disaster in Germany. The letter was addressed to General Henry T. Allen, former commander of the American Forces in Germany, and read:

"The breakdown in currency and the rapidly spreading unemployment in Germany is such that hunger and undernourishment are already spreading among the poorer classes in the large towns and manufacturing districts.

"It is always the children who are ground in the mills of international disputes. I know that many will feel it is a fault of one side or the other, or of some person or another that these things have come to pass amongst the German people. Whoever may be at fault, it is not the people who must go hungry, and honest charity inquires no further than that.

"Yours faithfully,
"Herbert Hoover."

Encouraged by this endorsement of his own view in the matter, General Allen started a new drive to feed German children through the American Society of Friends.

On December 8, 1923, Secretary Hoover again expressed concern over the German situation in a letter to Congressman Hamilton Fish, Jr., member of the House Committee on Foreign Affairs:

"In accordance with your request of December 1st, I send you herewith a report on the German food situation, made by our staff in Germany. This report is necessarily objective as any discussion of causes lies, of course, outside of this department. In short the situation is this:

"Germany is confronted with three major difficulties in her food supply. First, the breakdown in currency has caused a breakdown in the distribution of the last harvest, inasmuch as the farmers will not accept the practically worthless paper money. Second, German merchants are unable to finance the full annual margin of imports necessary to meet the usual deficit in domestic production because diminished exports reduce the available supply of foreign exchange, which is also to some extent being hoarded abroad because of economic chaos at home. Third, the widespread unemployment, as a result of which millions of the workers in the urban and thickly manufacturing areas are unable to purchase sufficient food even if it were in the markets.

"The normal processes of distribution from farm to town are breaking down and shops are gradually closing. The agricultural population is amply supplied with food, and to a less extent the smaller towns in agricultural districts, which are able to barter with the farmers. The better-to-do people of the larger cities and the more expensive hotels and restaurants are also supplied. Thus the whole burden of economic failure lies upon the working population, the old and disabled, and the professional groups in the larger cities and manufacturing districts comprising about 20,000,000 people.

"Germany must at all times import a certain amount of food. The margin of imports needed during the current harvest year based upon last year's experience (assuming that domestic distribution can be re-established) is apparently about 50,000,000 bushels of bread grains, 700,000 tons of pork fats, dairy produce and vegetable oils and oil seeds.

"Unemployment has long been almost complete in the Ruhr and will be only gradually restored at best. Outside the Ruhr an actual majority of the town workers are either unemployed or are employed part time and unemployment is increasing. Suffering is already considerable and failure of adequate measures will make a very grave situation indeed. As is universal in food shortages, the burden falls most upon children because their essential food in dairy produce and fats is always the most largely diminished.

"This situation is one of acute economic breakdown. Some imports will no doubt take place in the return for the diminishing exports but further measures will be necessary.

"The most constructive solution is the creation of a foreign commercial credit for food supplies, permission for which is now being sought by the German government. Such a credit operation would not only provide increased imports but through the domestic sale of these imports by the government it would give more substantial background to the new experimental currency and from such imports the unemployment doles and charitable public feeding could be conducted. Such a measure would of course be temporary, for the ultimate solution lies only in settlement of political relations, the re-establishment of currency and the rehabilitation of productive industry. This would require time in any event.

"Yours faithfully,

"Herbert Hoover."

The question of international debts, which had already cast menacing shadows over the economy of the world during the Harding Administration, kept plaguing President Coolidge, who assumed office on President Harding's death on August 2, 1923, as it did later the Hoover Administration which began in 1928. America had changed from a debtor to the world's largest creditor nation. Mr. Hoover as Secretary of Commerce was naturally deeply concerned and, indeed, officially involved, at least indirectly so.

Various addresses made his position known. The excerpts from speeches which now follow are reproduced because the Allied Powers attempted again and again to base their pleas for the cancellation of their debts on Germany's incapacity to pay reparations. Mr. Hoover stuck consistently to his opinion that there was no connection between the two and that it was morally wrong to construct such a junctim.

Speaking on "European Debts to Our Government" at New York on March 16, 1926, under the auspices of the Export Managers' Club he said:

"The most commonly remarked revolution in our foreign economic relations is our shift from a debtor to a creditor nation upon a gigantic scale. It is the father of much speculative discussion as to its future effect upon our merchandise trade. Alarm has been repeatedly raised that repayment of the war debts must necessitate the increase of imports of competitive goods in order to provide for these payments—to the damage of our industry and workmen. These ideas are out of perspective. Our war debt when settled upon our own views of the capacity to pay will yield about $300,000,000 per annum, although as yet the actual payments are much less than this. The private foreign loans and investments today require repayments in principal and interest of about $600,000,000 annually, or nearly twice the war debt. I have heard of no suggestion that interest and repayment of these private debts will bring the disaster attributed to the war debt."

In an address on "The Repayment of European Debts to Our Government," made in Toledo, Ohio, October 16, 1926, in support of the election of United States Senator Simeon D. Fess, he argued:

"Proposals have been repeatedly made over the last three years that the loans from our government to foreign countries during the war should in part or in whole be canceled, either for moral reasons or in the interest of economic stability. Less sweeping proposals have been made that the payments of interest and installments as required by Congress should be further postponed or moderated.

"These loans are often spoken of as debts to our Government. They are, in fact, debts owing to our taxpayers. These loans were made at the urgent request of the borrowers and under their solemn assurance of repayment. The loans were individual to each nation. They have no relation to other nations or other debts. The American taxpayer did not participate in reparations and acquired no territory or any other benefits under the treaty, as did our debtors. There is no question as to the moral or contractual obligation. The repudiation of these loans would undermine the whole fabric of international good faith. I do not believe any public official, either of the United States or any other country, could or should approve their cancellation. Certainly I do not. . . .

"America earnestly wishes to be helpful to Europe, but economic matters require a degree of realism that will do justice to the American people, as well as be helpful to peoples abroad."

Two weeks later, on October 30, at the convention of the California Federation of Republican Women's Clubs, held at San Bernardino, he said:

"One of the great recent problems in reconstruction has been this question of settlement of our foreign debt. It has been vital to the growth of stability and international commerce and international relations that we should arrive at some basis, some settlement or agreement by which we could dispose of that question, and with our government in the United States assailed by some individuals on the ground that the debt settlement has been too generous and assailed by some individuals that we are a Shylock on the ground that we have refused to cancel the debts, it might be generally believed that somewhere between these two extremes we have followed a fairly just and moderate course.

"To those who consider our settlements are too generous I might express the view of the American Debt Commission which has been supported so far by the ratification of Congress, that we should not hold the debtors to the bond which they signed but that we should make the settlements in the same common-sense relationship which should be maintained between debtor and creditor, whether governmental or private. Such a view requires that we should act generously to that point that would bring those payments within the reasonable capacity of the borrowers to pay. Such of those citizens who advocate that we should exact the full payment of the bond are asking that we undertake the impracticable, or that we enter into the land of injustice. Neither policy is consistent with American sentiment or American traditions, for we are anxious for the stability of all nations. On the other hand, those of our citizens who have advocated that we should cancel these debts, perhaps do not realize the reality of these obligations because they are an obligation of the American taxpayer and any derogation of them is but an increase in his burdens."

Meanwhile it was becoming increasingly clear that a new crisis was impending in Europe over the German Reparations question. The European creditors of Germany desired that a Commission be appointed to consider whether or not German reparations obligations should be revised, and they requested American participation in such a committee effort.

What ensued when this wish was transmitted to the American government is contained in a memorandum dated November 5, 1923, and written by Mr. Hoover:

"This morning Secretary Hughes asked for a conference of Secretary Mellon and myself over a proposal that an American should sit upon a Commission appointed to advise upon revision of German Reparations. We agreed that as we received no part of the reparations there should be no official participation, but it was desirable, in order to assist in solution, that Americans should sit on the Commission. We canvassed possible membership and agreed upon suggesting General Charles G. Dawes as the head of the Americans, with Henry Robinson and Owen D. Young.

"Mr. Hughes mentioned that the French demanded that the Commission should not reduce the $33,000,000,000 total of German reparations. He was doubtful whether with this limitation the Commission could be of any service whatever. I suggested that the Commission had better go as they would probably ignore the French demand as preposterous; that the situation in Germany was near breakdown and starvation again imminent; that persistence in these policies would some day bring destruction to France. The French had only one of two courses, to support democratic government in Germany or to face implacable hate and constant danger. In any event the Commission could do something in a desperate situation which was affecting the economic life of the whole world. Hughes said properly that the French policies were totally dominated by fear—and from their experience no wonder—but they had lost all sense of reality."

From the deliberations of this committee resulted the Dawes Plan, presented to the world on April 9, 1924. It provided for a reorganization of the German Reichsbank, the national bank of issue, under Allied supervision. Reparations payments of one thousand million (one billion in American terms, one milliard in

German) gold marks were to be made annually for five years. At the end of that period the payments were to be increased to 2,500,000,000. To enable Germany to make her first payment, a loan of 800,000,000 gold marks was to be granted.

The German government on April 16 accepted the Plan and the Reichstag somewhat later passed the enabling legislation. A conference of the interested Allied governments in London which sat for a month beginning July 16 also adopted it.

Most of the loan—$110,000,000 of an approximate $190,000,000, figuring the value of the gold mark at $0.24—was taken up in the United States. The rest was subscribed in Europe. S. Parker Gilbert, Jr., of the banking firm of J. Pierpont Morgan and Company, New York, was appointed Agent General for Reparations.

Germany's acceptance of the Dawes Plan was hailed with a sense of relief by the people of America. It looked as though German solvency were at last restored. The price paid for it, however, as far as the German people were concerned, included the repudiation of government bonds and old war loans. This act of their government wrought much hardship, especially in the middle-class citizenry.

Criticism was vociferous in some American circles to the effect that General Dawes had failed to insist upon a speedy withdrawal of the French armies of occupation from the Ruhr Valley and that the Dawes Commission had neglected to fix either a final figure or else the final date after which no reparations were to be paid. Accordingly, various political rivals of the general, to whom vice-presidential and presidential aspirations were ascribed, deemed it inexpedient to come out publicly for the Dawes Plan.

Secretary of Commerce Hoover, who knew how difficult international negotiations are, alone of all members of the Coolidge Cabinet had the courage to endorse the Plan in public, saying:

"The greatest single barrier to the economic recuperation of the world has been the unsettlement of German reparations. Malign forces have flown from it in unemployment, continued great armaments, disturbance of world finance, instability of exchange—all in a multitude of directions.

"Restoration of courage, enterprise and confidence in Europe, increase in industrial production, decrease in unemployment finally may react beneficially to our own people. The consumption of foodstuffs that will follow decreased unemployment will benefit the American farmer."

In his *Memoirs* Mr. Hoover commented: "The Dawes Commission succeeded beyond our hopes. It seemed as though Europe might be on the way to peace and progress."

While the formulation of the Dawes Plan, its presentation by the Commission on German Reparations, and its acceptance by debtor and creditor nations were under way, negotiations for a treaty of commerce between Germany and the United States were progressing slowly and painfully. This treaty had been preceded, during the Harding Administration, by the formal proclamation of peace with Germany and Austria in July, 1921, the treaty restoring friendly relations with Germany in November, 1921, the recall of the last American occupation troops from the Rhineland in January, 1923, and the subsequent return of Alien Property to the former enemy countries.

Under constant prodding by the Secretary of Commerce and his assistants, who desired a return to normal business relations with the Reich, the Treaty of Commerce was finally ratified at Washington on February 10, 1925, and by Germany half a year later, on August 20.

The treaty contained a most-favored-nation clause which forbade the imposition of import or export duties higher than those imposed on any other country. Only the previous customs agreements of the United States with Cuba and the Panama Canal Zone were to be exempted from this understanding.

When ratification of this instrument by the Senate was proclaimed, the new Rentenmark was again at par in Germany. The old Reichsmark had reached an all-time inflationary low on November 19, 1923, when an American dollar bought 4,200,000,000,000 marks. Now the fixed rate was 4.20 marks to the dollar.

The Dawes Plan, although its operation had made a temporary recovery of Germany possible, nevertheless proved inadequate to cope with the Reparations problem. Owen D. Young, who had been a member of the Dawes Commission, was invited by the interested nations to serve as chairman of an international committee to re-examine and, if possible, finally dispose of the Reparations question. His appointment became effective January 19, 1929.

This committee came up with the Young Plan on June 7, 1929. It is not apparent that Mr. Hoover had much to do with it directly. In fact, it joined debts and reparations, a junctim against which the Secretary of Commerce had fought energetically.

This Plan, too, proved its inadequacy two years later. By then Mr. Hoover was in his second year of the Presidency, and it devolved upon him to cope with the situation. This will be dealt with in the chapter on the Hoover Moratorium.

A thumbnail sketch of the provisions of the Young Plan is here inserted from William L. Langer's *Encyclopedia of World History:*

"Responsibility of transferring payments from German marks into foreign currency was to be undertaken by Germany and was to be made under a new institution, the Bank for International Settlements at Basel. On the directorate of this bank all the principal central banks were to be represented.

"Germany was to pay annuities ending in 1988 and increasing gradually for the first thirty-six years. But only 660,000,000 Reichsmarks were unconditionally payable annually. The transfer of the rest of the annuity might be postponed for two years.

"These safeguards were meant to cover any possible crisis in transfer. The unconditional annuity was secured by a mortgage on German state railways.

"The total annuity of 1,707,000,000 Reichsmarks was less than Germany had been paying with apparent ease under the Dawes Plan, so that experts and diplomats had no doubt that the Young Plan was a permanent settlement."

The plan was accepted by the German government on August 31, 1929, but upon demand of the nationalist right wing of the Reichstag had to be submitted to a popular referendum. The proponents looked for its defeat by the voters. Their calculation proved wrong: the electorate, too, approved it.

Shortly before his services as Secretary of Commerce were ended, Mr. Hoover had occasion to honor two young Germans and an Irish airforce commander who had accomplished the daring feat of the first nonstop flight from Europe to America in a heavier-than-air machine. They were Captain Hermann Koehl of the German navy and Commander James Fitzmaurice of the Irish airforce, accompanied by Baron Günther von Hünefeld, a German army flier.

They made the crossing in a Junkers monoplane, the *Bremen,* named after the city from which Koehl and Hünefeld took off for America via Dublin, where Fitzmaurice joined them. Starting on April 12, 1928, they had to make a forced landing thirty-six hours later in Labrador. But the fact remained that their plane had been the first to cross the ocean successfully in a westerly direction.

In Washington and New York they were showered with honors. At a banquet in New York the two Germans were seated on either side of the Secretary of Commerce.

Baron von Hünefeld proposed a toast to Mr. Hoover, saying: "You, sir, were the first after the war to give food to the German people. It shall never be forgotten in the Fatherland."

5

AMERICA'S THIRTY-FIRST PRESIDENT

On June 14, 1928, Herbert Hoover was nominated for the Presidency of the United States. He resigned as Secretary of Commerce, an office which had given him more than seven years of Federal Cabinet experience.

Three weeks before his election, his thoughts were once again directed toward Germany by the arrival, on October 15, 1928, of the lighter-than-air dirigible, the *Graf Zeppelin,* on its maiden voyage to America. Mr. Hoover sent a message of welcome to the bold aeronauts as the cigar-shaped aircraft spanned the Atlantic.

The day after the *Graf Zeppelin*'s arrival Mr. and Mrs. Hoover received Dr. Hugo Eckener, Captain Ernst A. Lehmann, Count Alexander von Brandenburg-Zeppelin, and several junior officers, as well as the American Lieutenant Commander Charles E. Rosendahl, furloughed from the dirigible *Los Angeles* to take part in the venture as an observer.

After Mr. Hoover had expressed his high appreciation of the successful trans-Atlantic flight, Captain Lehmann at the bidding of modest Dr. Eckener replied. "Had it not been for you, sir," he said to Mr. Hoover, "and your efforts for the relief of Germany after the war, thousands upon thousands of our people would have starved to death."

Dr. Eckener described the meeting and especially its political consequences in his *Im Zeppelin über Länder und Meere* (*In the Zeppelin over Lands and Oceans*):

"Hoover was very friendly and expressed some flattering thoughts about our ocean crossing. The photographs [of our meeting] appeared the next day in all larger newspapers. At that time I already knew enough about campaign propaganda to realize that Hoover's election strategists expected a favorable reaction to this picture on the part of the voters. An authoritative source was to confirm this to me two days later.

"I had been invited to a big banquet of the American steel industrialists and was seated next to Charles Schwab, the well known head of the Bethlehem Steel Works. Mr. Schwab, a convinced Republican, had seen the picture in the papers and asked me whether I had also been photographed with 'Al' Smith, the Democratic presidential candidate. I replied, 'No, Al Smith did not invite me to visit him.'

" 'Excellent,' Mr. Schwab exclaimed, 'that will cost him at least 200,000 votes.' "

Whether or not Charles Schwab was right can never be proved; however, that the so-called German vote had some relation to Herbert Hoover's overwhelming victory over Al Smith would seem to be further indicated by another occurrence described by Edwin Emerson in his *Hoover and His Times:*

"Hoover's last long speech in the campaign was made in the Coliseum at St. Louis in Missouri. There, seated beside him on the platform, was seen among others the tall figure of Charles Nagel, not long ago [William Howard] Taft's Secretary of Commerce and now a successor of the late Carl Schurz in the affections of the Germanic citizens in the United States. . . .

"Nagel's unexpected adherence to Hoover at the very close of the campaign won away many thousands of Missourians from the leadership of Senator James A. Read, one of Hoover's bitterest opponents in the Middle West. It also cost Alfred E. Smith many hundreds of thousands of votes, especially among women, in all the states known to have a large Germanic population."

Another man of prominence with a background of experience in Germany who urged Mr. Hoover's election was Alanson B. Houghton, Ambassador to Germany from 1922 to 1925 and to Great Britain from 1925 to 1929. Again quoting Mr. Emerson: "In a speech at Carnegie Hall before several thousand voters of Germanic descent Mr. Houghton recalled how Hoover almost alone had broken the hunger blockade against Germany, kept up by the Allies after the Armistice so as to cause the deaths of innumerable women, children and aged folk. Mr. Hoover, he said, put a stop to the iniquity and with the help of the Quakers fed 1,500,000 starving children a day. 'This was not politics,' concluded the speaker, 'but humanity.'"

Came the November election. Herbert Hoover received 21,392,190 popular votes as compared with Alfred E. Smith's 15,016,443. He carried all but eight of the forty-eight states. Of the electoral votes, he received 444, Smith only 87.

As they learned of the American election results, many Germans remembered who Herbert Hoover was and what he had done for them, and said so in letters to the President-elect. For those who had forgotten or whose memory needed refreshing, there were multitudinous reminders in the German press.

One of the weeklies with the then widest circulation in Germany was the *Berliner Illustrirte Zeitung*. On November 18, 1928, it commented:

"Herbert Hoover is not a man of the people compared to Al

Smith over whom he achieved an unparalleled victory; he is not a man of words, but of deeds. The slogan he chose for his Presidential candidacy was prosperity (*Wohlstand*).

"Everyone knew what he had done for increasing the prosperity of America during seven years as Secretary of Commerce under Presidents Harding and Coolidge. Indeed, during the past seven 'fat' years many Americans almost forgot what Herbert Hoover had already accomplished earlier. Europe, however, still remembers it most vividly. That's why in Germany, too, people realize that the President-elect of the United States is not only an outstanding leader in commerce and industry, but also a strong moral and ethical personality. It was Hoover who during the German occupation of Belgium organized and administered American food aid to Belgium. It was upon his initiative that American relief was started after the war for the hungry children of Europe. As organizer of this aid he rendered an unforgotten service to Germany."

The democratic *Vossische Zeitung* of Berlin editorialized on November 8:

"Herbert Hoover has been chosen President of the United States by an overwhelming majority. Hoover is an American, a 100% American. Nevertheless it was he who organized aid to Europe in a grandiose style. His will-to-do, his boundless energy, his technical know-how have won him the reputation of being a helper in need also in his native land.

"Big words do not impress him; simplicity does. The fact that Germany does not follow the apostles of doom, but went to work despite disaster, has elicited Hoover's praise and increased his interest. Long before his nomination for the Presidency he expressed his sympathy for Germany in decisive terms. . . . He declared that of all European countries he had the greatest faith in the development of the German people and the German republic."

The Center (Catholic) Party's *Germania* of Berlin had this to say on November 7: "Germany will never forget the debt of gratitude she owes Mr. Hoover. The war generation of underfed children have him to thank for the life-giving nourishment that reached their neglected bodies just in time. This accomplishment, in a measure and at a speed unprecedented in history, justifies the opinion that Mr. Hoover is a working machine which by speeding up can be brought to any desired degree of efficiency for the realization of any desired end."

The middle-of-the-road *Kölnische Zeitung* of Cologne opined on November 8: "This much can be said already today: a strong and pronounced personality will enter the White House—a personality which will place its stamp upon the foreign and domestic policies of the United States. . . . In questions of foreign policy Hoover will take a strictly American stand. . . . The only exception to his neutrality in principle will be Russia. Only recently he told a Russian delegation, 'The Republican Administration is not willing to recognize the Soviet Government, not only because we are opposed to Socialism, but also because we know that *de jure* recognition of the Bolshevists through the United States of America would give them new courage, whereas our refusal to recognize them would render a real service to Russia and hasten the end of the drama.' "

The nationalist *Tägliche Rundschau* paid this tribute: "Hoover's executive ability and administrative capacities are internationally recognized. In the Department of Commerce at Washington he has proven himself a statesman and organizer of highest caliber."

The *Vorwärts,* official organ of the Social Democratic Party of Germany, on November 8 predicted that the Hoover Administration would be characterized by "political aloofness from Europe and the League of Nations, concerning which the platform of the Republicans again expressly declared that America would not join it, whereas collaboration in technical and humanitarian work is to continue."

At the time of the 1928 election Adolf Hitler's National Socialist German Workers' Party, soon to be dubbed the Nazis for short, was beginning slowly to gain momentum. Its Berlin organ, *Der*

Angriff (*The Attack*), edited by Dr. Joseph Goebbels, on November 12 devoted only a few disparaging lines to the American election: "This much is already quite clear: if we don't liberate ourselves from the yoke of reparations by our own efforts, we won't be helped, as some optimists imagine, either by Mr. Hoover, America's newly elected president, or by any change in the French Government, such as has been necessitated by the sudden resignation of Poincaré."

To these excerpts from the German press could be added many extracts from letters written by German individuals of whom Mr. Hoover had never heard before, expressing their gratitude for aid extended, and by organizations such as the Association for Aiding German War Orphans of Essen, remembering his child-feeding program.

The German situation, which had demanded Mr. Hoover's watchful attention during his service as Secretary of Commerce, continued as a key international problem throughout his own Administration.

In the second volume of his *Memoirs*, in a chapter dealing with general peace policies, he included the following items among the "specific proposals" he made "in many directions" during his four years as chief executive:

Efforts to sustain representative government in Germany;

The moratorium on intergovernmental debts;

The "standstill" agreement upon German private debts;

A world economic conference to stabilize currencies and reduce trade barriers.

As regards the "efforts to sustain representative government in Germany," the President's guiding maxim in his dealings not only with Germany but also with other nations was contained in his inaugural address of March 4, 1929:

"The United States fully accepts the profound truth that our own progress, prosperity and peace are interlocked with the progress, prosperity and peace of all humanity. . . .

"The recent treaty for the renunciation of war as an instrument of national policy sets an advanced standard in our conception of the relations of nations."

The President here referred to the Briand-Kellogg Pact, also known as the Pact of Paris, for the outlawry of war, concluded in Paris during the Coolidge Administration on August 27, 1928. Fifteen nations were signatory to it originally, but the last of their ratifications was not deposited until July 24, 1929, after President Hoover had been in office for nearly five months. He then immediately issued a proclamation making public the terms of the pact, "to the end that the same and every article and clause thereof may be observed and fulfilled with good faith by the United States and the citizens thereof."

Germany was a contracting party of the Pact of Paris. In fact, the Weimar Republic is mentioned directly after the United States in the Presidential Proclamation, which begins with the words, "Whereas a Treaty between the President of the United States of America, the President of the German Reich. . . ." Had Mr. Hoover followed the English alphabetizing instead of the French, the King of Belgium and the French Republic would have preceded mention of Germany's President. Or, even if he had adopted the French alphabetizing in an American document intended for the American people—a procedure hardly thinkable in as rugged an American individualist and patriot as Herbert Hoover—according to which *Allemagne* comes first, nobody would have thought it out of place that he named France directly after the United States inasmuch as French Foreign Minister Aristide Briand, with Secretary of State Frank B. Kellogg, drafted the Pact.

The conclusion seems obvious that, in placing the President of the German Reich ahead of all other cosignatories, Mr. Hoover meant to call special attention to the fact that "representative government" now obtained in Germany, and that this was one of his "efforts to sustain" it.

The Pact which the United States and Germany as well as other nations signed was short and simple. It consisted of only two articles:

"Articles I. The High Contracting Parties solemnly declare in the name of their respective peoples that they condemn recourse to war for the solution of international controversies, and renounce it as an instrument of national policy in their relations with one another.

"Article II. The High Contracting Parties agree that the settlement of all disputes or conflicts of whatever nature or of whatever origin they may be, which arise among them, shall never be sought except by pacific means."

Thirty-one additional nations, including Soviet Russia, adhered to the Pact as of July 24, 1929.

In August of 1929 Mr. Hoover sent a friendly message of congratulation to President Paul von Hindenburg on the occasion of the observance of Constitution Day, August 11, as a German holiday. Hindenburg replied, thanking him for the "kindly thought."

While this exchange was taking place, Dr. Hugo Eckener had started on the first round-the-world flight of an airship with his *Graf Zeppelin.* Upon its successful completion the President on August 29 invited the "Columbus of the Air," as the American press dubbed the bold aeronaut, to the White House, and addressed these words of official welcome to him:

"It gives me great satisfaction personally to congratulate you upon this noteworthy attainment. It shows that the spirit of high adventure still lives. Its success has been due to the eminent scientific and engineering abilities of the German people, translated by your own skill and courage.

"You have already witnessed the universal appreciation of the American people of your accomplishment. You have given a most valuable service to aviation; you have added to the luster of your countrymen and have lifted the spirits of men with renewed confidence in human progress."

In a personal vein he then extemporized: "I had thought that the era of the great adventurers, like Columbus, Vasco da Gama and Magellan, was a thing of the past. Now I see such an adventurer before me. I am happy to note that the American people greeted you warmly."

During the Coolidge Administration Jacob Gould Schurman,

former President of Cornell University, had represented the United States as Ambassador to Germany. A man of grace and culture, he had "clicked" especially well with the Weimar Republic's internationally famed foreign minister, Dr. Gustav Stresemann, co-winner with Aristide Briand of France of the 1926 Nobel Peace Prize.

Dr. Stresemann died on October 3, 1929, after a tempestuous career marked by violent opposition of the German political parties of the supernationalistic right to his policies of international reconciliation. These were epitomized by:

The adoption of the Dawes Plan (1924) which took German Reparations out of politics;

The conclusion of the Treaties of Locarno (1925) wherein Germany, France, Great Britain, Belgium, and Italy bound themselves to respect, in the event of conflict to arbitrate, and mutually to guarantee the Franco-German and Belgo-German frontiers, besides ensuring Poland and Czechoslovakia against possible German aggression;

The admission of Germany into the League of Nations (1926) as a major power, with a permanent seat in the League's Council;

The end of the Interallied Commission of Military Control in Germany (1927);

The acceptance of the Young Plan to supersede the Dawes Plan (1929);

The pledge (1929) of the Allied Powers to evacuate the Rhineland in 1930, five years earlier than was envisaged in the Treaty of Versailles.

Despite these triumphs of Stresemann's diplomacy, Germany's economic and financial problems kept mounting catastrophically. President Hoover believed that a man with an industrialist's and financier's economic approach should now represent the United States in Berlin. Early in 1930 he sent Frederick Moseley Sackett to the German capital to succeed the seventy-six-year-old Ambassador Schurman, who had resigned some months previously.

Mr. Sackett had started his professional life as a lawyer, then had switched over into business, first as president of both the

Louisville Gas and the Louisville Light companies, and later as president of the Pioneer Coal and the Black Star Coal companies —all four of Louisville, Kentucky. His public service had included the positions of federal food administrator for Kentucky, president of the Louisville Board of Trade, director of the Louisville Branch of the Federal Reserve Bank, and United States senator from Kentucky.

Fortunately for Germany, the cordial relationship which had existed between Dr. Schurman and Herr Stresemann was now duplicated in the attitudes of Ambassador Sackett and Chancellor Heinrich Brüning toward each other. It had its beneficent impact upon the Hoover Moratorium and the "Standstill" Agreement, discussion of which follows in Chapters VI and VII.

The bicentenary observance of the birth of General Friedrich Wilhelm von Steuben (1730–1794) in the summer of 1930 by the German nation led President Hoover on July 16 to address to President von Hindenburg the following cable of appreciation for what George Washington's chief of staff had done for the cause of American Independence: "I am happy to have this occasion to address your Excellency personally and to convey to you the friendly greetings of the American people. General von Steuben's invaluable service in the cause of Independence is taught in every American school and is gratefully remembered by every American citizen. The people of the United States have also never forgotten the other great contributions to our National life that have been made by men of German birth or German blood in this country. They have influenced our educational ideals and methods, our scientific and technical thought, and our cultural and artistic life. They have greatly served the land of their adoption and have done honor to the land of their origin."

President Hoover's battles with German militarists and Allied chauvinists for feeding women and children during and immediately after the First World War appear to have been so deeply ingrained upon his memory that he offered a suggestion which, had it been adopted, would have rendered unnecessary the creation, in December of 1940, of the National Committee on Food for the Five Small Democracies, whose purposes will be explained in Chapter IX.

The President's proposal, in a nutshell, was that "food ships should be made free of interference in times of war" and should be placed "on the same footing as hospital ships."

The occasion for launching the suggestion was Armistice Day, November 11, 1929, when the President spoke in the Washington Auditorium on "Preparedness for Peace and Immunity for Food Ships."

During the address President Hoover pointed out that the "age-old controversy" about "freedom of the seas" in reality simmers down to "simply the rights of private citizens to trade in times of war, for there is today complete freedom of the seas in time of peace." He argued that "if the world succeeds in establishing peaceful methods of settlement of controversies, the whole question of trading rights in time of war becomes a purely academic discussion. Peace is its final solution."

Then came his proposal:

"But I am going to have the temerity to put forward an idea which might break through the involved legal questions and age-old interpretations of right and wrong by a practical step which would solve a large part of the intrinsic problem. It would act as a preventive as well as a limitation of war. I offer it only for consideration of the world. I have not made it a governmental proposition to any nation and do not do so now. I know that any wide departure from accepted ideas requires long and searching examination. No idea can be perfected except upon the anvil of debate. This is not a proposition for the forthcoming naval conference, as that session is for a definite purpose, and this proposal will not be injected into it.

"For many years, and born of a poignant personal experience, I have held that food ships should be made free of any interference in times of war. I would place all vessels laden solely with food supplies on the same footing as hospital ships. The time has come when we should remove starvation of women and children from the weapons of warfare.

"The rapid growth of industrial civilization during the past half century has created in many countries populations far in excess of their domestic food supply and thus steadily weakened their natural defenses. As a consequence, protection for overseas or imported supplies has been one of the most impelling causes of increasing naval armaments and military alliances. Again, in countries which produce surplus food their economic stability is also to a considerable degree dependent upon keeping open the avenues of their trade in the export of such surplus, and this again stimulates armament on their part to protect such outlets.

"Thus the fear of an interruption in sea-borne food supplies has powerfully tended toward naval development in both importing and exporting nations. In all important wars of recent years, to cut off or to protect such supplies has formed a large element in the strategy of all combatants. We can not condemn any one nation; almost all who have been engaged in war have participated in it. The world must sooner or later recognize this as one of the underlying causes of its armed situation, but, far beyond this, starvation should be rejected among the weapons of warfare.

"To those who doubt the practicability of the idea, and who insist that agreements are futile for the purpose of controlling conduct in war, I may point out that the Belgian Relief Commission delivered more than two thousand shiploads of food through two rings of blockade and did it under neutral guarantees continuously during the whole World War. The protection of food movements in time of war would constitute a most important contribution to the rights of all parties, whether neutrals or belligerents, and would greatly tend toward lessening the pressure for naval strength. Foodstuffs comprise about twenty-five percent of the commerce of the world but would constitute a much more important portion of the trade likely to be interfered with by a blockade."

The thoughts and energies of the statesmen of the world as well as of the peoples whom they represented were apparently so centered upon their economic worries—the Great Depression was just around the corner—that the "anvil of debate" for which the President pleaded was not invoked to discuss the suggestion. Also, at that time the idea of another world war seemed too fantastic to bother with an issue like immunity for ships in time of war.

Instead, hundreds of thousands of innocents unconnected with Hitler's challenge to the world were to perish.

One further incident in Herbert Hoover's relationship to Germany deserves mention before the facts about the Moratorium and the Standstill Agreement are told.

On February 2, 1932, a world disarmament conference convened at Geneva for a five-month session attended by sixty nations, including the United States and Soviet Russia. It failed to achieve tangible disarmament results, chiefly because of the divergence of views between France and other Powers. It did, however, produce a declaration in favor of equality of rights for Germany. The inherent inequality, which stemmed from Germany's being virtually disarmed under the provisions of the Treaty of Versailles, was being used day in, day out as one of Adolf Hitler's main arguments for winning adherents to his avalanching Nazi Party. The American delegation, under repeated instructions from President Hoover, worked for recognition of the German viewpoint. So strongly did the German delegation feel on this point that it abstained from further participation in the conference when the efforts of the British and American delegates to meet the German view were counteracted again and again.

An acceptable formula was finally agreed upon, following preliminary drafts by the British Prime Minister, Ramsay MacDonald, and his Foreign Minister, Sir John Simon. The head of the American delegation, Norman H. Davis, with the approval of

President Hoover, joined the other chief representatives of the "Big Five" in the following Declaration dated December 11, 1932:

"(1) The Governments of the United Kingdom, France and Italy have declared that one of the principles that should guide the Conference on Disarmament should be to grant to Germany, and to the other Powers disarmed by Treaty, equality of rights in a system which would provide security for all nations, and that this principle should find itself embodied in the Convention containing the conclusions of the Disarmament Conference.

"This declaration implies that the respective limitations of the armaments of all States should be included in the proposed Disarmament Convention. It is clearly understood that the methods of application of such equality of rights will be discussed by the Conference.

"(2) On the basis of this Declaration, Germany has signified its willingness to resume its place at the Disarmament Conference.

"(3) The Governments of the United Kingdom, France, Germany and Italy are ready to join in a solemn reaffirmation to be made by all European States that they will not in any circumstances attempt to resolve any present or future differences between the signatories by resort to force. This shall be done without prejudice to fuller discussions on the question of security.

"(4) The five Governments of the United States, the United Kingdom, France, Germany and Italy declare that they are resolved to cooperate in the Conference with the other States there represented in seeking without delay to work out a Convention which shall effect a substantial reduction and a limitation of armaments with provision for future revision with a view to further reduction.

"(Signed) J. RAMSAY MACDONALD, *Chairman*,
"NORMAN H. DAVIS
"JOHN SIMON
"J. P. BONCOUR
"C. VON NEURATH
"ALOISI"

6

THE HOOVER MORATORIUM

On May 6, 1931, our American Ambassador in Berlin, Frederic M. Sackett, arrived in New York on an urgent mission camouflaged as a vacation leave. President Hoover in the third volume of his *Memoirs* disclosed its nature:

"World commodities and securities continued to decline in the markets. On May 7th, our Ambassador to Germany, Frederic M. Sackett, arrived in Washington on an urgent mission. His purpose was to inform me that Chancellor of Germany Brüning had disclosed to him a detailed account of the disastrous financial crisis then developing in his country. Mr. Brüning had outlined the increasing economic strain as shown by the flight of capital, currency difficulties, unemployment, drying up of credits from abroad, pressures for payment of debts, and refusal to give renewals of accounts due from German banks to foreigners. The Chancellor had also set forth the danger from the Communist and Nazi elements, and the old military groups, now rallying to Hitler, all bent on destroying the representative government. However, Mr. Sackett thought that there was no danger of political or economic crisis in Germany before autumn.

"Aside from any economic repercussions which might affect us, it seemed to me that the United States had a broad interest in supporting the efforts of liberal-minded men in Germany, Austria, and Eastern Europe to sustain their representative governments against the political forces besetting them. These democratic governments were the foundation of any hope of lasting peace in Europe.

"I informed the Ambassador of my convictions and assured him of my desire to help, although I had the direst forebodings of the economic effect their situation might have upon the United States."

The President did not share his Ambassador's optimism that the crisis could be staved off until autumn. He considered the German Chancellor's message of such grave consequence that from May 7 on and through July 22 he kept a day-by-day diary of his discussions and actions to find a solution. This *Diary of Developments of the Moratorium,* hereafter referred to as the *Diary,* will act as guide through the intricate negotiations which resulted in what came to be known as the Hoover Moratorium on Inter-Governmental Debt Payments. It will be underpinned, as it were, by further documentary evidence in the form of quotations from cables and memoranda exchanged and statements issued. The *Diary* as well as copies of cables, memoranda, and statements are preserved in the Hoover Archives at Stanford.

According to the *Diary* the President told Mr. Sackett that "we, of course, were vitally interested, but it was difficult to see what could be done as we were not a party to reparations; that I felt that one of the fundamental difficulties of all Europe was the increasing armament, which had now reached the stage where the total expenditure of the civilized nations was nearly $5,000,000,000 per annum; that this sum amounted to many times the whole debt weight of the world, but that this did not so much directly concern Germany. I asked him if he thought a suspension of reparations under the Young Plan would do any good. He thought it would help.

"I undertook to make a study of this situation and to discuss the matter with him when he returned at the end of the month."

The President moved with speed. Dr. Julius Klein, Assistant Secretary of Commerce, was instructed to "furnish me with various memoranda showing the relation of war debts of the different countries; the inter-governmental debts; the military expenditures; the movement of imports and exports into and out of European countries in relation to the United States and between themselves."

Similar pertinent information, especially on "the interrelation of in and out payments of inter-governmental debts of the various countries" was, according to the *Diary,* requested from the Department of State.

Silas H. Strawn, Chicago banker, who had been president of the American Bar Association, but at this time was both president of the United States Chamber of Commerce and vice-president of the International Chamber of Commerce, was asked to draw out the delegates from Germany to the International Chamber of Commerce, meeting in Washington, as to their opinion concerning the situation in Germany. Mr. Strawn reported they took the gloomiest view.

The President on his part invited the Belgian delegates to a dinner at the White House. These men described conditions in Germany as very bad, both socially and economically.

Secretary of State Henry L. Stimson was apprised of the situation. The President "suggested to him that we might give thought to the fact that both the American debt settlements and German reparations were predicated upon capacity to pay in normal times; that of course there was no relationship between reparations and the debts due to the American government, as the American debt had been settled irrespective of any income of the Allied Governments from reparations, but that it began to look possible that the depression had reached such depths as to make the whole fabric of inter-governmental debt beyond the capacity to pay under depression conditions."

He told Secretary Stimson that payments for reparations and war debts totaled more than $1,000,000,000 a year between governments, of which the United States annually received about $250,000,000 by way of payments of war debts.

Conversations with Chairman Eugene Meyer of the Federal Reserve Board indicated that he and his colleagues were unusually optimistic about the world financial situation. They even intimated that Mr. Hoover was "seeing ghosts so far as the United States was concerned," and assured the President that nothing was going on that they and the American private banks could not easily handle.

According to an entry in the *Diary* for May 20: "Chairman Meyer informed me that there were very large amounts of German trade bills held all over the world, of which considerable amounts were held in the United States; that these bills are self-liquidating by the countries to whom the goods had been sold, and were therefore safe. He pointed out the very wide distribution of German Government and local bonds in the United States, and that the French Government had deposits in various American banks of probably six or eight hundred millions of dollars, the movement of all of which might be affected by difficulties in Central Europe. He felt our system could handle the shock; that the Federal Reserve could at any moment expand the credit facilities by the purchase of more government bonds, etc."

Meanwhile the first great financial crash had occurred in Austria, where the Creditanstalt, the most important banking house in the old Austrian Empire, had failed. A conference of economic experts from the various Allied Powers, assembled in Geneva, Switzerland, to consider methods of ending the depression, had terminated without any constructive suggestion. Chancellor Heinrich Brüning had announced that he would visit British Prime Minister Ramsay MacDonald at Chequers to discuss the situation.

The American Chargé d'Affaires in Berlin, George A. Gordon, had cabled: "Lately there have been many rumors in the press of Berlin to the effect that Germany was about to agitate for some definite alleviation of reparations obligations. The rumors, which have been cumulative during the past days and probably cabled to the United States by American correspondents, follow the lines that (1) [British Foreign Minister Arthur] Henderson was responsive to the idea at Geneva, (2) the visit of [German Foreign Minister Julius] Curtius and Brüning to Chequers will provide an opportunity for discussion, and (3) subsequent to the Chequers visit concrete steps will be undertaken by the German Government."

Also, the time had come for Ambassador Sackett to return to his post in Berlin. Before he sailed on June 2, the President, according to his *Diary*, "explained to him that I felt we would need to assist in the crisis, and that he could assure the German Ministry that we would endeavor to be helpful. I told him of my view that the whole reparations and debt complex could well be temporarily reviewed in the light of capacity to pay under depression conditions, and that he might advise upon his arrival the reaction of the German Government."

By June 5, scarcely one month after Mr. Sackett had delivered his alarming message, President Hoover was ready with a concrete plan. His *Diary* reveals:

"I asked Secretaries Stimson, Mellon and Undersecretary [Ogden L.] Mills to attend at the White House. I explained to them that I felt the European situation had been degenerating much faster during the past month due to the failure of the Creditanstalt; that we were endangered by a general financial collapse in that quarter; that while the Germans as yet had made no move I felt that their situation was weakening and that the political forces in motion might result in revolution and overthrow if any financial crisis should develop; that it seemed to me the drift of gold to the United States was paralyzing central banking institutions the world over.

"I stated that the idea which I had discussed with Stimson during the past two weeks of a re-examination of capacity to pay under depression conditions would not work fast enough. I had a definite proposal to lay before them. That was that we should postpone all collections on Allied debts for one year in consideration of all the Allies making similar postponements of reparations and all claims during the same period.

"I further explained that the world needed some strong action which would change the mental point of view and that I felt perhaps such an action might serve the purpose of general re-establishment of courage and confidence. I read them a rough memo I had prepared.

"Mr. Stimson favored it. Mr. Mellon stated his unqualified disapproval. Mr. Mills stated that there was no executive authority except so far as payments on principal were concerned amounting to less than $80,000,000 out of the $250,000,000. . . .

"I reiterated my position but said I thought it desirable to make further inquiries. . . . I stated that I feared we were in the presence of a great crisis."

As yet no mention of the plan was made beyond the highest officials concerned and outside the most trusted nongovernmental personalities. Meanwhile the situation was being aggravated by Chancellor Brüning's statement to the press in London that Germany must have assistance.

Senator Dwight D. Morrow, whom the President took into his confidence at this stage of his efforts, reported that New York bankers were panicky over the situation in Germany and Austria. According to Mr. Hoover's *Diary* of June 9 the senator believed that "the rapidly developing situation in Germany would bring the world to a realization that something real must be done. [He cautioned, however, that] we must allow it [the situation] to develop a little before we could present my [the President's] plan to political leaders on both sides and to the governments of Europe with any hope of success."

Other advisers were more urgent than Senator Morrow. Owen D. Young, Ogden L. Mills, and S. Parker Gilbert urged immediate action without even waiting for consultation with political leaders. They pointed out that the statements made in London by the German cabinet members had precipitated runs on Central European banks. Secretary Mellon, now in Europe, reversed his position and telephoned urgently that action must be taken immediately. The American Embassy in London cabled on June 15 that Montagu Norman, Governor of the Bank of England, believed immediate relief was needed for Germany.

The President decided that he could not act without approval of the leaders of both political parties if he hoped to secure the necessary cooperation by Congress. He enlisted the aid of Bernard M. Baruch to line up the Democrats.

Also, he had Secretary of State Stimson suggest to Ambassador Sackett that "a clear-cut statement signed by the highest German authority of the need of action" was most desirable.

The German authorities readily obliged. The message, signed by President von Hindenburg and dated June 20, 1931, reached Mr. Hoover as he returned from several speaking engagements in the Middle West. Its wording follows:

"The need of the German people which has reached a climax compels me to adopt the unusual step of addressing you personally.

"The German people have lived through years of great hardship, culminating in the past winter, and the economic recovery hoped for in the spring of this year has not taken place. I have, therefore, now taken steps, in virtue of the extraordinary powers conferred upon me by the German Constitution, to insure the carrying out of the most urgent tasks confronting the Government and to secure the necessary means of subsistence for the unemployed. These measures radically affect all economic and social conditions and entail the greatest sacrifices on the part of all classes of the population. All possibilities of improving the situation by domestic measures without relief from abroad are exhausted. The economic crisis from which the whole world is suffering hits particularly hard the German nation which has been deprived of its reserves by the consequences of the war. As the developments of the last few days show, the whole world lacks confidence in the ability of the German economic system to work under the existing burdens. Large credits received by us from foreign countries have been withdrawn. Even in the course of the last few days the Reichsbank has had to hand over to foreign countries one third of its reserves of gold and foreign currency. The inevitable consequence of these developments must be a further serious restriction of economic life and an increase in the numbers of unemployed who already amount to more than one third of the total number of industrial workers. The efficiency, will to work, and discipline of the German people justify confidence in the strict observance of the great fixed private obligations and loans with which Germany is burdened. But, in order to maintain its course and the confidence of the world in its capacity, Germany has urgent need of relief. The relief must come at once if we are to avoid serious misfortune for ourselves and others. The German people must continue to have the possibility of working under tolerable living conditions. Such relief would be to the benefit of all countries in its material and moral effect on the whole crisis. It would improve the situation in other countries and materially reduce the danger to Germany due to internal and external tension caused by distress and despair.

"You, Mr. President, as the representative of the great American people, are in a position to take the steps by which an immediate change in the situation threatening Germany and the rest of the world could be brought about."

Later, in an address in Madison Square Garden, New York, on October 31, 1932, Mr. Hoover characterized the message from the German chief of state as "an appeal of a character without precedent in diplomatic history. That appeal was for the preservation of a great people, that I should use the good offices and prestige of the United States for their rescue."

From now on, day in, day out and far into the night, President Hoover and his associates, especially Mr. Baruch, Senator Morrow, Secretary Stimson, and Under-Secretary Mills, patiently explained the Moratorium Plan to senators and congressmen. Minute details as to who saw whom and what the various reactions were, are to be found in the President's *Diary*.

Presidential Secretary Theodore G. Joslin in his *Hoover off the Record* commented on this phase of the negotiations: "The President . . . went immediately to work lining up members of Congress right and left in behalf of the proposal he was about to make. One by one, those senators and congressmen who happened to be in Washington were called to the office, where, with infinite care, he told them in confidence of the situation, of the proposal he was to make and asked for their help. They lined up with him. Without this assurance, he could not convincingly pledge the American Government, for Europe had seen Congress upset agreements before.

"Interspersing these conferences were telephone calls throughout the country and beyond its borders. Effort was made to find every member of Congress who was away from Washington. The operators were given the lists of names and told to go to it—first come, first served.

"If anyone thinks it is an easy matter to locate senators and congressmen during a recess, try it once. A few were reached quickly, others only after the greatest difficulty. Some were actually hours' rides from the nearest telephone. Messengers had to be sent to them. They had to come in to the nearest telephone. Of course, those difficult to run down were the ones it was most essential to find. They were in the mountains, or at the seashore; on motor trips or out of the country. In some instances, the investigating services of the Government were used to track the members down. We cornered one senator in Canada and got him to a drugstore telephone. Some were taken out of meetings they were attending, from hotel lobbies, off the golf courses and the streets.

"One after another they came on the line and were connected with the President. To each of them he told the story with the same care as if they were sitting down with him in his office. For hours upon hours he sat at the telephone on his desk, and for more hours in his study at night.

"The response was all that could be hoped for. Some members tried to welch afterward, but they came through at the time. They were thoroughly frightened, whatever they may say today. They forgot political considerations. They saw the necessity of action. They agreed to give the proposal their support."

To prepare the public for what was in the offing, the President on June 19 issued a press release:

"Since my return from the Central West yesterday I have conferred with those leaders of both political parties who are present in Washington with respect to certain steps that we might take to assist in economic recovery both here and abroad.

"These conversations have been particularly directed to strengthening the situation in Germany. No definite plans or conclusions have yet been arrived at, but the response which I have met from the leaders of both parties is most gratifying.

"Any statement of any plan or method is wholly speculative and is not warranted by the facts."

What ensued from there on is described by Mr. Hoover in the third volume of his *Memoirs:*

"As soon as I was sure of enough Democratic votes in addition to the Republican to pass legislation, I instructed the Secretary of State to communicate the proposal to the different governments.

"Although I had urgently impressed upon all members of Congress that the subject must be confidential until we had had time to lay it before the other governments, Senator [William H.] King of Utah told it 'off the record' to reporters with the result that a garbled and antagonistic account went out to the press both at home and abroad. I was, therefore, compelled either to risk displeasing the other governments by not giving them the courtesy of a few days for consultation or, alternatively, to have my proposal discussed by their people in a garbled and destructive form. Therefore, on the 20th of June I issued a statement to the press for release the following morning."

Because of its transcendent importance the full text of the proposal is here reproduced, except that between the first paragraph and the rest of the statement there was interposed a long list of names of members of the Senate and House who had by then approved. These names have been omitted.

The Moratorium Plan:

"The American Government proposes the postponement during one year of all payments on inter-governmental debts, reparations and relief debts, both principal and interest, of course, not including obligations of governments held by private parties.

"Subject to confirmation by Congress, the American Government will postpone all payments upon the debts of foreign governments to the American Government payable during the fiscal year beginning July 1 next, conditional on a like postponement for one year of all payments on inter-governmental debts owing the important creditor powers.

"The purpose of this action is to give the forthcoming year to the economic recovery of the world and to help free the recuperative forces already in motion in the United States from retarding influences from abroad.

"The world wide depression has affected the countries of Europe more severely than our own. Some of these countries are feeling to a serious extent the drain of this depression on national economy. The fabric of intergovernmental debts, supportable in normal times, weighs heavily in the midst of this depression.

"From a variety of causes arising out of the depression such as the fall in the price of foreign commodities and the lack of confidence in economic and political stability abroad there is an abnormal movement of gold into the United States which is lowering the credit stability of many foreign countries. These and the other difficulties abroad diminish buying power for our exports and in a measure are the cause of our continued unemployment and continued lower prices to our farmers.

"Wise and timely action should contribute to relieve the pressure of these adverse forces in foreign countries and should assist in the reestablishment of confidence, thus forwarding political peace and economic stability in the world.

"Authority of the President to deal with this problem is limited as this action must be supported by the Congress. It has been assured the cordial support of leading members of both parties in the Senate and the House. The essence of this proposition is to give time to permit debtor governments to recover their national prosperity. I am suggesting to the American people that they be wise creditors in their own interest and be good neighbors.

"I wish to take this occasion also to frankly state my views upon our relations to German reparations and the debts owed to us by the allied Governments of Europe. Our government has not been a party to, or exerted any voice in determination of reparation obligations. We purposely did not participate in either general reparations or the division of colonies or property. The repayment of debts due to us from the Allies for the advance for war and reconstruction were settled upon a basis not contingent upon German reparations or related thereto. Therefore, reparations is necessarily wholly a European problem with which we have no relation.

"I do not approve in any remote sense of the cancellation of the debts to us. World confidence would not be enhanced by such action. None of our debtor nations have ever suggested it. But as the basis of the settlement of these debts was the capacity under normal conditions of the debtor to pay, we should be consistent with our own policies and principles if we take into account the abnormal situation now existing in the world. I am sure the American people have no desire to attempt to extract any sum beyond the capacity of any debtor to pay and it is our view that broad vision requires that our government should recognize the situation as it exists.

"This course of action is entirely consistent with the policy which we have hitherto pursued. We are not involved in the discussion of strictly European problems, of which the payment of German reparations is one. It represents our willingness to make a contribution to the early restoration of world prosperity in which our own people have so deep an interest.

"I wish further to add that while this action has no bearing on the conference for limitation of land armaments to be held next February, inasmuch as the burden of competitive armaments has contributed to bring about this depression, we trust that by this evidence of our desire to assist we shall have contributed to the good will which is so necessary in the solution of this major question."

The third from the last paragraph was included because a flood of propaganda had inundated America, urging that the United States cancel the war debts.

This propaganda was not confined to our country. As early as December 13, 1929, S. Parker Gilbert, the Agent General for Reparation Payments, sent a revealing cable from Paris to the American Secretary of State. Discussing the Young Plan Conference scheduled for The Hague, Holland, January 3, 1930, Mr. Gilbert wired: "The fundamental object of [Chancellor of the Exchequer Philip] Snowden and the British Treasury is the same already stubbornly pursued for many years by the British Treasury, viz., to bring about at the expense of the United States the all-round cancellation of war debts and reparations. For this reason Snowden and the Treasury have always opposed the Mellon-Baldwin debt funding agreement and the Dawes Plan, the two principal commitments to the policy of debt collection. They will for the same reason oppose the final acceptance of the Young Plan as long as any chance exists of precipitating a situation in which the whole debts and reparations question could be reopened in such a way as to put the burden on the United States. Throughout the five years of the Dawes Plan the Treasury has hoped for an economic crisis in Germany, its theory being that such a crisis would put pressure on the United States to reopen the debt question and that the growing volume of American investments in Germany would greatly increase this pressure. . . ."

Before recording how the Moratorium Plan was received by the American public and the foreign Powers concerned, a passage in Joslin's *Hoover Off the Record* merits attention:

"Throughout this period, Mr. Hoover was putting in eighteen-hour days. Tense though he was, he controlled his emotions. Only once when conditions were darkest did he remark: 'It is a cruel world.'

"But the more difficult the problem became, the more determinedly he settled down into the harness, all of this without the slightest intimation of what he was doing getting to the public. Until now put into words, it has not been known. The reason was he had to be absolutely sure of his facts and his plan before anything was said at all. Otherwise, better no effort at all.

"It soon became apparent that the action he had been contemplating absolutely had to be taken. I found him engaged in writing one evening when I entered his office to make a report. I started to leave, but he asked me to wait. He kept on writing. As was so often the case whenever he was engaged on something out of the ordinary, he pressed down hard on the pencil, breaking the lead. He tossed it aside, took another and repeated the process again and again. Looking up finally, he said:

" 'This is perhaps the most daring statement I ever thought of issuing.'

"Then he read it to me. It was the original draft of the moratorium proposal. And let me say right here that it differed little in construction from the formal announcement he made public some weeks later. He already had decided what he was going to say and do—if he could get the necessary cooperation. In that as all other instances, a considerable part of his labors had to be, not in initiating the activities, but in getting others to go along with him so he could project them for the common good."

The American press hailed the proposal with astonishing relative unanimity. Moreover, in thousands of telegrams and letters reaching the White House, Americans from all walks of life endorsed the President's proposal.

In England a much read and much commented-on editorial in the *Week-End Review* had alerted the British public to the seriousness of the situation in Germany only shortly before President Hoover announced his Moratorium Plan. The editorial predicted that a revolution was likely to come in Germany unless relief were brought quickly. It continued:

"What would a revolution mean to us? It would be, we must assume, either a Nazi or a Communist enterprise. If it were Communist, the position becomes only too clear. Communist Germany joins Communist Russia, and with them go Lower Austria, Latvia, Estonia, Lithuania, Poland, and probably several more. Europe as we have known it disappears.

"The Soviet frontier is brought nearer London than Newcastle is. The hypothesis, moreover, is much less remote than is commonly supposed. That the Communist bogey is exploited by a somewhat selfish propaganda must not be allowed to prejudice appreciation of the reality behind it.

"Assume, though, that it is the Nazis and not the Communists who bring about a *putsch* in the autumn. Hitler does not look like a Mussolini, but a Nazi government could only survive by producing one. It would be clearly forced to adopt Fascist methods with more than Fascist severity in order to keep powers in a Germany whose blight next winter must, in any event, require strong measures. If the Nazis succeed they become more extreme Fascists; if they fail, the Communists take over from them. In either case Europe has lost a civilizing, progressive element, whose disappearance must bring permanent impoverishment.

"Suppose all the same that neither of these things happens and that the present state survives. On the present basis it will survive only by sacrificing all that means anything to it or Europe. It will become the materialist, irritable and dangerous Germany which already can be seen emerging in Nazi and Communist crudities, but without the courage of its convictions or the power to give effect to them."

After warnings like these, to which should be especially added those of Montagu C. Norman, Governor of the Bank of England, the British press and public were quite ready to endorse the Plan.

Not so the French. They were peeved, to begin with, that they were informed only shortly before President Hoover, because of a "leak" to the press, made his plan public. They also inferred from Secretary Mellon's visit to London that the Americans and British were "ganging up" against France.

Secretary Stimson, as a matter of fact, had informed all nations concerned before the Plan was released for publication and had explained why the interval between communicating it to them and to the press had been so short.

As to their fears of collusion between Washington and London, he assured the French government that "no preliminary discussion of this Plan has been had with any other nation." He further informed the French through our Embassy that the President had requested Mr. Mellon to go to Paris to "make it clear to the members of the French Government that his conversations in London were directed only to discovering the extent and urgency of the difficulties in the financial situation in Germany and not to making any plans of any nature for the President to act." He requested of the American Ambassador, "When Secretary Mellon arrives, please show him this telegram."

Mr. Stimson also cabled directly to Mr. Mellon in London concerning the misgivings of the French that "it is also important that they should know from high authority how the critical developments in German withdrawals on Friday and Saturday in the end forced the President's action. We are informed that there would have been a financial disaster in Germany today had he not acted as he did. France should be reassured by these facts and they should prevent her from entertaining any idea that she has been left out of any carefully calculated plan intentionally."

French press reaction was summarized in a telegram from Ambassador Walter E. Edge in Paris to the Secretary of State dated 11.00 P.M. June 23, 1931:

"The French press continued today with a few exceptions to turn a deaf ear to President Hoover's proposal for a one year debt and reparations moratorium. The tone of the majority of newspapers was frankly hostile; in some instances it was hysterically abusive; but on the other hand as contrasted with yesterday's unanimity there were a few suggestions, notably in *Le Temps* and *Le Matin,* that it would be well to consider the American proposal and perhaps support it under certain conditions.

"The opposition in the press centered increasingly on the issue of unconditional reparations payments. It was argued that for France to forego the sums involved in these payments would mean not only serious material sacrifice but a death blow to the Young Plan. French opinion was so intransigent on this point that many editors pointed out that it would be political suicide for the Laval Government to ignore the general criticism.

"Aside from the specific reproach the cumulative effect of President Hoover's sudden Moratorium announcement, following so soon upon the *Anschluss* and the Chequers Conference and made, as the press claimed, without prior warning to the French Government, contributed a storm of newspaper criticism so severe that many editors feared its possible effect on the Government."

[By *Anschluss* is meant the union of Austria with the German Reich. On March 20, 1931, the two countries had agreed, as a first step toward a merger, to establish a customs union. There were violent protests by France, Italy, Czechoslovakia, and other states against this project, which the objectors held were contrary to certain treaty obligations. A decision of the World Court at The Hague was invoked, which interdicted the *Anschluss.* The Chequers Conference was a meeting, already referred to earlier, between German Chancellor Brüning, Foreign Minister Curtius and their experts on the one hand, and British Prime Minister MacDonald and his co-workers on the other, held on June 7, 1931, at the country home of British prime ministers, Chequers, near London.]

In Germany there was jubilation and gratitude. German statesmen, especially in times of crisis, were exceedingly meticulous about giving interviews. They usually insisted on having every word read back to them or subjected to their scrutiny, and often upon having the Federal Press Department check upon journalistic form and content.

All the more surprised was I when, on the Sunday (June 21) on which the text of the Moratorium Plan appeared in the German Press, Dr. Curtius, a cautious, careful statesman and lawyer, spontaneously expressed his views to me for publication by The Associated Press. Acting on a tip from a minor Foreign Office functionary, that Dr. Curtius was taking a stroll in Berlin's popular Tiergarten, comparable to New York's Central Park, I finally traced him through the fact that a team of secret service men, placed at intervals and endeavoring hard to camouflage their identities by a somewhat strained casualness, acted as "markers" for me, indicating the direction in which the Foreign Minister was taking his Sunday constitutional.

The story which resulted was released by The Associated Press. It was the type of "exclusive" that is the dream of every journalist. The text follows:

"BERLIN, June 21 (AP)—Foreign Minister Julius Curtius, in a statement to the Associated Press today, expressed the gratitude of his whole nation at President Hoover's proposal.

" 'He has placed his finger on the sore spot,' said this usually unemotional statesman, 'and now comes one of those rare moments in history when all reserve should be thrown aside. I can only say that we endorse with unqualified joy the heroic declaration which President Hoover has made.'

"Dr. Curtius smiled broadly and gestured with animation as he described the President's offer as a 'gift from Heaven.'

" 'It is a heroic act for him completely to swing the helm and mobilize America's indomitable will in the solution of the world crisis. What I admire particularly is the President's realization that what is needed now more than anything else is restoration of confidence.

" 'I don't care what people say about lower prices and such-like economic factors—at the bottom of it all is lack of confidence. That is the decisive factor, and Mr. Hoover has been quick to see it and to realize that that is where decisive action is needed.

" 'Through you and for the German people, I express our deep appreciation for the services of Ambassador Frederic M. Sackett in bringing about this action. This wise, quiet man long has advocated solution along the lines which Mr. Hoover now proposes.

" 'We Germans know how he worked on our problem in his unobtrusive, statesmanlike manner.'

"Dr. Curtius turned then to the work of the German Government itself.

" 'I think,' he said, 'the time has come to say that our foreign policy of conciliation and of international cooperation is now fully justified.

" 'It took an iron nerve to hold out when on every side there was clamor for haste.

" 'Chancellor Brüning and his whole Cabinet have clung tenaciously to the position that the United States was the deciding factor and that nothing should be done to check the efforts of the American Government.

" 'Our conference with Prime Minister MacDonald at Chequers now is shown to have been more than justified, for by a providential coincidence your Secretary of the Treasury, Mr. Mellon, reached London almost immediately after we had left.

" 'There is one more thing I want to tell you,' said Dr. Curtius. 'That is, that we must not forget that next to the United States, France makes the greatest sacrifice in accepting President Hoover's plan.

" 'I do not hesitate to recognize this truth fully and appreciatively, and everything possible will be done by Germany to make it easy for France to accept. We have but one wish—to put an effective stop to the world economic crisis, and we want to cooperate with France toward that end in every possible manner.' "

Two days later Chancellor Brüning presented the German government's official position in a radio address in which he coupled gratitude to the President of the United States with a warning that the Moratorium was not a panacea. Also, he addressed an appeal to Europe and especially to France for cooperation:

"All peoples of the world are deeply impressed with the historic steps taken on Sunday by the President of the United States to meet the tremendous crisis which has struck almost all nations and to bring aid to those who are in danger of succumbing.

"The German people and the German Government have accepted the proposals of President Hoover with heartfelt gratitude. We see a new hope arising for Europe and Germany from these proposals. They bring help to Germany at a decisive moment in its history, at a time when difficulties have piled up to the *n*th degree.

"The first effective step into a better future has been taken. The Reich Government must warn, however, that this Plan of the American President, if accepted by all nations concerned, will not help us over the totality of the many problems besetting us. The Government is aware that the year 1932 will in all likelihood bring the culmination of our financial difficulties. . . .

"The German people would forfeit all sympathies and confidence in the [rest of the] world were it not to cling resolutely to the principle that the public finances must unconditionally be placed on a healthy basis at whatever sacrifice. Sound financing is one of the most important preconditions to the creation of confidence.

"The assumption of confidence which underlies the world-historic step taken by President Hoover can bring forth fruit only if the German people are fully determined on their own strength to continue to walk the path of greatest economy in all fields. . . .

"The well-being of Europe and the world depends upon the determined resolution and far-sightedness with which on both sides those whom a tragic fate has made enemies during the world war, will pull themselves together and arrive at the necessary decisions demanded of all governments and peoples by the needs of the hour. . . .

"The German Government is ready to cooperate with every means at its disposal for the attainment of this objective of the American initiative. It is animated by the honest desire in cooperation with the other governments to approach a solution of questions important for the pacification of Europe from the political angle also. . . .

"The German Government is aware that an especially important factor in all this will be the future relationship between Germany and France. . . . The tasks confronting France and Germany are too immense and urgent not to make it possible to find a common basis after trustful and honest exchanges of views for tackling these problems with a prospect of success."

The German press displayed the Moratorium Proposal prominently. On the whole, however, and probably at the suggestion of the German government, it refrained from editorial comment while the Hoover message was being examined and debated in the chancelleries and parliaments of the other nations concerned. The usual jarring note, of course, was injected by the Nazis, who always and at all times used every available means for undermining the Weimar Republic.

Hitler's personal organ, the *Völkischer Beobachter* of Munich, commented on the Moratorium Plan in these words on June 22: "It must be emphasized that all that it amounts to is a breathing spell for the milchcow Germany. For the moment they [the Allies] are, after all, dealing with a 'fulfillment' cabinet and not with an awakening national-socialist German people."

Hitler's *Gauleiter* for Berlin, the poison-penned Dr. Joseph Goebbels, in his daily *Angriff* was even more vehement. His across-the-page headline in fifteen-millimeter type read: "Germany the Victim of a New American Bluff." Editorially the "*kleine Doktor*" observed:

"Germany has become a victim of the Dawes Plan and a victim of the Young Plan. It won't for a third time be lulled to sleep by the phrases of the Hoover Plan, however attractive it may appear at first blush. . . . It does not provide a solution, but merely the postponement of any decision for a year. . . .

"The underlying thought is that the advancing national opposition movement can be hindered and arrested by this maneuver.

. . . That means that for us there is nothing else to do but doggedly and defiantly to continue to fight against the international enslavement of the German people."

The proclamation of the Moratorium Plan was one thing; its acceptance by the governments concerned was quite something else and not easy to obtain.

In a campaign speech delivered in New York's Madison Square Garden on October 31, 1932, President Hoover reviewed the anxious weeks that followed his proclamation in these words:

"Immediately after this act, for the first time in the history of the world, I made personal, hourly use of the newly installed trans-Atlantic telephone and talked with our Ambassadors in the presence of the leaders of the nations. I received wholehearted and immediate response from Signor Mussolini of Italy; the same sympathetic response from the Prime Minister of England. Furthermore, the Governments of Belgium and Poland, which you might think would have retained more bitterness from the war than any other nations, responded instantly.

"The arrangements were not easy, as existing contracts were complicated in their relationships between many nations and it involved unequal sacrifices. Day after day, night after night, I was in communication first with one ambassador and then another, proposing methods to meet difficulties which arose, building up adjustments amongst different nations, until finally that year of postponement was secured.

"And it was not merely a postponement of a year in the payments on debts for which I was seeking. I was seeking for a year in which Europe could solemnly consider the situation into which she was drifting. I was seeking to remove from the mind of the world the fears of debacle in civilization which were breaking down all security of credit and to bring to their attention the healing powers of international cooperation."

The French government proved to be the most difficult of all to deal with. The President stated in his *Memoirs,* Volume III:

"That government raised a host of technical and fictitious

difficulties and continued to raise fresh ones as fast as we met them.

"They kept this up for more than three weeks. Discouragement and destructive forces again began to haunt the world. Further runs on Central and Eastern European banks became prevalent, and further gold poured out of Europe."

One such "fictitious" argument was that a moratorium was tantamount to cancellation of existing obligations. Secretary Stimson on instructions from the President met it in a telegram to the American Embassy in Paris dated June 23, 1931: "It has not been suggested that there should be any change in any international agreement either in relation to our debts or to reparations —only that the application of the agreements shall be suspended for one year; that such contracts being in full force and effect, payments would be resumed at the end of the year in the normal fashion. We cannot see the validity of the contention that the agreements in any fashion are destroyed by failure to maintain current payments, and obviously if the French wish to require it, all parties should confirm the fact that the agreements are in no way invalidated by the postponement."

Another argument was to the effect that the German government might use the year of grace to build up her armed strength with the money saved on the Moratorium. The President met it by instructing Ambassador Edge to present to the French government a copy of the following statement by Chancellor Brüning, delivered to the American government by German Undersecretary Bernhard von Bülow via Ambassador Sackett and released to the American press on the afternoon of July 5:

"In view of the fears which have sprung up in some circles that the amounts released in the German budget by the relief from reparations payments might be used to increase armaments, I declare that an increase in the appropriation for the army and navy during the holiday year has never been contemplated nor will it take place. The aggregate alleviations accruing to Germany from the Hoover Plan are required and will be used in their entirety to cover the deficits in revenue which are to be expected, to consolidate financial conditions, and to save German economic life.

"(Signed) Brüning."

After almost a month of wrangling over details of the Plan and French reservations thereto, President Hoover's patience was exhausted. He instructed Ambassador Edge to tell the French government that there was now sufficient approval of the Plan by the other countries concerned to make the inclusion of France unnecessary—they could take it or leave it.

The President's forceful, energetic language worked. The French fell into line. Mr. Hoover eased their situation by accepting the face-saving reservation that the Germans must make the annuity payments to France characterized in the Young Plan as unconditional, but that France would immediately plow them back into the German economy as a loan repayable in ten annual installments beginning July 1, 1933. The German government agreed to this.

The French acquiescence in the Plan was communicated to Mr. Hoover in the form of a Memorandum handed to Secretary Mellon, who telephoned it across the Atlantic to the President for his approval at 2.50 P.M. on July 6. It read as follows after the White House had made one minor correction which was readily accepted by the French conferees:

"The French Government states that it is in agreement with the United States on the essential principles of President Hoover's proposal and on the following proposition which may be expressed as follows:

"1. The payment of intergovernmental debts shall be postponed from July 1, 1931, to June 30, 1932.

"2. The Reich will pay the amount of the unconditional annuities. The French Government agrees insofar as it is concerned that the payments thus paid by the Reich shall be placed by the B.I.S. [Bank for International Settlements] in bonds *of the German*

Railroad. [The original text read "guaranteed by the German railroads."]

"3. All suspended payments shall be subjected to interest in accordance with the conditions suggested by the American Government, payable in ten annual installments, beginning with July 1, 1933.

"4. The same conditions shall apply to the bonds to be issued by the German railroads."

President Hoover authorized Mr. Mellon to initial the Memorandum and instructed him to accompany this act with this statement: "The President considers that the understanding arrived at today comes within the spirit of the American proposal. It is, of course, subject to approval of the other interested powers, for whom the American Government cannot speak."

At long last the President was able to make a historic public statement on the conclusion, subject to ratification, of the Moratorium Agreement. He made it even though he felt that, as revealed in his *Memoirs*, "irreparable damage had been done" by the French cabinet "by its delays and its propaganda." Herewith excerpts from the statement:

"I am glad to announce that the American proposal for one year's postponement of all intergovernmental debts and reparations has now been accepted in principle by all of the important creditor governments. . . .

"The acceptance of this proposal has meant sacrifices by the American people and by the former Allied Governments, who are with all others suffering from world-wide depression and deficits in governmental budgets. The economic load most seriously oppressing the peoples of Germany and Central Europe will be immensely lightened.

"While the plan is particularly aimed at economic relief, yet economic relief means the swinging of men's minds from fear to confidence, the swinging of nations from the apprehension of disorder and governmental collapse to hope and confidence of the future. It means tangible aid to unemployment and agriculture.

"The almost unanimous support in the United States is again profound evidence of the sincere humanity of the American people. And in this year, devoted to economic upbuilding, the world has need of solemn thought on the causes which have contributed to the depression. I need not repeat that one of these causes is the burdens imposed and the fears aroused by competitive armament. Contemplation of the past few weeks should bring a realization that we must find relief from these fundamental burdens which today amount to several times the amount of intergovernmental debts."

Having announced the Agreement Mr. Hoover, according to his *Memoirs,* "breathed easier in the hope that it might still save the situation. There was again a momentary lift in the economic world—but it lasted less than a week."

The reason for the but "momentary lift" is explained in the next chapter.

The German Government almost immediately—on July 7—issued a formal declaration:

"The far-sighted and statesman-like initiative of President Hoover has been crowned with success. The psychic relief and the hope for economic improvement inherent in this result release joyous and friendly feelings everywhere. The [President's] decision to act quickly and decisively opens far-reaching possibilities for the world's restoration to health.

"The German people know very well that the execution of the Hoover Plan will bring them, as the people bearing the greatest burden, the relatively greatest relief. Agreement concerning the year of grace could be attained only through the understanding cooperation of all concerned, among them some states which had to accept an increase of their own difficulties and considerable inconvenience in the interests of a general solution.

"The noble renunciation on the part of the American people has, however, found a commendable echo. We acknowledge with gratitude that in the hour of our greatest economic difficulties there was such understanding for Germany's situation. Even after the year of grace begins, Germany will in no wise be relieved of her economic and financial problems. While alleviating certain hardships, our country cannot use what resources are left to reduce the sacrifices which the government has had to demand of the population. We must not lessen our all-out effort. All alleviations which the Plan will bring to Germany will be needed and used to the last pfennig for consolidating the public finances. Whatever easing of the money and credit markets will result herefrom must inure to the benefit of German industry.

"An increase of expenditures by the Reich during the year of grace in any realm, whatever it may be, will not be possible. On this point the Reich Chancellor has made an unmistakable declaration.

"The Hoover year is to be devoted to the rehabilitation of the German economy and beyond that to the economic recovery of the whole world. In order that this hope may become a reality and the goal reached within the time envisaged, close cooperation of the peoples of the earth is essential. The ensuing months will furnish an opportunity for such cooperation.

"The common goal which must be set by the statesmen and the peoples as they solve the even greater tasks of the ensuing year must be the healing of the wounds of this crisis and the adoption of measures for preventing a recurrence of a similar world catastrophe."

President von Hindenburg cabled President Hoover: "Now that the Paris negotiations have been brought to a conclusion and the year of grace proposed by you has begun, I desire to give expression to the feelings of gratitude of the German people toward you and the American people. May the entire world, thanks to your initiative, be led into a new era of peaceful and trustful cooperation. This is my sincere wish."

Our Chief Executive replied: "I have received with great appreciation your communication of July 7. It is my sincere hope and expectation that this proposal which has been presented to you and accepted by the nations of the world will revive confidence and promote prosperity among all peoples."

At the same time Mr. Hoover sent appreciative messages to Secretary Mellon, Senator Morrow, and Undersecretary of State William R. Castle, Jr., for their share in the negotiations. He had already felicitated and thanked Secretary Stimson, Ambassador Sackett, and Undersecretary of the Treasury Ogden L. Mills.

Adolf Hitler's counterblast to the German government's declaration came in his *Völkischer Beobachter* of July 8: "The French-American Agreement signifies full victory for the French. All essential French conditions have been fulfilled. Germany must pay the unconditional annuities totalling eight hundred millions. Whether they will immediately be made available again to the Reich with an interest charge and on the basis of proper guarantees is purely an 'assumption.' In addition, Paris demands political guarantees from Germany, i.e., the ceding of further sovereign rights insofar as there are any left to cede. Brüning has already been in a hurry, by his declaration to the American ambassador, to do everything possible to satisfy the French, so that the real essence of the Hoover Plan becomes revealed more and more clearly: under the camouflage of a grandly conceived but in reality purposeless Moratorium, Germany once again is humiliated and degraded to the role of shoe-shine for French and High Finance."

Dr. Goebbels seconded his master with this editorial comment in the Berlin *Angriff:* "Germany missed her chance. Whosoever does not understand even now that Germany's fate is not to be determined from the outside but solely from within, and that others, *men,* must take that fate into their hands, has forfeited even the right to complain, once he has become a 'tribute coolie.'"

The non-Nazi press, with the exception of the Communists, supported the stand taken by the Brüning government. Even the *Vorwärts,* official organ of the Social Democratic party which was in opposition to Brüning, commented on July 5: "The Hoover proclamation has evoked a feeling of deliverance. It was actually a case of help at the last moment. . . . The German public has looked upon the help given by Hoover's action as upon a miracle. But as is the case with all miracles, the public has over-estimated the extent of the miracle. . . . It took fourteen days . . . before a provisional agreement between France and America became discernible. . . . These fourteen days . . . must be charged up against France. They cost Germany dearly . . . and had an unfavorable bearing upon the psychological effect envisaged by Hoover as likely to result from his action."

The liberal-democratic *Berliner Tageblatt* on July 7 editorialized:

"Last night agreement was achieved in Paris concerning the Hoover Plan. The firmness of Hoover and of his deputy during the Paris negotiations . . . after a long struggle against French opposition has put the Plan through with a few changes which do not depreciate its value.

"It should be emphasized that the opposition did not stem from Premier Laval or Briand, but from other members of the Cabinet who again and again thwarted the negotiations. Now the Plan can be put into operation. The tremendous nervous tension, which finally brought the German financial structure into a very dangerous position, has eased; the danger may be regarded as having been averted. Yesterday's result has already had its effect upon today's foreign exchange market."

Other German editorial opinion could be cited.

As to the author of the Plan himself, his optimism remained unbroken despite the calamitous situation of German finance and economy which made new negotiations necessary virtually the moment the year of grace began.

Upon ratification of the Plan by the American Congress Mr. Hoover said on December 23, 1931:

"I have signed the Act authorizing the foreign debt postponement for one year. I am gratified at the support it received in the Congress as indicated by the approval (including those absent yet who expressed their views) of 79 Senators as against 15 opposed, and the approval of 317 members of the House of Representatives as against 100 opposed. It is further gratifying that both political parties strongly supported this proposal. . . .

"In saving the collapse of Germany by the year's postponement the American people have done something greater than the dollars and cents gained from the maintenance of our agricultural markets, the prevention of panic and unlimited losses. They have contributed to maintain courage and hope in the German nation, to give opportunity for the other European countries to work out their problems."

In one of his last major addresses before the 1932 election, delivered in St. Louis, Missouri, on November 4, the President reaffirmed his faith, strengthened by his experience with the Moratorium Plan, in the idealistic impulses of mankind. He closed his speech with the words:

"I know that the proposal of the Moratorium diverted the entire current of thought and changed the history of what otherwise would have been a tragedy to the whole of civilization. It brought to new understanding the realization of the burdens under which Germany had been laboring.

"Under the impulses of these agreements and the recognition at least of the peril in which they stood, there came out of this agreement a great measure of redemption to the German people, a sense of greater security to the world from the agreements at Lausanne.

"That agreement and the human sympathies which were evoked by that new understanding of the postwar difficulties in the world has served greatly in the healing of the wounds of the great war.

"There lie in many events of the last three years great dramas, great tragedies. . . . But overriding all those incidents, the world has witnessed the courage of men and the willingness to place their fate and their political future at stake for the world's progress. No man can go thorough these episodes without belief that there is a great regeneration in the courage, confidence, and intelligence of men for the guidance of this world back toward stability and common interest in the development of human welfare."

Spelled out in terms of nations involved, the Moratorium meant a year's relief for fifteen countries over and above all others, which now had time to do constructive thinking as to how to meet the problems facing them after the year was over. The countries directly enmeshed in these intergovernmental debts were Austria, Belgium, Czechoslovakia, Estonia, Finland, France, Germany, Great Britain, Greece, Hungary, Italy, Latvia, Lithuania, Poland, and Roumania.

The significance of the Moratorium Plan was obvious also to nations not as directly involved in the vicious circle as were these fifteen. Accordingly, Australia, Bulgaria, Canada, India, Japan, New Zealand, Portugal, and the Union of South Africa accepted the Plan, although they had no government debt relation with the United States, the initiator of the Plan.

A third group was that of nations holding government pledges to repay obligations arising from relief extended beyond that of a charity character. These countries, Denmark, the Netherlands, Norway, Sweden, and Switzerland, also declared adherence to the Plan.

With so many creditors willing to abstain from pressing their claims, President Hoover had expected that the private debts could be adjusted without government action.

His hopes were disappointed.

7

THE "STANDSTILL" AGREEMENT

The feeling of relief which permeated Europe when President Hoover's Moratorium Plan was first announced had dissipated rapidly when one obstacle after another to its acceptance was interposed. France's grudging final adherence came too late to forestall the wholesale closing of Central and Eastern European banks. As Mr. Hoover expressed it in his *Memoirs*, Volume III:

"During the French delay, the spirit of panic had gained force and the drains upon Germany, Hungary, and Eastern European countries severely depleted the gold reserves against their currency. But something worse was impelling the crisis. By July 15, 1931, practically all Austrian, German, Hungarian, and European banks farther east had been closed. Various meetings between government representatives were taking place in Europe, but they got precisely nowhere. . . .

"I suggested . . . to the British Government that they call a conference in London on the European financial situation. I requested Messrs. Mellon and Stimson to attend. The meeting was set for the 20th of July. On the 16th and 17th, however, at an intermediate meeting in Paris of various government representatives, including Secretary Stimson, it was proposed by the French that the British, French, and American governments should lend Germany $500,000,000. I informed Secretary Stimson (who urged it) by telephone that the United States Government could not join in such a plan, as in my view it would be totally ineffective even if Congress were called into session and approved it."

This intermediate meeting had come about at the insistence of the French government, which had also made it a condition of attending the London Conference that the German delegation first come to Paris. It meant the cancellation of a visit to Berlin by British Prime Minister MacDonald and Foreign Minister Henderson, scheduled to take place directly preceding the London Conference.

On instructions from the President, Acting Secretary of State William R. Castle, Jr., on July 17 telephoned Ambassador Sackett, requesting him to see Chancellor Brüning before he started for Paris and to brief him on what was likely to be in the offing. Mr. Castle said in part:

"The French, you know, have evolved a plan for supplying a lot of money on long term loans to Germany. That is a plan which necessitates government guarantees to the bonds of the United States, Great Britain, and France. As you know, this country cannot give any government guarantees. We also know the British will not do it, because if they do, they must guarantee bonds for India and elsewhere, and they won't do it.

"The whole scheme of the French is a false one. They are putting something up to Germany which they know cannot go through and I think the Germans ought to realize that very strongly before they go there. I do not believe the French Government would guarantee the bonds themselves. You know that no German bonds could be sold in the New York market at the present time."

The meeting of Chancellor Brüning and his delegation with representatives from the United States, France, Great Britain, Italy, Japan, and Belgium took place in Premier Laval's office. The picture which the American conferees gained concerning the situation in Germany was cabled to the Department of State by Ambassador Edge:

"Its budget is stabilized as a result of radical, almost brutal financial restrictions. The Government has done everything in the domestic field to remedy the situation. It has bolstered the Darmstädter Bank; has taken drastic steps to curb the flight of capital; has decreed that all bearers of foreign currency must notify the Reichsbank; has held up bank payments for several days; has increased the circulation of paper currency; has taken measures to broaden the scope of bank credits; and has arranged a system of mutual guarantees, grouping forty German banks.

"If Germany were to declare an external moratorium tomorrow it would imperil the financial structure of all Europe. Many European nations would be obliged to follow the moratorium and suspend foreign payments. . . . To meet the situation Germany must have, not short term credits alone—that would not in any sense be sufficient—but it must be assured that the capital already withdrawn will be replaced by new capital."

President Hoover had been watching the private banks' international operations with anxiety for some months. As early as January 21, 1931, Ambassador Sackett had sent a confidential dispatch which described the visit of the chief representatives of Lee, Higginson & Company of New York to Germany, in the course of which they had floated a loan of $125,000,000. Mr. Sackett stated that he was shocked to learn from George Murnane, one of the Lee, Higginson men, that the Chase Bank and the Guaranty Trust Company of New York had loaned to Germany respectively $190,000,000, and $90,000,000 which, he estimated, was nearly one-half of the capital of these banks. The Sackett dispatch continued:

"I am led to feel equally strongly, if these figures are approximately correct, that American investments in this country under existing political and financial conditions have attained perhaps dangerous proportions as short term obligations in separate ownership. They are largely the result of competitive effort by American banks working independently of each other to secure attractive earning power for surplus funds showing only meager returns in the home market. . . . I mean to differentiate between short and long term obligations. The latter could be funded. . .

"Murnane admitted short term German credits in the United States could not be called or renewals refused without great danger to the financial situation in the United States, because if even 25% of these loans were not renewed there would be no way of Germany carrying on, as they could neither pay nor borrow elsewhere."

The immediate reason for President Hoover's asking the British government to call a conference was an urgent telegram from Ambassador Sackett, sent on July 11 after a conference with Chancellor Brüning and Staatssekretär Bernhard W. von Bülow of the Foreign Office. The two statesmen, according to Sackett, reported "a further development today was in runs on deposit accounts of two D-Banks and other large deposit institutions as well as on savings banks. This was spreading to all parts of the country and was not confined to Berlin.

"The very last resources are being thrown in tomorrow, the vice-president of the Reichsbank said, but that at the latest these cannot carry beyond Monday noon, after which a panic was considered inevitable by my visitors. Closing of banks, the failure on the part of industry to meet payrolls, and people being thrown into the streets would result from this. They declared that actual revolution is implied."

[Four of Germany's largest financial institutions were called D-

Banks because their names began with the letter "D": Darmstädter Bank, Deutsche Bank, Diskontogesellschaft, and Dresdner Bank. Reference here is to the Darmstädter and Dresdner Banks.]

As a preparatory step to the London Conference President Hoover sought to ascertain the facts as to America's involvement in the bank closings in Central and Eastern Europe. He was informed by a banker friend that many American banks had bought German trade bills and bank acceptances. The trade bills had as their security the bills of lading covering goods shipped; the bank acceptances were backed by no collateral whatsoever. In the parlance of Wall Street they were "kited" bills.

Mr. Hoover's inquiry from the Federal Reserve Bank as to what amounts of these bills were held by American banks and business drew the reply that American banks held no more than $500,000,000 of them, and that they could be handled easily.

The President was not convinced. In his *Memoirs* he confided:

"Worrying over the matter during that night I was somehow not satisfied with this report, and in the morning I directed the Comptroller of the Currency to secure an accurate report on such American holdings direct from the banks. Twenty-four hours later I received the appalling news that the total American bank holdings probably exceeded $1,700,000,000; that certain banks having over $1,000,000,000 of deposits held amounts of these bills which, in case of loss, might affect their capital or surplus and create great public fears. Here was one consequence of the Reserve Board maintaining artificially low interest rates and expanded credit in the United States from mid-1927 to mid-1929 at the urging of European bankers. Some of our bankers had been yielding to sheer greed for the 6 or 7 per cent interest offered by banks in the European panic area.

"Worse still, the Comptroller informed me that these European banks were already in default on many bank acceptances and were frantically endeavoring to secure renewals. He thought the 'acceptances' comprised a major part of American bank holdings and informed me that some of the 'trade bills' did not have the collateral documents attached.

"When the Comptroller's information began to come in, I sent for Secretary Mills who was also fearful, and requested him to ask his friends in the Bank of England by telephone what they knew about the volume of these bills. In a day or two they replied, in alarm, that there might be $2,000,000,000 in the banks of Britain and the Dominions, together with Sweden, Norway, Switzerland, Holland and Denmark. They also stated that there were quantities in Latin-American and Asian banks. They said the German and other Eastern European banks were frantically trying to renew the bank acceptances and were being refused.

"It looked at this time as if Germany, Austria, Hungary, and other Eastern European countries had as much as $5,000,000,000 of these short-term bills afloat. The Germans had also, over the years since the war, floated many long-term loans by their governments, their municipalities, and their business houses. It looked as if the German total external debt alone, excluding reparations but including long-term debt, might possibly exceed $5,000,000,000. They not only had paid all their reparation instalments to the Allies out of this borrowed money, but had paid for reconstruction of German industry and their budget deficits. It was obvious that they and the others could not meet their short-term obligations, at least for the present.

"Thus, the explosive mine which underlay the economic system of the world was now coming clearly into view. It was now evident why the European crisis had been so long delayed. They had kited bills to A in order to pay B and their internal deficits.

"I don't know that I have ever received a worse shock. The haunting prospect of wholesale bank failures and the necessity of saying not a word to the American people as to the cause and the danger, lest I precipitate runs on our banks, left me little sleep.

"The situation was no longer one of helping foreign countries to the indirect benefit of everybody. It was now a question of saving ourselves."

The President decided to parallel the Moratorium Plan with one to meet the new catastrophic situation. He drafted a proposal for a "standstill" or "hold everything" agreement among all banks everywhere which possessed German and Central European short-term notes.

The gist of his plan was cabled to Secretary of State Stimson at Paris. The President's *Diary* under date of July 18 records a negative reaction: "Mr. Stimson apparently did not react to the plan, still insisting that we had to work along with the French. I insisted that there was no genuinity to the French proposals, that they were the road to a political morass and the demoralization of Germany. On discussion with Mills and Castle I resolved to place the matter in a formal note which could be presented at the London Conference and asked Mills and Castle to formulate such a note on the basis of the telegraphic plan of yesterday."

Before cabling it to Secretaries Stimson and Mellon in its final form, however, for presentation to the London Conference, he called in Acting Secretaries Castle and Mills, Senator Morrow, and the American Ambassador to Great Britain, Charles G. Dawes, who happened to be in Washington. That was on July 19, 1931. All of them fully agreed to the proposal.

All also agreed that, after the intergovernmental relief of Germany had been accomplished by the President's Moratorium action, the German position was now solely a banking crisis. Stimson, they feared, was being headed in Paris into an utterly impossible situation of political entanglements.

The salient portions of the "Standstill" Plan, as transmitted to Messrs. Stimson and Mellon and released to the press, follow. For the convenience of the nonspecialist in financial affairs the paragraphs containing the core of it have been placed in *italics:*

". . . The general uncertainty which has prevailed for the last few weeks resulted in such a loss of confidence that the German banking and credit structure was subjected to a very severe strain. This strain took two very definite forms, both of which resulted in a drain of banking resources and the depletion of German gold and foreign exchange holdings.

"In the first place there was a flight from the mark within

Germany. In the second place there was a withdrawal of foreign deposits and a curtailment on the part of foreign banks of outstanding lines of credit.

"(a) As to the first, namely, the internal flight from the mark, this can be and is being successfully combated by the vigorous action of the German Government and the Reichsbank. Once unreasonable fear has been eliminated, it is certain that the patriotism of the German people can be relied on to prevent the destruction of the credit of their own country.

"(b) As to the external credits, *we believe that the first approach to this problem is the development of a program that will permit the maintenance for an adequate period of time of the present outstanding lines of credit.* In this connection it is our understanding that *this volume of credit,* together with the freed reparations and the natural gain from the allayment of the panic, *should be adequate to meet the needs of German economic life for the immediate moment.*

"On the other hand, it must be apparent that, unless provision is made for the maintenance of these credits, an attempt to provide new ones, whether of short- or long-term character, would be ineffective. In the development of such a program the governments of the countries having principal banking centers, including the United States, Belgium, France, Great Britain, Holland, Italy, Japan, and Switzerland, and other important banking centers, might well undertake to encourage their bankers so to organize as to permit the maintenance for an adequate period of time of present-day outstanding lines of credit to Germany.

"The responsibility for working out the details of such a program and the methods of making it effective with due regard to the protection of the banks and the needs of German economy should be left to the banking communities of the respective countries and the central banks could, we believe, be relied on to furnish the necessary leadership, cooperation and direction.

"Such voluntary arrangements should be supplemented, for the time being, by strict control of all foreign exchange transactions

by the Reichsbank so that the integrity of the program can be maintained and the banks that are participating can be assured that there would be no arbitrary withdrawal either from within or without Germany.

"It is our belief that if such a program could be made promptly effective it would result in an immediate restoration of confidence and that in a comparatively short time the necessity for restrictions of this character would disappear and normal conditions would once more prevail."

For the carrying out of the details involved, the Plan envisaged the creation of a committee, preferably selected by the Bank for International Settlements.

Besides cabling the official text for presentation, President Hoover sent his two negotiators in Paris a brief in which he analyzed the whole situation, anticipated possible objections, and offered American government aid to help meet the German crisis by an undertaking to finance, up to a sum of $120,000,000, raw materials in wheat and cotton "at the same terms that credit is extended to Germany by other nations" (see Point 5 of the brief).

The brief was signed by Acting Secretary of State Castle on behalf of President Hoover, and was communicated to the American Embassy at London for Messrs. Stimson and Mellon on July 19. It read, in the usual paraphrase of the State Department of messages originally sent in code:

"The following considerations may come up in the discussions:

"One. Although the American proposal is simply a first step, it is possible that it will be held that it is inadequate to take care of the present situation. In this regard the banking world has no information of a convincing or satisfactory nature. Naturally it is felt in Germany that more credit is needed; but without further evidence it will be impossible to satisfy the banking centers on this point.

"Two. It should be understood in Germany that because of their crisis the entire world of finance has been placed in a very precarious position and that it is much more difficult now to provide further credit than would have been the case three months ago. It is necessary first of all to bring back confidence even though for a certain length of time Germany should be short of working capital. Furthermore, Germany should realize that at present the entire world is short of capital, and that each nation is now endeavoring to bolster up its own economic structure.

"Three. On the 20th of June when Mr. Hoover made his offer, there was a practical cessation of the external run on Germany, but unrest developed again both in Germany and abroad as a result of the delays on the part of the French in accepting. In consequence, from various quarters there has been a demand on Germany to furnish exchange against a large proportion of its short term credit. The Hoover proposal has been undermined as a consequence of these demands. According to information which has come to us, the banks in the United States have stood up to a very large percentage and certain of these banks have even complied with demands for additional aid. The French, on the other hand, are said to have reduced their holdings of German short term credits by more than two hundred million dollars. Moreover, the banks of Italy, Holland, Denmark, and Switzerland are said to have done the same thing. The present situation has come about principally because of the action by these groups of banks; and it is morally up to them to assume their share of the world burden and restore these credits. Such a result can be obtained in either one of two ways: each nation should bring back its situation with respect to Germany to what it was on June 20 or, alternatively, each country should restore its credit up to the same proportion of its June 20th credit as the proportions which have been maintained by the American and British banks to date as compared with June 20th. That is to say, if American credits were decreased during this period by 20 per cent, then the other nations of the world ought to restore these credits to 80 per cent of what they were on June 20th. The reply to this suggestion will doubtless be to the effect that these matters are private transactions; to which we can say that American and British credits have been held open through governmental influence which would have been equally effective and can still be made effective in other banking nations.

"Four. It can not be said that the American banks would not consider making some additional short advances; but they are entitled to know that other foreign banks have restored proportionately the situation and that any new load that may be necessary will be borne by them in their just proportions.

"Five. It might be well for you to suggest, at some point in the discussions, that if other nations agree to maintain and build up credits to the amount of $120,000,000, the Government of the United States will agree to finance raw materials in cotton and wheat for such an amount at the same terms that credit is extended to Germany by other nations. Otherwise expressed, the American Government, instead of providing banking credits, would be able to open credits to Germany for the purpose of buying these raw materials from American governmental agencies. This kind of service amounts to the same thing as the extension of credits by banks.

"Six. With regard to the assertion of the French Government to the effect that it is the only government which is showing any willingness to face the situation, you can answer effectively by the following:

"The United States has put up already by the Hoover proposal two and one-half as much as France has put up. Over one-half of the entire burden of Germany's short term credits is carried by American banks; while less than 5 per cent is carried by the French. Ever since President Hoover's offer was announced the French have further embarrassed the situation by reducing their credit. It would be of advantage if the French would agree at the conference to restore these credits in the same proportion as the credits still held by Americans, who had maintained their short term holdings at the request of the President. The Government of the United States is willing to help extend German credits either through increasing the outstanding American banking credits or, in any case by supplying raw materials as stated above, on condition that other banking nations agree to render assistance in proportion. In order that these various matters could be considered, we made our suggestion in telegram No. 218 of a committee.

"Seven. According to indirect information received from the officials of the Reichsbank, we are of the opinion that the immediate needs of the moment can be provided for by keeping the lines of credit outstanding at present open. There is no doubt that the situation can be handled successfully if other banking nations will build up their credits to the same level proportionately as that maintained by the Americans now in comparison with their June 20th level. The American Government is afraid, however, that if the success or failure of the conference is considered dependent on whether or not a new sum of money is provided for Germany, the entire world will be on edge until such a loan is consummated; and it should be remembered moreover that the loan may prove a failure. If, on the other hand, is taken the immediate step of keeping open the lines of credit which now exist, there will be a general feeling throughout the world that stabilization of the situation has been achieved. The world will begin to regain its confidence; and from this restored confidence will arise the possibility of taking additional measures.

"Eight. In view of the fact that France has already withdrawn all but a very small portion of its short term credits, you will appreciate the fact that, if other nations agree to maintain these credits, we can for the present save Germany without the help of France. Moreover, the force of public opinion, which ultimately made it impossible to turn down the Hoover offer, will once more force her to join with us. For these reasons, we are not dependent on action by France; nor do we need to agree to any demands of a political nature which the French may make of the Germans, nor need we be involved by the French in any manner unacceptable to us.

"There is no doubt that, in case France was willing to give

money to Germany in exchange for political guidance and if these conditions were accepted by Germany, confidence in Germany would be completely destroyed, and her collapse would be precipitated. Consequently we are not in sympathy with encouraging France to put out money for Germany under the conditions set forth in the French proposal; nor would Germany gain anything by accepting money under political conditions such as these, which would cause the confidence of the rest of the world to be lost. In brief, the London Conference is not subject to French dictation."

As regards the wheat and cotton offer contained in Point 5 of the brief, Mr. Castle in a telegram sent two days earlier had explained to Secretary Stimson that "the farm cooperatives, financed by the Farm Board, could supply 1,100,000 bales of cotton and 70,000,000 bushels of wheat to Germany on payments over two or three years. This would comprise a year's supply of these commodities. The total aggregate amount of assistance to Germany by so doing would be about $120,000,000." The offer was accepted by Germany following completion of the Standstill Agreement.

The French delegation to the London Conference countered the President's Standstill Proposal with a repetition of its plan for a joint government loan of half a billion dollars to Germany. Secretaries Stimson and Mellon again urged strongly that the President approve of this measure. Mr. Hoover remained adamant. Again quoting from his *Memoirs:*

"I replied that this was a banker-made crisis, and that the bankers must shoulder the burdens, not our taxpayers; moreover, that the amount proposed would not be a drop in the bucket. It was merely partial relief of banks at government expense. Or even if a loan to Germany was provided by American, British, and French and other banks themselves, it would be a wholly inadequate solution. I again informed them by telephone in detail of the situation as to German and other Central European short-term obligations in the United States and abroad. I also stated that such a loan would not even take care of the American situation alone.

"At this point I instructed Mr. Mills to ask a friend in the Bank of England by telephone what their idea was of the French loan proposal. He quickly learned that the Bank of England did not approve of such a loan. Also, the British Treasury officials had no faith that it would meet the crisis. The affair began to take the color of the usual attempt of European political officials to make us the first to refuse something and therefore the scapegoat for anything that happened. Indeed, one reason given to me by Messrs. Stimson and Mellon for American governmental support of a loan was fear of just that. I finally telephoned them emphatically that we would not participate in such a loan and that I was publishing the gist of the standstill proposal to the world that very minute. They protested against the publication as undiplomatic. I issued it nevertheless."

Publication of the proposal in the press of the world, plus the President's unyielding veto of the French counterproposal, led to the acceptance of the essence of the plan the following day. The Bank for International Settlements at Basel was delegated to administer it.

The fight was not over, however. A group of American bankers balked. In the President's words: "a group of New York banks informed me that they could not agree to the Standstill Plan and that the only solution was for our government to participate in a large international loan to Germany and other countries. My nerves were perhaps overstrained when I replied that, if they did not accept within twenty-four hours, I would expose their banking conduct to the American people. They agreed."

Mr. Hoover was able at last, on July 23, 1931, to release to the press a public statement expressing satisfaction with the acceptance of his plan by the London Conference. It read in part as follows:

"The London conference has laid sound foundations for the establishment of stability in Germany.

"The major problem is one affecting primarily the banking and credit conditions and can best be solved by the voluntary cooperation of the bankers of the world rather than by governments with their conflicting interests. Such a basis of cooperation is assured.

"The program supplements the suspension of intergovernmental debts already in effect. The combined effect should enable the German people with their resources, industry and courage to overcome the temporary difficulties and restore their credit."

Secretary Stimson upon his arrival in New York on September 3 also made a statement, saying:

"The month which has elapsed since the close of the Seven Power Conference in London has given us a chance to begin to appraise the result of that conference and of the various meetings which preceded and have followed it. From the information which has come to me I believe that Germany has received a new spirit of courage and confidence. The result of the recent plebiscite in Prussia; the fact that on the day when the German banks reopened, the deposits exceeded the withdrawals, together with many other similar indications, all point to more hopeful conditions and spirit.

"Even more encouraging have been the meetings of the French and German ministers and the friendly and conciliatory spirit in which Prime Minister Laval and Chancellor Brüning have begun to discuss the vital political questions which divided their countries. The same is true of the meetings which have been held between the ministers of Germany and Britain, and of Germany and Italy. Such informal meetings constitute the most effective method of approaching and discussing these political problems, and until they are thus approached in such a spirit, any thorough economic rehabilitation of Central Europe is almost impossible.

"I think there is now good reason to believe that these European statesmen, taking advantage of the respite granted by Mr. Hoover's Moratorium as well as the recommendation of the London Conference, are beginning gradually to lay the foundations of political good will, upon which a lasting structure of peace and economic prosperity can finally be rested. It was very evident in each of the countries I visited that the spirit and policy of the President's Moratorium was highly appreciated and was proving helpful in many directions."

A third person with authority in these matters who gave his estimate of President Hoover's accomplishment was Thomas W. Lamont, senior partner of the banking House of Morgan. It was in the form of a personal letter to the President, dated July 27, 1931, from which the following is excerpted:

"I have been waiting until things quieted down before sending you this word of congratulation upon what you have accomplished in the German situation and in other situations closely interwoven with it. . . . I hope that you realize and take comfort in the excellent progress that has been made since you first put your hand to the plow in this matter. The great fact remains that $400,000,000 has been lifted for at least one year off Germany's back; and as the days and weeks go by the public will come to have a fuller appreciation of the service that you have rendered and of the benefits of it to the whole world. . . .

"Now while we cannot make any prophecy, the storm seems to be dying down. The Germans are the ones upon whom the responsibility chiefly rests for the solution of their own internal difficulties. I suppose that many of them are tired, somewhat rattled and with poor judgment. But they must pull themselves together, and in both the financial and political fields must do the sort of job that will restore public confidence. They must, as has been so often stated before, handle their public finance much more prudently and vigorously. . . .

"I think that we can afford to settle down now for a while and see what else they are doing over there in Europe among, by and for themselves. But please don't forget that, despite all the discouragements and delays, your plan has been a great thing for your country and for the world. . . . Please accept again my warm congratulations."

A year later the world learned what an underestimate the figure was which experts had supplied President Hoover concerning the German external indebtedness, excluding reparations but including long-term debts. They had thought it might possibly exceed $5,000,000,000. The Bank for International Settlements in its annual report stated that "the total amount of short-term international [private] indebtedness which existed at the beginning of 1931 aggregated more than $10,000,000,000." Mr. Hoover's contention that a $500,000,000 loan would be "totally ineffective" was thus proved to have been completely justified.

Herbert Hoover's over-all evaluation of the effects of the Moratorium and Standstill Agreements, after a passage of time of twenty-one years, is contained in the third volume of his *Memoirs:*

"With the combined moratorium on inter-governmental payments and the standstill agreement, we had avoided a panic in the United States. With both these measures, the world breathed more easily again, and recovery began to show itself in the market places. It was only a momentary breathing spell, for the larger forces . . . had now begun to gnaw like wolves into the financial vitals of Britain.

"When this economic earthquake spread to our shores, Americans were to learn about the economic interdependence of nations through a poignant experience which knocked on every cottage door."

The question of intergovernmental debts and of Germany's capacity to pay continued to occupy Mr. Hoover's mind for the rest of his Presidency. On November 19, 1931, anticipating the expiration of the Moratorium, the German Government requested the Allied Powers to send a committee to reinvestigate the Reich's capacity to pay reparations. The Allies agreed to do so. The committee held sessions for over two weeks and reported that for two more years Germany would be in no position to make reparations payments.

A call was sent out to all who were entitled to reparations for a meeting in Lausanne, Switzerland, beginning January 18, 1932, a date that was later changed to June 15. The United States declined to take part, as we had no claim to German reparations.

After three weeks of haggling—Franz von Papen had meanwhile become German chancellor and led his country's delegation—the Lausanne Conference on July 8 announced that its labors had resulted in a reduction of German reparations to about $700,000,000 (the hypothetical figure of what she owed was estimated at $30,000,000,000).

That sounded like a great step forward, except that it was not the whole truth. A secret gentlemen's agreement stipulated that the Lausanne result would become operative only if America canceled the Allied war debts owed her.

When President Hoover learned of it, he instructed Acting Secretary of State Castle to issue this statement:

"The American Government is pleased that in reaching an agreement on the question of reparations, the nations assembled at Lausanne have made a great step forward in stabilization of the economic situation in Europe.

"On the question of war debts to the United States by European Governments there is no change in the attitude of the American Government which was clearly expressed in the President's statement concerning the proposed moratorium on intergovernmental debts on June 20th of last year."

Despite this restatement of the American position, Mr. Hoover pointed out, "we were soon to see the European debtors ganging up against us. On July 14th the British announced an agreement with France for a 'solid front' on war debts. . . . Our debtors took open joint action in December, 1932."

This "joint action" consisted in a notification by our war debtors that they intended to demand deferment of payments due the United States on December 15, 1932, at which time the Moratorium was to expire, and that they would propose an entire readjustment of the debts.

President-elect Franklin D. Roosevelt declined to collaborate with the outgoing Chief Executive in the attempt to salvage what might be saved by a reduction of war debts commensurate with the debtors' capacity to pay. The end result, under these circumstances, was the repudiation of war debts to the United States by Great Britain, France, Belgium, Italy, and all other European debtors except Finland, which continued faithfully to fulfill its obligations.

8

UNINTENDED MEETINGS WITH NAZI LEADERS

During February and March of 1938 Herbert Hoover undertook what he termed a "sentimental journey" to the countries of Europe with which he had been especially associated as their food provider. Accompanying him were Perrin C. Galpin, president of the Belgian-American Educational Foundation, Paul C. Smith, editor of the San Francisco *Chronicle,* and John Hartigan, a Pacific Coast public relations man.

The itinerary included Belgium, Northern France, Austria, Czechoslovakia, Poland, and Finland. Germany was omitted because Adolf Hitler was ruling there with an iron fist. Only when it became necessary to touch Berlin in transit from Prague to Warsaw was one day allowed for an incognito stopover. Instead, the stay lengthened to three days. Of this more to be described later.

Wherever Mr. Hoover went in the democracies of Central and Western Europe he was given the "red carpet" treatment. Honorary degrees and other honors showered upon him included doctorates from universities in Lille, Vienna, Prague, and Helsinki; medals from the Universities of Brussels, Ghent, and Liège, the city of Lille, and a dozen communities in Northern France; streets named after him in Brussels, Lille, Valenciennes, and Prague; and illuminated "addresses" from many organizations and societies in the countries visited.

Even a planet discovered by the Brussels Astronomical Observatory was named Herberta in his honor. But when the International Astronomers' Union ruled that planets must be named after Greek gods, Mr. Hoover, as he dryly remarked, "had to move off of Olympus."

In an address delivered soon after his return in the War Memorial House of San Francisco on April 8, Mr. Hoover referred to these honors in these words:

"These hospitalities proved the occasion for great demonstrations of affection and respect for America.

"No American can remain unmoved when tens of thousands of school children line the streets with their cheerful yells of 'Long live America,' with the frantic waving of thousands of American flags.

"No American can remain unmoved when tens of thousands of common people gather in city squares and remove their hats to the American National Anthem.

"No American can remain unmoved by the fervent expression by men of immense responsibilities of hope and almost prayer that America shall stand fast in liberty, that it shall not perish from the earth."

In an article entitled, "The Life of an Ex-President," published in *Collier's* of March 24, 1951, Mr. Hoover revealed how he came to see Hitler on March 8, although he had in no way sought to establish contact with the Nazi dictator:

"In Berlin we expected to remain only a day, but were detained by urgent invitations of the Nazis, including Hitler. I was not enthusiastic about seeing Hitler, as I had long since formed a great prejudice against the whole Nazi faith. The American ambassador, Hugh Wilson, felt, however, that there was no escape; in fact he was delighted, as he had never seen Hitler except in parades.

"We were supposed to be with him for a few moments' formal call, but he kept us for considerably over the hour. My impressions were that he was forceful, highly intelligent, had a remarkable and accurate memory, a wide range of information and a capacity for lucid exposition. All this was contrary to my preconceptions based on books which tried to make him out a dummy.

"I was soon convinced that this was the boss himself. My adverse reactions to his totalitarian aspects were, however, confirmed by minor items. From his clothing and hairdo he was obviously a great deal of an exhibitionist. He seemed to have trigger spots in his mind which when touched set him off like a man in furious anger.

"The conversation touched on Communism, whereupon he exploded and orated. I silently agreed with his conclusions so did not mind. A moment later the discussion spread to democracy, and he began to explode again, whereupon I remarked that I could not be expected to agree as I was one of those myself. The subject was dropped and we went on to some less controversial topics.

"I of course did not then know that Hitler had already determined upon his barbarous invasion of Austria four days later. He certainly did not confide in me."

In his brief personal diary of the "sentimental journey," which he used as the raw material for the *Collier's* article, Mr. Hoover diagnosed the "trigger spots" in Hitler's mind as "an emotional streak that goes off into a mental loss of control like furious anger." He regarded this streak as "of utmost importance."

The "less controversial subjects" discussed are indicated in the diary notes to have been "housing; the economic situation in the world."

Ambassador Wilson gave a luncheon in the former President's honor directly after the Hitler interview. Wilson had arrived in Berlin only a short time previously and was the chief beneficiary of Mr. Hoover's visits with Hitler, Göring, and Hjalmar Schacht. Diplomatic formalities, such as Mr. Wilson was bound to observe when he paid official visits, were waived as Mr. Hoover was not "official."

Baron Konstantin von Neurath, who only a short time previously had been succeeded by Joachim von Ribbentrop as German Foreign Minister, was seated next to Herbert Hoover on one side and quite near Dr. Paul Schmidt, Hitler's chief interpreter, on the other.

The *Collier's* article, already quoted, relates:

"This gentleman [Dr. Schmidt] proceeded in undertones to give Von Neurath an apparently amusing account of the minor clash between these two 'high priests' of rival faiths. I noticed two American newspaper correspondents at the opposite side of the table, listening intently. They hardly waited to be civil in their excuses for departure.

"I did not at the moment know what their haste was about. But they had smelled from the Schmidt-Von Neurath conversation that a fight had taken place between myself and Hitler and proceeded to telegraph such a story to the American press. The next thing I knew Schmidt came to see me, much perturbed, and asked me to make the statement that my impressions of Hitler had been most favorable. Schmidt's anxiety was, of course, for himself. I could not assist him. He later squared himself by giving the impression that the story was manufactured by Paul Smith, one of my secretaries—who was not present at the meeting at all."

One of the newsmen referred to was Pierre J. Huss, Berlin correspondent for International News Service. My colleague has kindly supplied me with a copy of his story which caused the furor, as published on March 8, 1938, with permission to reprint it as well as to quote from the exchange of letters between him and his home office that ensued:

"For the first time in his career, Adolf Hitler today heard from an American statesman a forthright denunciation of Nazism as a practical and enduring force in world affairs.

"The detractor, speaking straight from the shoulder, was Herbert Clark Hoover, thirty-first President of the United States, who spent forty minutes in private audience with the Führer.

"Hitler barred Hoover's personal press attaché from the meeting, but a reliable source revealed to this correspondent their conversation developed into one of the most remarkable ideological clashes in recent times.

"Hoover bluntly informed Hitler the United States will never become reconciled to understanding or even having the slightest tolerance for Nazism as a political and national creed.

"He declared further American democratic ideals reject the fundamental principles on which the Nazi regime is based and on which it flourishes.

"Hoover, according to this well-informed source, went so far as to even boldly intimate his own doubts as to the durability of the Nazi ideology within the borders of Germany itself.

"Hoover expressed keen interest in the German housing program. The Führer thereupon painted a glowing picture of Nazi progress within the past five years.

"Hitler took occasion to reassert the peaceful aims of the Nazi regime, while insisting on Germany's right to full equality. It was during this stage of the conversation that Hoover reportedly voiced his own strong opinion about Nazism. . . ." (There followed a breakdown of Mr. Hoover's other engagements.)

When a dispatch by a rival nonagency correspondent indicated that both Mr. Hoover and Hitler were "intensely annoyed" at the Huss version of what happened, the latter's editor, Barry Faris, asked for an explanation.

"Pete" Huss replied in part on March 21:

"For your confidential information, Hitler hit the ceiling Wednesday night, when he heard that the Hoover conversation with him had leaked out. . . . Because of the unfavorable tenor of the Hoover conversation, the Nazis were anxious to keep this story quiet. I felt it my journalistic obligation to send this important American story after it had been specifically okayed in every word. . . . I was given the alternative of summarily leaving Germany or withdrawing the story, but the whole matter was cleared up in my favor. . . . The story was true and I stood on it as such.

"That evening Hoover let it be known from Warsaw that he would publicly go to bat for me if necessary. He refused before leaving Berlin to give any denial to the Foreign Office on my story, although the Foreign Office sent a man to the station with him, specifically instructed to get that denial. . . ."

International News Service headquarters not only accepted the explanation but commended him for "the stand you took and the manner in which you followed through to prove your integrity."

After the Ambassador's luncheon Herbert Hoover was visited by Dr. Hjalmar Schacht, Hitler's Reichsbank President and his former Minister of Economics (he later went into the underground opposition to the Nazi regime). The entry in Mr. Hoover's brief diary on this visit is:

"That afternoon Dr. Schacht called and sent for other leading German industrialists, economists and others to come in and discuss matters. I had known Schacht ever since 1914.

"The Carl Schurz Foundation gave a banquet and reception in the evening. This is undoubtedly a fake 'association' conducted by the Government solely to entertain visiting Americans. [The *Vereinigung Carl Schurz* was founded in 1926 during the government of the Weimar Republic as a truly democratic institution for the fostering of good relations between Germany and the United States, with Reichstag Deputy Anton Erkelenz, a noted German trade union leader and member of the Democratic party, as its president. When the Nazis came into power, they seized it, dismissed Herr Erkelenz, and converted it into what Mr. Hoover termed a "fake association."]

"Schacht told me the University of Berlin would like to confer an honorary degree on me out of recognition of my services after the Armistice and while President. I got out politely by not having time to stay another day."

The principal German speaker at the Carl Schurz dinner was Dr. Schacht. It was a rather stiff, stodgy, strained affair, inasmuch as the guests were obviously at variance ideologically with their hosts. No one knew whether he might not be sitting next to a Nazi secret agent.

Dr. Schacht toasted Mr. Hoover as a "protagonist of the conscience of humanitarianism and international understanding," and averred that "there is a certain tragic element in the fact that a man who had the noblest ideas and the most humanitarian thoughts, through the mistakes and consequences of post-war times could not bring those ideas to full fruition."

My brief diary notes of March 8 contain this passage, *inter alia:* "Had long talk with Hoover. Referring to Nazism's regimented, dictated economy he observed: 'You can probably get greater efficiency and less waste, but don't other things go by the board in the process? Liberty? Freedom of thought and speech? Isn't this what it grows upon?' His conclusion seemed to be that the U.S.A. should stay out of Germany and Europe. 'We get no thanks,' he commented."

A day later the Hoover party were the guests of Field Marshal Hermann Göring, the Number Two man in the Hitler dictatorship. This episode is described by Mr. Hoover in the *Collier's* article of March 24, 1951:

"I received an urgent invitation from Field Marshal Goering to attend a luncheon at his hunting lodge, Karin Hall, some miles from Berlin. The American ambassador was all for it, for he had never seen the No. 2 Nazi either, except in parades.

"The only affinity of Karin Hall to a shooting lodge was the imitation shingles on the roof. It was an immense structure, with rooms half as large as a Waldorf dining room, crammed with hundreds of thousands of dollars' worth of furniture, paintings and art, including two or three busts of Napoleon. Goering came from an impecunious military family and had never legitimately enjoyed more than a general's salary.

"When our cars entered the courtyard we were stopped by a sentry for no apparent reason. In a few moments there emerged from a side door 12 or 16 men dressed as huntsmen and armed with French horns. They played the Siegfried's Hunting Call the most beautifully I have ever heard it. I certainly knew we were in a Wagnerian atmosphere.

"We went to lunch each attended by at least one butler and a footman. Perhaps some were secret service men in livery to prevent visitors doing bodily harm to our host. In any event some of them were always within reach. In the middle of the table was a life-sized bust of a lady wearing a string of pearls. Curiosity drew my eye to it in contemplation of whether it was brass or gold. Göring noted this and remarked, 'My first wife. It's pure gold.' His second wife, Emmy, was somewhere in the house."

Added interesting details of the Karin Hall visit are to be found in Mr. Hoover's diary for March 9:

"We stayed over this day, as Goering had sent word he would like to see me. We went to lunch to his 'hunting lodge,' Karin Hall. I was accompanied by the American Ambassador, Galpin, Paul Smith, and John Hartigan.

"A shooting lodge! Rooms as large as a Waldorf dining room; millions of dollars in building, furniture, painting and art objects; huntsman's call from *Siegfried;* reminiscent of 'Beggar on Horseback' with his 12 butlers, each with 12 footmen. Request for information on 'rationalization' and on mineral resources of Russia; familiarity with my background—from a memorandum; map of Czechoslovakia illuminated by electric lights—'Dagger at Germany's heart.' Lunch with younger nobility. Gold bust of former wife studded with pearls. Shown the portion built by William II, about 2% of the present structure. We were there for five hours, probably three hours of conversation. Very brilliant, conservative, ruthless. 'I can do that before ten o'clock.' Probably cruel. Polite."

Perrin C. Galpin also wrote up his impressions in his privately circulated *Random Notes—Personal and Confidential,* from which a few excerpts are here quoted as they emphasize certain details other than those noted by Mr. Hoover:

"The trip from Berlin takes about one hour. After passing a small village, which seemed to be well equipped with military guards, we turned on to a road with game preserves on either side which at one place at least had an electric connection in the road which notified of the approach of any vehicle.

"Karin Hall is a so-called hunting lodge set in a forest or game preserve, with a large park, well wooded, but in excellent condition, and a good sized lake at least half a mile long. . . .

"About eighteen people attended the luncheon and were all assembled in the Great Hall to await the coming of the *Hausherr,* General Göring. The party was planned to be informal and ladies were present, although Mrs. Göring was not there as she is expecting a baby in June. Sherry and Port were served in the Great Hall by men servants dressed in a modified uniform of Frederick the Great's soldiers—knee breeches, buttoned gaiters, etc., coats with tails buttoned back to show the lining. Very handsome.

"The dining room was thoroughly modernistic. The walls were made of parchment and illuminated from the far side. All the other lighting was concealed. One long table was decorated with silver flowers and in the center a bust, apparently solid gold, of the General's first wife, named Karin. This bust, I understand, had a detachable necklace and could be turned on its pedestal so that a visitor could see the profile and head from every angle.

"An excellent meal, fairly simple, was served. I understood later that the meal and some of the waiters came from Horcher's in Berlin. After luncheon we walked through another passage where the outside wall was quite thick and had been turned into a combination flower garden and aquarium. I should say that the fish had a place about 200 feet long in which to swim and 2 feet wide, so that one looked through plate glass into the aquarium and on to daffodils and flowers which were also growing there.

"We moved on for coffee into a large room with a great many trophies of the hunt on the walls, each carefully labelled. This room was similar to what one might find in a Canadian hunting lodge and was quite well done. One of the Germans told me that he had been at Karin Hall three times, but this was the first time he had ever seen this particular room. The whole view outside reminded me of Canada or Maine. Under each animal's head on the wall were the particulars, date and place of the kill.

"When it was time to go the General had arranged for from 12 to 16 huntsmen in green uniforms, each with his hunting horn, to assemble in line in the courtyard and play the Hunting Song from Siegfried. It was a magnificent sight and we did not know whether to salute, stand at attention, or, as we did, get in the automobile and drive away.

"General Göring has a number of personal aides, all of whom are flyers, as he himself was an aviator in the war. Each personal aide has 'General Göring' embroidered on his coatsleeve. One of the aides told me that the General was a fine man. 'He gave me my house, he gave me my automobile, he gave me my plane. I like the General,' he said.

"Planes have been developed, we understand, with a very slow landing speed which will enable the General's aides to go quickly to Berlin and back when it is necessary.

"The General, who spoke no English, spent a good deal of time with Mr. Hoover after luncheon discussing questions of elimination of waste. He had read the books put out under Mr. Hoover's authority in connection with the campaign when Mr. Hoover was in the Department of Commerce. The General also took great pleasure in talking about the 'substitutes' program for textiles, oil, foods, etc. etc. . . .

"On comparing notes after the luncheon we all decided that Karin Hall would put to shame the wildest dreams of any Hollywood magnate. The whole place was built in a year and one could estimate the cost of the whole thing, including the art, at anywhere from three to six million dollars.

"Paul Smith was particularly affected at luncheon at having a German companion say to him, 'we are the party of the people.'"

Mr. Hoover summed up his impressions of his unscheduled stay in Germany in his *Diary:* "My impressions of Germany are perhaps best indicated by a distinct lift of spirit the moment we crossed the frontier going out. One feels a dreadful, repressive atmosphere; the men I have known for years, [Theodor] Lewald, former Minister of the Interior; [Christian Otto] Fischer [banker]; Dr. [Hermann] Schmitz of the Chemical Trust; [Dr. Bruno] Bruhn, former director of Krupp's; Schacht and others would not talk anything but banalities in each other's presence. But each wanted a few minutes alone, which I was able to arrange. They then all took a gloomy view of the situation and the future. None of these men were Nazis."

Mr. Galpin in his confidential notes added this further observation on the Hitler type of tyranny: "One feature of this sort of government is the continual uncertainty regarding the personal relationships of the dictator. When Mr. Hoover saw Mr. Hitler on March 8 there was even more excitement among the Germans as to what had been said than there was among the newspaper people. What Mr. Hitler says is the German doctrine."

On his arrival in New York on March 19 Mr. Hoover received the representatives of the Fourth Estate. He expounded his general conclusions, based upon his travels in fourteen countries, but declined to expand upon his conversations with Hitler and other European leaders.

In a newsreel talk on March 29 he emphasized that American policy in his opinion should be one of "inflexible determination to keep out of other people's wars and Europe's age-old quarrels. Our job is to cleanse our democracy, raise our moral standards, and keep alive the light of free men in the world."

Seven months later one of the most disgraceful acts in the history of the German Reich was perpetrated by Adolf Hitler and his minions. Using the assassination of a young diplomat in the German Embassy at Paris by his exceptionally intimate Jewish friend as a pretext, the Nazis engaged in wholesale destruction and plundering of Jewish shops, the burning of synagogues, the maltreatment of individual Hebrews, and wholesale arrests of non-Aryans.

Jews were forbidden to possess arms. The Jewish Community—such as there was left of it after mass emigrations during the preceding years—was fined the colossal sum of 1,000,000,000 Reichsmarks to "atone" for the Paris assassination, a sum that virtually amounted to the confiscation of all remaining Jewish assets. The Jews of Germany were forbidden to own or administer commercial undertakings or to engage in independent handicraft. Membership in a cooperative ceased automatically.

A further "atonement fine" consisted in the exclusion of Jews from German schools and higher institutions of learning and from attendance at cultural functions, including motion-picture showings, and in limitation to the use of designated streets. At concerts of their ghettolike groups they were forbidden to render the works of Aryan composers such as Bach, Beethoven, and Brahms.

Herbert Hoover could not remain silent as the world learned of these atrocities. On November 13, 1938, The Associated Press carried the following story: "Palo Alto, Cal., Nov. 13—(AP)—Former President Herbert Hoover issued a public statement today expressing his indignation at the treatment of Jews in Germany.

"The statement prepared at the request of the Federal Council of Churches [of Christ], was addressed to Samuel McCrae Cavert, general secretary of the federation, New York City.

" 'I am glad to again evidence my own indignation and to join in an expression of public protest at the treatment of the Jew in Germany,' the statement said.

" 'It is not the German people at large who are to be blamed for this action. The blame is squarely up to the political agencies in power. These individuals are taking Germany back 450 years in civilization to Torquemada's [Thomas Torquemada, inquisitor general of Spain] expulsion of the Jews from Spain. They are bringing to Germany not alone the condemnation of the public opinion of the world. These men are building their own condemnation by mankind for centuries to come.

" 'They are destroying every effort of the friends of the German people who have sought to be of aid to them. And I believe I have more than a usual right of protest. I have held inalterably to belief in the great contribution the German people have made to civilization in the past and to the necessity for civilization that they be given opportunity to take again their place in the forward march of the world.

" 'With these views I labored to reduce the injustices of the treaties both before and after they were signed. I insisted upon saving their people from famine after the armistice. I have participated over the years in many official actions to aid in their recovery from war. I had hoped that recent events might be the end of the action by the party in power which endangers the whole world.

" 'It is still my belief that the German people if they could express themselves would not approve these acts against the Jews. But as they cannot so express themselves, it is the duty of men everywhere to express our indignation not alone at the suffering these men are imposing on an innocent people but at the blow they are striking at civilization itself.' "

9

CONCLUSIONS DRAWN FROM A FOURTEEN-NATION JOURNEY

In his press interview of March 19, 1938, and his newsreel remarks on March 29 Herbert Hoover had touched only briefly upon the conclusions at which he arrived during his "sentimental journey" as a result not only of personal observations in fourteen countries, but also, as he put it, of the opportunities he had "to discuss the forces in motion with more than a hundred leaders whose friendship I had enjoyed in the past and probably another hundred whom I met for the first time."

In two prepared speeches, one before the Council on Foreign Relations in New York on March 31, the other during a Homecoming Welcome in his honor in San Francisco on April 8, he outlined his position in detail.

Regarding Hitler's National Socialism—a form of Fascism—he said in New York:

"In Germany Fascism has had its most complete development under the iron rule of the Nazi party. In order to understand the Nazi regime we must not overlook its apparent accomplishments. It has brought about a gigantic mobilization of a materialistic system at the hands of the government. Great industrial wastes in strikes and materials have been eliminated. Great efforts have been obtained from the people in work and sacrifice of comfort. Progress has been made toward self-sufficiency. Some sort of employment and economic security has been brought to all who comply. And concentration camps give security to the balance. New houses, jobs and more recreation have been brought to the underprivileged. The support of a gigantic growing military machine has been successfully squeezed out of an already skimpy standard of living. Germany has been restored to a first class military power. It is today feared throughout the world. Germany today burns with a prideful sense of restored self esteem. Youth has been fired with new hopes and high emotions.

"So far as material things are concerned the average German is today better off than five years ago. Yet to a lover of human liberty there is another side to even this picture. All the remaining democracies in Europe have made sounder and greater recovery from the depression than has Germany or any of the Fascist states in the same period. And the standard of living is higher in all the Democratic states than in any of the Fascist states.

"But for us there are deeper issues in all this. Under this regime the spirit of man is subordinated to the state. The individual must be developed into conformity with the national will as expressed by the leaders. Whatever is deemed by them as good for the state becomes the standard of justice, right, and morality. That has become the basis of law.

"And Fascism has demonstrated a way to fool all the people all the time—by suppression of all criticism and free expression; and by drilling children and youth, stage by stage, to a governmentally prescribed mental attitude. A controlled Press and organized propaganda have poured this new faith into the adults. It has stamped out, or controlled, every form of independent association from Trades Union to Universities. It has instituted a form of terrorism, for the fear of concentration camps is ever present. Its darkest picture is expressed in the heart-breaking persecution of helpless Jews. Intellectual sterility and deadened initiative and individuality are its inevitable results. It is becoming a gigantic spartanism. And let no one believe it is about to collapse."

These observations about Nazi Germany must be measured, however, against the background of Mr. Hoover's general conclusions concerning Europe. In New York he said:

"Seven obvious forces or factors have come to the forefront in Europe over these nineteen years.

"The first of these is the rise of dictatorships—totalitarian, authoritarian or centralized governments, all with so-called Planned Economies. Nationalism, militarism and imperialism have certainly not diminished in nineteen years. . . . Today there are 30,000,000 less people living under liberal institutions than there were before the War.

"The second great movement today, partly cause and partly effect, is the race to arms. Every nation in Europe . . . is now building for war or defense more feverishly than ever before in its history. . . . Europe today is a rumbling war machine, without the men yet in the trenches.

"The third process in motion is increased government debts and deficits. There is hardly a balanced budget in Europe—that is, if we strip off the disguises of words. . . .

"The fourth movement is: every nation is striving for more and more self-sufficiency in industry and food production for either military reasons or to meet the necessities of 'Planned Economy.' . . . New and far more effective walls have been erected around each nation by quotas, exchange controls, internal price fixing, clearing agreements, and inter-governmental agreements on both purchases and sales.

"The fifth factor is the failure of the League of Nations as a potent force for peace, and its complete replacement by the old shifting balances of power. And they are certainly shifting.

"The sixth of these forces is fear—fear by nations of one another, fear by governments of their citizens, fear by citizens of their governments, and the vague fear of people everywhere that general war is upon them again. And there is the fear of the promised massacre of civil populations from the air.

"The seventh force is the steady increase in some nations of brutality, of terrorism, and disregard for both life and justice. Concentration camps, persecution of Jews, political trials, bombing of civil populations are but the physical expressions of an underlying failure of morals terrible to contemplate. All in all, it is an alarming and disheartening picture. . . .

"These are the visible, apparent tides and moving storms. There are still deeper currents beneath them. I need hardly catalogue them. They comprise all the inheritances of the war and in fact of history. There were the injustices and unrealities of the Peace Treaties. There were the debts and post-war inflations that led up to the European financial collapse in 1931 with its enormous unemployment and misery, both to themselves and to us.

"There has been one blunder after another. Not the least of them have been the lack of cooperation by the Allies with the struggling democracy of Germany; the rejection of the American proposals of disarmament in 1932, and the destruction of the currency conference of 1933. . . .

"There sounds constantly through this labyrinth the shrill note of new philosophies of government and the echo of old orders of society disguised in new phrases. There are democracy, socialism and communism of fifty-seven varieties; there is Fascism with its variations from soft to hard; there are autocratic forms all the way from disguised democracy through authoritarianism, totalitarianism to dictatorships and unlimited monarchy.

"And these movements contain as many dangers for the American people as either the military forces or trade barriers of Europe."

An illuminating variation of this theme and its implied application to Hitler's Nazism is to be found in this passage of Mr. Hoover's San Francisco address:

"While outwardly the incidents of life go on much the same everywhere, underneath Europe is seething with change which will yet affect the whole destiny of human institutions and the ways of human life. Europe is giving birth to a new philosophy of government and of life.

"That has happened at other periods in history. Within the Christian Era we have seen the rise of Christianity, the rise of Mohammedanism, the rise of Feudalism, the rise of the Reformation, the rise of Liberalism and its philosophy of free men, and the rise of Communism. And each of these great ideas has carried a train of human conflict.

"I am not going to take your time to discuss or describe this new European philosophy or what it means today or to the future.

"But let no man underestimate the dangers to free men. It not only represents the mobilization of racial instincts and racial yearnings for glory and power. It not alone represents ruthless economic organization at the sacrifice of all personal liberty. It represents the extinction of pity and mercy which Christianity gave the world. It represents an upsurge of abhorrent brutality of which the Jews are helpless victims. Its method is that any end justifies the means. And that justifies every perversion of intellectual honesty and government morals."

Mr. Hoover in many warnings following his "sentimental journey" made it evident that he did not believe in what his successor, President Franklin D. Roosevelt, described as "quarantine action" against dictatorships. In his New York address he argued:

"I find in many quarters of Europe and some in America an insistence that, as Democracy is endangered by the rise of dictatorships and authoritarian governments, therefore democracies should join in some sort of mutual undertaking for protective action. These ideas were greatly stimulated and encouraged by the word quarantine from these shores. Such proposals, if sincere, involve more than mere good words. Anything honest in that direction implies the pledge of some sort of joint military or economic action by the United States with other powers. We may as well be blunt about it.

"If we join with the two other powerful democracies, Great Britain and France, we are engaging ourselves in an alliance directed against Germany and Italy and all the satellites they can collect. But we are doing more than this. Great Britain has her own national and imperial problems and policies. Any commitment of ourselves will mean that we are dragged into these policies. France has her own special alliances and her own policies, including an alliance with Communist Russia. We would be supporting Stalin.

"But more than all this, we would be fostering the worst thing that can happen to civilization, that is, the building up of a war between government faiths or ideologies. Such a combination of democracies would at once result in combining the autocracies against the democracies. It could have all the hideous elements of old religious wars.

"We should have none of it. If the world is to keep the peace, then we must keep peace with dictatorships as well as with popular governments. The forms of government which other peoples pass through in working out their destinies are not our business. You will recollect we were once animated by a desire to save the world for Democracy. The only result that time was to sow dragons' teeth which sprang up into dictatorships. We can never herd the world into the paths of righteousness with the dogs of war.

"While we should reject the whole idea of pledging our military or economic forces to any scheme for preserving peace by making war, we have both the obligation and the interest to organize and join in the collective moral forces to prevent war. I know I will be told again that moral forces do not weigh much in a world of soldiers and battleships. But the greatest force for peace is still the public opinion of the world. That is a moral force. I will be told again that it has no weight. But I found everywhere an anxiety for the approval of world opinion. Every consequential nation supports at great expense a propaganda bureau for that purpose. The dictatorships especially devote themselves to it.

"And why? Because the desire of nations for the good opinion of mankind is not dead. Secretary Hull's eloquent denunciation of international lawlessness was echoed in every newspaper in the world. Decency is still news."

After making a number of concrete suggestions for the mobilization of the moral forces of the world for peace, Mr. Hoover reverted to the fulminations of Adolf Hitler:

"The leader of German Fascism in a speech last week hurled the taunt to democracies that 'not a single decent nation has died for the sake of democratic formalities.' To the extent that races do not actually die because they forfeit individual liberty, that may be true. But what is far more important is that when true Liberty dies, then Justice and Truth die. And intellectual progress and morality die also.

"I have no doubt that Fascism will fail some time, just as Marxian Socialism has failed already. The stifling of intellectual progress, the repression of the spirit of men, the destruction of initiative and enterprise, will offset all the efficacies of planned economy. Even economic life cannot succeed where criticism has disappeared and where individual responsibility is constantly shirked for fear of the state. Even in Fascist countries liberal ideas are not dead and will not be downed. Every despotism today lives with fear of liberty at its heart—or there would be no concentration camps.

"And I may add that, having listened in many countries to eulogies of Planned Economy and Fascism and of their benefits to the common man, I detected in every case the hope that some day liberty might return. The spirits of Luther, of Goethe, or Schiller, of Mazzini and Garibaldi are not dead.

"Moreover there has been nothing shown me in Europe in elimination of wastes or better housing or security to workers or farmers or old age that we cannot do better under democracy if we will. Though I had little need for confirmation in my faith, I pray God that this nation may keep its anchors firmly grounded in intellectual liberty and spiritual freedom."

On October 26, 1938, our thirty-first President, responding to an invitation to address the Eighth Forum on Current Problems conducted by the New York *Herald Tribune,* chose as his subject "America and the World Crisis."

This address climaxed in an unequivocal "no" to the question, "If there should be a war between the Western European Democracies and the Despotisms, is there sufficient reason why we should join?" Mr. Hoover reasoned as follows:

"The call to join is based upon the preservation of personal liberty in the world. Free economic life is not built on war. Any major war means that our country must be mobilized into practically a Fascist government. It will be so organized. It went some distance in the last great war, although we did not use that term at the time. It would have gone much farther if the war had extended longer. The lowered vitality of free enterprise and the necessity to subordinate our enormous peace-time national debt both enter into the improbability of after-war demobilization of a further centralized power.

"Those who would have us go to war to save liberty might give a little thought to the preponderant chance that we should come out of such a struggle with personal liberty restricted for generations. Moreover it is even less likely that the European Democracies would emerge as Democracies.

"If European war should take place between Liberal and Totalitarian countries the only hope for survival of democracy is for us to stay out of it and keep the lamp of liberty alight in this world.

"The second reason for staying out is the futility of American intervention in Europe. We can make war but we do not and can not make peace in Europe.

"Our people do not have the knowledge and the willingness to compromise ideals and principles which meet their necessities. There is the ever present factor of a thousand years of European history that on a score of boundaries there exist zones of mixed populations, each with its own age-old hates and its aspirations. Whatever way these boundaries may be drawn, some people will be separated from their 'fatherlands.' These agitations are the key to much European war history. There are also economic factors which necessitate the joining of peoples of diverse races. In war-fed fears and hates there are certain to evolve balances of power for their defenses. There is no clear base of idealism or principle for making peace in Europe. It is a matter of compromise.

"And the third reason for keeping out of the European situation lies in the fact that there is no clear call of liberty from Europe. France has her own special alliances and her policies, including an alliance with dictatorial Russia. She believes that is necessary for her defense and we have no right to criticize. But if we are involved, far from standing on the side of Liberty, we should be standing on the side of Communism. And Russia is certainly not a Democratic state.

"And as great a Democracy as is the British Commonwealth and as vitally important as it is to the continuance of civilization, she also has interests of her own that we can scarcely be called upon to defend."

Came the Second World War. It was unleashed, despite all peace efforts on the part of men of good will, by the aggressive acts of Adolf Hitler, who in due time was joined by Benito Mussolini and the militarists of Japan.

As the pressures mounted for the United States to enter the fray, Herbert Hoover delivered a warning on October 31, 1940, in the Colosseum of Lincoln, Nebraska, which was broadcast over the NBC Blue Network:

"The over-riding question is: Is fanned war psychosis the sort of statesmanship that makes for peace of our country?

"This fanned hysteria has reached the danger point where reason may be lost. Every polite caution and sober warning is met with the yell of 'Hitler sympathizer,' 'appeasement,' 'the Fifth Column,' 'isolationist,' 'pacifist.'

"We might dismiss these political maneuvers and these unbalanced statements were it not that they push this country steadily closer to war. And to these hysteria raisers I would like to give a word of caution on the consequences of war between the United States and Asia or Europe.

"If we go to war, that war must end either in a stalemate and compromise, or alternatively it must be ended by the actual invasion of the enemy country and its disarmament. . . .

"If we get into this war it is not an eighteen months' action. It is more likely to be another Thirty Years' War.

"And might I add something about ideological wars in general, as that is the kind of war we are being urged to get into. Ideological wars are no more capable of settling anything than the thousand years of religious wars of the Middle Ages. If we won such wars by exhaustion of the enemy we would be incapable of establishing democracy in its place. The way of life of a people must come from within; it cannot be compelled from without. The Communists are the most likely beneficiaries."

As the war progressed, the danger of wholesale starvation mounted alarmingly in five little nations in Europe—Finland, Norway, Holland, Belgium, and Central Poland—comprising 37,000,000 people, of whom about 15,000,000 were children.

In August of 1940 Mr. Hoover was appealed to for help by leaders of these small nations. He revealed to the students of Vassar College how he reacted. On November 15 he told them:

"Some three months ago leaders of these little nations asked that I raise a voice to the world on their behalf. They asserted that devastating famine and pestilence would be upon them with winter. No man can receive such an appeal of human misery without action.

"I proposed a plan as the basis of agreement by the war governments.

"These proposals were that the Germans, on one hand, agree

(a) not to take any of the domestic products of these people and to furnish the equivalent of any food that may already have been taken; (b) to permit such imports as can be had from other parts of Europe; (c) to allow free passage of food without attack.

"On the other hand, the British to raise the blockade so as to allow one food ship at a time to pass so long as the guarantees are fulfilled.

"And finally both sides to agree to adequate control of distribution by a neutral organization to assure that these agreements are carried out."

Anticipating an objection which he felt was sure to come, he continued:

"There is a group of persons who close their minds with the idea that the Germans would get the food and that it would help the Germans to win the war and that therefore the subject should not be further discussed. They obstinately refuse to believe the fact that such an effort was successfully managed in the last war, and that the occupying army did not benefit. They do not realize, moreover, that such an operation is conducted in such a way that there would be only a small stock of food supplies on hand in the occupied area at any one time. This stock would not exceed 120,000 to 140,000 tons. The German nation consumes about 1,400,000 tons a month. If they seized it all, they would be getting only a three days' food supply. That would not prolong the war very much. In any event, under any such violation the whole work would have to stop as hopeless.

"Driven from these positions, this sort of people then falls back on the argument that agreements made now would be less likely to be respected than those in the last world war. But agreements with belligerents during war are not to be based only upon altruism, humanitarianism, or good will. With people who are desperately fighting in a great war, agreements must be based on self-interest.

"When the food supply falls to famine levels, people don't lie down and die from starvation. Long before they get to that point their physical resistance is so lowered by malnutrition that they die of disease. The children weaken first, the women and old men next. The common cold turns to pneumonia. Influenza seems to become very much more virulent and deadly in its passage through non-resistant populations. Typhoid and smallpox are more prevalent because of lowered resistance. Typhus always appears, for when a population is approaching famine levels, it will eat all of its fat supplies and thus deprive itself of soap. Soap is the greatest disinfectant that the human race has discovered. With the absence of soap, lice at once spread, and from lice comes typhus.

"It is to the interest of the German Army that these cesspools of disease and contagion are not created. And it is to the interest of the whole world that they are not created. For contagion, once it starts from such cesspools, will spread irrespective of borders or nations or ideologies. You may remember the malignant influenza epidemic during the last war which first appeared in starving Central Europe and spread over the whole world. Such an operation as this is in the interest of Great Britain and America. If confidence in the ideals of democracy is to be upheld in these peoples now is the time to hold it.

"There is another group who say that the British Blockade is the great instrument in the fight against totalitarianism and that it must not even be opened for a single ship. This idea is based upon an illusion. That is that a blockade is a sort of earth embankment and that if a single hole is permitted it will automatically enlarge until the embankment is swept away. A blockade is nothing of the kind. It is a notification that traffic cannot pass except by permission. That permission is in the control of the dominant sea-power. It can be extended and withdrawn at will, ship by ship."

Our Elder Statesman closed his argument with this appeal: "Can you believe that American public opinion or the spiritual leadership of America has so lost its bearings as to be opposed to even an effort to aid those who lie in the ditch?

"To show that American opinion is not indifferent to their sufferings is their only hope today.

"There are things in this world that are not silenced by ideological argument or armchair strategists or declamation as to who is responsible. They are not to be settled that way because of the teachings of Christ which have resounded down these two thousand years. That teaching gave to mankind a new vision and part of that vision was mercy and compassion."

In an article which appeared in *Collier's* of November 23, 1940, entitled, "Feed Hungry Europe," he again pleaded for the little nations, caught between German occupation and British blockade: "Their normal supplies are stopped by the German occupation on one side and the British blockade on the other. Unless some sort of method can be set up with the belligerent governments by which aid may be extended to these victim nations, the world will witness this winter a death roll from famine far greater than during all the four years of the last World War. It will witness the death or stunting of millions of children who surely have a right to live. Death will come to the weaker in the men and women.

"As famine and disease rise with the winter, the cries of these people will ascend above any press censorship, any war hysteria, or any government official. And in America we have 10 or 12 millions of citizens who are of these racial stocks, many of them with actual relatives in these countries. These racial groups have long since organized themselves into a multitude of relief committees seeking aid for their people. They will not be silenced. Throughout the world in the colonial possessions and in other neutral countries are millions of people of these racial groups. They are not content to see their families suffer without effort to save them.

"This problem has been under debate in all parts of the world during the past few months. No man or group of men can end this question by saying, 'Hush, hush.' Nor can it be ended by emotional controversy over who has the responsibility for this situation. My views upon that subject are probably as strong as those of anyone. But the starving people will be there just the same."

Again he appealed to the American conscience in the article: "We hear much of the purposes for which this war is being fought. They include the upholding of the standards of Christianity. One of the major distinctions of the Christian faith is mercy and compassion. The parable of the Samaritan has played a large part in the moral foundations of all these nations and has a live hold upon the hearts of their people and our people. And compassion is part of the woof and warp of democracy. From this ethic has sprung our vast fabric of benevolent institutions, the relief of our unemployed, our hospitals, our solicitude for the weak and the unfortunate. Today the Christian world is confronted with preserving the lives of 10 or 15 million people.

"We cannot as a Christian nation dismiss our concern that some solution be found by which they may be saved. And the parable of the Samaritan has pungent implications other than the compassion of the Samaritan alone. Perhaps some will remember the condemnation, which has echoed over centuries, of the priest and the Levite who passed by on the other side. And perhaps some will remember that the Greatest Teacher of all time did not allow His immortal vision to be clouded by a debate on the previous sins or the ideology of those who "stripped him of his raiment and wounded him . . . leaving him half dead. . . . He had compassion on him."

The passions aroused by the war raging in Europe were already running so high that the proposal for feeding the little countries at first met with skepticism and even outright hostility.

The relief organizations of the countries mentioned in Mr. Hoover's proposal rallied to the support of its proponent and issued a joint statement. They reiterated Mr. Hoover's suggestion, submitted data to prove its practicality, and argued that "an international commission should be set up to manage shipping, to import, safeguard, and distribute the food." The statement concluded with the words: "We are putting the vital question to the American people: 'Should Great Britain and Germany enter into agreements with a neutral commission which would protect the native food supplies from seizure and allow these little countries to save the lives of millions of their men, women and children from their own money, by their own ships and under safeguards that assure that they alone shall eat their food?' "

The signers of the joint statement included Chauncey McCormick and Maurice Pate, president and vice-president, respectively, of the Commission for Polish Relief; Edgar Rickard and Perrin C. Galpin, president and vice-president, respectively, of the Commission for Relief in Belgium; Hendrick Willem Van Loon, chairman of the Queen Wilhelmina Fund; and Johannes Westergaard, acting chairman of the Norwegian Relief Fund.

One principal opponent of the plan was the British government. Lord Lothian, His Majesty's Ambassador in Washington, on December 10 issued a statement setting forth Great Britain's official view that adoption of the "short-sighted" Hoover Plan would prolong the war and that it was Germany's responsibility to feed the little democracies. The statement argued:

"Under present conditions any such scheme must be of material assistance to Germany's war effort and would thereby postpone the day of liberation of these peoples from German subjugation. . . .

"The risk of starvation has been greatly exaggerated. It would be of no service to these people to send in food if it means the prolongation of their slavery. Moreover, any shortage of food from which they may suffer is solely due to German action. Until they were conquered by Germany they had ample food for their own needs. In conquering them and installing German control Germany has assumed responsibility for their welfare. . . .

"Now that Germany is in control of the food supplies of almost all the Continent west of Russia, the introduction of food from outside would add to the total amount of food available to Germany for whatever purposes she decides to allot it. Nor can it be forgotten that the German Government convert foodstuffs on a large scale into valuable war material.

"Moreover it must be remembered that the war against Great Britain is being actively and ruthlessly prosecuted from the countries under German occupation which border on the North Sea and the Atlantic. . . .

"It is certain that the Germans will not allow starvation to disorganize the social and economic structures upon which an important portion of their war effort depends. Equally, it is clear that any food which was allowed to pass the blockade would merely permit the diversion of yet more of the indigenous stocks to Germany or for the use of the German troops of occupation. . . ."

By December, 1940, Herbert Hoover had won his point. A National Committee on Food for the Five Small Democracies, numbering 1,000 leading citizens, was formed under his honorary chairmanship. This Committee was supported by more than 500 religious, educational, and civic leaders and 2,000 local committees.

Among its officers and members were General John J. Pershing, former Vice-President Charles G. Dawes, former Philippine Islands Governor-General Theodore Roosevelt, Jr., former Secretary of the Navy Charles Francis Adams, Admiral William V. Pratt, and many others, including state governors, former diplomats, and others who had served in high government positions.

The National Committee stated that its purpose was "to raise a voice on behalf of these people so that agreements may be made by the German and British Governments with a neutral organization: a.) by which their domestic food supplies can be protected from the occupying armies; b.) by which supplemental supplies can be imported through the German and British blockades and protected; c.) to secure the efficient operation of such a neutral organization."

Mr. Hoover was not heard from again publicly until May 11, 1941, when he made a Statement to the American People upon the Immediate Relation of the United States to This War. It opened with these words: "For the last six months I have remained aside from the controversy on whether we should join in this war. I have been waiting to see the progress of our preparedness. I have wanted to see the situation abroad develop more fully."

He reminded the American people of President Roosevelt's promise of October 23, 1940, ". . . We will not participate in foreign wars and will not send our army, naval or air forces to fight in foreign lands outside the Americas except in case of attack." Again he counseled keeping out of the war. He made it unequivocally plain, however, that he was in no sense of the word on the side of Hitler and Mussolini. He continued: "I do not need to express again my abhorrence of the whole totalitarian movement or its dangers to the world. That there be no misunderstanding, let me state at the outset that I support provision of the maximum tools of war to Britain; that I am convinced we can give this maximum during her next critical months only if we keep out of this war; that putting our navy into action is joining this war; that the whole European war situation is in transformation; that America is as yet unprepared even for adequate defense; that our people are not united. To go in now is neither wise nor for the interest of either Britain or ourselves."

On June 29 Mr. Hoover delivered a radio broadcast, "A Call to American Reason," to the nation from Chicago, saying at the outset:

"Six weeks ago I made a statement to the American people upon the relation of the United States to this war.

"That address has received large approval. It has naturally been disliked by the extremists. That is the psychosis of war. That disease has two outstanding symptoms. Those who catch it lose their reason in the fever of emotion. And in that fever intolerance rises to a pitch where it seeks to frighten men from free speech by defamation."

His chief attack was centered upon those who advocated America's entry into the war because "we must destroy the whole dictator ideology and impose the four freedoms on other nations." His argument ran in part:

"In the last seven days that call to sacrifice American boys for an ideal has been made as a sounding brass and a tinkling cymbal. For now we find ourselves promising aid to Stalin and his militant Communist conspiracy against the whole democratic ideals of the world. Collaboration between Britain and Russia will bring them military values, but it makes the whole argument of our joining the war to bring the four freedoms to mankind a gargantuan jest.

"On August 22, 1939, Stalin entered into an agreement with Hitler through which there should be joint onslaught on the democracies of the world. Nine days later Stalin attacked the Poles jointly with Hitler and destroyed the freedom of a great and democratic people. Fourteen days later Stalin destroyed the independence of democratic Latvia, Lithuania and Estonia. Ninety days later on came the unprovoked attack by Russia on democratic Finland. Is that not aggression and is not every case a hideous violation of treaties and international law?

"Stalin has taken advantage of the very freedoms of democracy to destroy them with the most potent Fifth Column in all history. He contributed to the destruction of France. He has daily implanted class hate in America and a stealthy war against our institutions. . . .

"We know also Hitler's hideous record of brutality, of aggression and as a destroyer of democracies. Truly Poland, Norway, Holland, Belgium, Denmark, France, and the others are dreadful monuments. But I am talking of Stalin at this moment.

"One of the real compensations America received for our enormous sacrifices in the last war was from the large part we played in establishing the democracies of Finland, Poland, Estonia, Latvia, and Lithuania. We nursed them in their infancy. We spent hundreds of millions to help them grow to manhood. Does America feel quite right about aiding Stalin to hold his enslavement of them? That is where Power Politics has carried us. No doubt we will make good our promise to aid Russia. But the ideological war to bring the four freedoms to the world died spiritually when we made that promise. . . .

"Now let us explore the practical side of an ideological war. I agree that the world would be vastly better if the whole totalitarian idea were extirpated. But those who still cling to this as the mission of America should ask realistically how much of a job it is. Especially in the face of this revolution in military weapons and this actual military situation.

"Such a war means that Hitler must be defeated. It means Mussolini must be defeated. It means the War Party in Japan must be defeated. It means that Turkey, Spain and Portugal must be defeated. It means that unless Hitler first disposes of Stalin we must defeat him also. Does any sane person believe that by military means we can defeat two-thirds of the military power of the whole world in even years and years? It would be another Children's Crusade.

"We cannot slay an idea or an ideology with machine guns. Ideas live in men's minds in spite of military defeat. They live until they have proved themselves right or wrong. These ideas are evil. And evil ideas contain the germs of their own defeat.

"Hitler's real weakness would be in peace. His invasions have won not the loyalty but the undying hate of two-thirds of the people under his control. They have known self-government and liberty for centuries. They are people of great spiritual and intellectual resistance. They cannot revolt in arms against tanks and planes but they will never accept a new order based on slavery. And these aggressions have won the fear and hate of all the rest of the world. Conquest always dies of indigestion.

"The whole Nazi ideology and the Nazi economic system are based upon coercion of the individual, the group or the class. Those coercions can be held in preparing for war or during war. They cannot be held in peace. Even if Hitler got peace the Nazi system will begin to go to pieces. Therefore, we do not need to despair that these evil ideologies will continue forever on this earth."

On October 19, 1941, Mr. Hoover once again took up the plight of the children in the small states of Europe. In a nation-wide address over the Mutual Network he traced the steps which the National Committee on Food for the Small Democracies, of which he was honorary chairman, had taken since its inception almost a year previously:

". . . We have made various proposals in an effort to find a solution. We proposed such methods and safeguards that there could be no military advantage to either side. We originally proposed that the same broad measures which were used in the last war should be adopted. It was to be administered by some non-official body. As this was refused we then proposed that we try a small experiment in Belgium to feed 2,000,000 children and 1,000,000 destitute adults. I clearly labelled it an experiment to determine what could be done. The Germans went a long way toward that agreement. The British decided against it, although it was to be safeguarded to meet their every military objection.

"After that time, American relations to the war so shifted that it was no longer possible for an American individual or any non-official body to conduct such negotiation or operations. To meet these changed conditions I therefore proposed last April to our State Department that our Government should enlist the services of some of the remaining neutral governments such as Switzerland, Sweden, Argentine or Ireland, to act as the trustee for these helpless people. I suggested that such a neutral government should with American encouragement negotiate with both of the belligerents such safeguards that would give no military advantage to either side. As a basis of such negotiation I proposed that the Germans, having a surplus of breadstuffs, should supply from their own stocks what breadstuffs were needed to save these children. I suggested that only the fats and special food for children which, due to the blockade, are deficient all over Europe, should be imported overseas. I proposed that the Germans should cease to take any of the native food products of these countries. I proposed that the trustee government should undertake to administer and safeguard the relief by its own agents. I proposed that the Administration take over the whole question. So far as I have been able to learn our Government took no steps in that direction."

Meeting once again the oft-heard objection that the food provided for the relief of neutral children would "benefit Hitler," he pointed out:

"The whole basis of our proposals is that the Germans cease to take food from the countries put under relief. And moreover, that they themselves furnish the breadstuffs taken from their own stocks. Their cooperation thus takes food from them, not to them.

"There are others who do not see how this process can be controlled even if agreed to. I, and three hundred living Americans know this can be done, for we did it twenty years ago. . . .

"It is not enough to plead international law. I agree Germany has the moral responsibility to feed them. There is a vague legal responsibility. But the overpowering fact is Germany does not, as the result of the blockade, have the kind of food needed for these women and children. They will not feed them. That stark fact faces the world. And these helpless people cannot eat morals and international law. Those Americans who deny moral responsibility cannot deny the obligations of compassion and self interest in the future of civilization. . . .

"I can say further to our own Government that last spring a number of the members of our Senate and House of Representatives became interested in this question. Jointly Democrats and Republicans introduced a resolution into both Houses, making a simple request of our Government that it should initiate negotiations for international action on this question. The resolution in the Senate was signed by 37 of its members, and I understand a majority of the whole Senate favors it. It was endorsed by a majority of members of the House. This resolution was endorsed by some 6,000 public bodies, church organizations, committees and other responsible groups throughout our country. Those resolutions alone represent the voice of at least 20 million people. Surely such an expression of American compassion deserves more adequate attention from our Government than to be dismissed by a curt letter from our State Department.

"There are lies spread that the Germans took the food from the Belgian Relief Commission in the last war. There were occasional infractions of those agreements. But these infractions were all remedied. And the officials of the British and French Governments, who contributed hundreds of millions of dollars to it, who had everything at stake, are on the public record time and time again expressing their satisfaction. And they based that satisfaction on the reports of their own agents."

Three weeks before Adolf Hitler by his declaration of war on the United States nullified all efforts on the part of Herbert Hoover and his followers to keep out of the European war, our Elder Statesman was invited to address the Union League Club of Chicago on November 19 on "Shall We Send Armies to Europe?" Again he counseled against entering the war unless attacked.

Regarding Hitler and Nazism he predicted: "There are certain things eating into Nazi vitals that will sometime end this travail to the world. The German people do not all believe in this evil ideology. Their victories have brought tidings of death and maiming to every fireside in Germany. The German people are living under privation and under strain.

"There is a widening gulf of friction between the right wings and the left wings in Germany as represented by the Army and Gestapo. The whole internal economic structure of Europe is degenerating.

"Even their great victories no longer seem to awaken enthusiasm in their people. There is a coming hopelessness of bringing the war to an end because their armies cannot cross the seas.

"Two hundred and thirty millions of people in 16 races which Hitler has overrun are seething with unquenchable hate. If he takes all Russia he will add another 100 million. His new order for Europe has met with no cooperation from these outraged peoples. They are not providing him consequential troops. I have never said, as some allege, that Hitler will be overcome by revolt of these unarmed peoples. But I am convinced that while he cannot be overcome by armies, by starvation or by air power, nonetheless the forces working within his regime will sometime destroy his dreams. Mine is therefore no gospel of defeatism.

"We want the end of these evil and brutal ideas of Nazism, Fascism, and Communism. The slogan of the day is to 'crush

Hitler.' The trouble with this world is far deeper than Hitler. He is only the symbol of these evil ideas which threaten civilization. He is the product of the miseries of the last war. A thousand Hitlers will rise when one falls unless these ideas are vanquished. All human experience shows ideas cannot be vanquished on the battlefield. These evils must die from within, if the world is to be delivered."

Adolf Hitler in a paranoiac mood challenged the United States to battle on December 11, 1941. Herbert Hoover accepted the situation loyally and from the richness of his experience offered ways and means for America to win. But he also looked beyond the end of the war and admonished his fellow citizens to prepare for peace even as they were straining every nerve to win the war.

In an address before the General Session of the Twenty-sixth Annual Assembly of the National Industrial Conference Board, Inc., of New York City, he said on May 20, 1942:

"The last time we did not prepare for peace-making.

"We were told: 'Destroy the Kaiser first. Discuss peace afterwards.' Today, again, it is 'Hitler, Mussolini and Tojo must be first destroyed; we cannot discuss peace until that is done.'

"We went to the Peace Conference in 1919 animated by the loftiest and most disinterested ideals, but we were totally unprepared for the specific problems and the ambushes that had to be met at the peace table. We did not secure much peace.

"There must be just as much preparedness for peace making as there is for war. And in many ways it is a more difficult job. Preparedness for war deals mostly with tangibles, men, guns, ships, planes, money, and with tactics and strategy. Preparedness for peace deals largely with intangibles, the setting up of moral, intellectual, economic and political forces over the whole world which will produce and hold peace.

"Nor is this alone the job of the several government departments now engaged upon it. If we are to make a better job of the peace this time than last it will be because intelligent public discussion develops more ideas and better ideas and because a public understanding of the problems is prepared to accept the solutions made.

"Unless we are to see again the aftermath of the Thirty Years' War, when one-third of the people of Europe fell before the Horsemen of Famine and Pestilence, we must have preparedness, not alone in America, but in every surplus food producing country, and unless there be food there will be no foundation for peace."

The fate of 50,000,000 starving people, among them 12,000,000 children, in the five little democracies of Europe never ceased to occupy Mr. Hoover's thoughts. British objections, as we have seen, had negated all attempts to put into practice the program which the National Committee on Food for the Five Small Democracies sponsored.

A ray of hope broke through the clouds of British resistance when His Majesty's Government in August of 1942 consented to opening the blockade for certain quantities of food to go to the suffering population of Greece. This relief action had been initiated by the Turkish government.

Herbert Hoover and his close friend, Ambassador Hugh Gibson, seized upon this action to renew the plea of the National Committee to come to the aid of the starving small-nation millions. They wrote an article, "Feed the Starving Now," which appeared in *Collier's* on February 20, 1943.

They praised the humane action of the Turkish government, then observed:

"Not only were the ships allowed to go through to their destination, but when experience proved that the operation involved no danger to the Allied armies, that it in no way benefited the Nazis, the volume of relief was increased, and financial facilities were provided by Britain and America. The whole operation was regularized by agreement set up by the Swedish and Swiss authorities and placed under the guardianship of the International Red Cross, exactly as the writers of this article had proposed eighteen months before.

"Civilization may well be grateful to the Turks for opening the door to reason and compassion. The whole problem was bogged down in governmental refusal to examine the possibilities of relief. This was all the more baffling because the whole question of relief had been thoroughly tested during the last war by the feeding of ten millions of Belgians and Frenchmen living under the German armies of occupation.

"Fortunately, the success of the Greek relief operation has served to confirm the experience of the last war and to demonstrate that it is possible to help our friends and allies without weakening the war effort. In the light of this, our Government has come out categorically to defend Greek relief against criticism with the soundest of arguments. We have no hesitation in approving and applauding these arguments which are those we have been advancing for over two years.

"With such a clear-cut governmental attitude having been adopted as regards the Greek problem, both compassion and loyalty dictate that we should try to do as much for other allies in desperate straits.

"Time will prove how tragic was our failure to institute suitable measures of relief while we could still have saved millions from tuberculosis, rickets, and physical and mental degeneration."

Herbert Hoover and Hugh Gibson, alas, pleaded in vain.

10

TWO HIGHEST-LEVEL MISSIONS

The ravages of the Second World War stagger the imagination. They marked a high point in human misery perhaps never before reached in the history of mankind. Millions upon millions of human beings faced starvation unless food came speedily. These millions were, in a large part, inhabitants of countries with which America had only just been involved in a life-and-death struggle. The passions of war were still running high.

President Harry Truman realized fully how difficult it would be to convince Congress of the necessity of pouring millions of dollars into the erstwhile enemy countries.

It was suggested that Herbert Hoover, who had fed millions of war-stricken human beings during and after the First World War, and who was respected by all nations as a great humanitarian and as a United States past President, might be persuaded once again to place his experience at the service of suffering mankind.

President Truman readily followed the suggestion. Mr. Hoover accepted. The first task to be performed was that of making a survey both of the world's nutritional needs and of the food supplies available. Upon announcement of the former President's acceptance of the chairmanship of the Famine Emergency Commission, Secretary of War Robert P. Patterson in a press release on March 7, 1946, stated: "I immediately called on Mr. Hoover and pledged full support and cooperation of the War Department. I am particularly pleased with the acceptance of Mr. Hoover, because his expert knowledge of world food problems and many years of experience in this humanitarian endeavor places the best qualified authority in a position to be of help." He further stated that "directives have been dispatched to impress all Army personnel with the gravity of the situation and enjoining the strictest economy and elimination of waste."

Accompanied by Hugh Gibson, Dennis A. FitzGerald, W. Hallam Tuck, Perrin C. Galpin, Maurice Pate, and Frank E. Mason, Mr. Hoover on March 17, 1946, started on a flight which took him clear around the world and led to an additional trip to South America to determine what food that continent might be able to provide.

The Hoover party reached Berlin on April 11, 1946. I was among the newsmen who reported on his stay in the battered capital, having been in Germany as a war correspondent since January 31, 1945. Among my papers I found, while working on this book, copies of the dispatches I filed with The Associated Press of America concerning Mr. Hoover's stay. Some excerpts follow:

"April 11. Hoover after one glance at the program tentatively outlined for him decided to eliminate the sight-seeing tours arranged for 12:30 P.M. and also an extended rest period which was to follow. Instead he asked to be enabled to go to work immediately.

"The officers of the Food and Agriculture Branch of OMGUS [Office of Military Governor, United States], scheduled to meet Hoover on the afternoon of April 12, were therefore ordered to come to [General Joseph T.] McNarney's residence on idyllic Schwanenwerder Island near Potsdam today to spend the afternoon with the Former President, giving him facts and figures. . . .

"One conducting officer commented: 'This is the first party I've ever met with which didn't want immediately to go sightseeing and souvenir collecting. This delegation actually wants to work first and play afterwards if there's any time left.'

"April 12. By the time that his first day in Berlin had ended, Former President Hoover already had assembled an enormous quantity of firsthand data on the food situation in Germany. From his arrival at McNarney's headquarters at noon until 7.00 P.M. Mr. Hoover almost continuously received experts on various phases of the German situation. His favorite method was that of being closeted alone with one or two visitors to whom he listened intently as he puffed away at his pipe.

"At 7.00 P.M. he left for Harnack House, the main entertainment headquarters of OMGUS, where he was McNarney's guest at dinner and where he continued to meet people in the know. . . .

"The indications are that Hoover is hopeful of an interzonal economic agreement between the Western Powers but that he does not expect the Soviets presently to join in such reciprocity. The Elder Statesman, however, is keeping his counsels and is saying nothing at this stage of his fact-finding expedition to Germany.

"April 14. The minister-presidents [premiers] of three Länder [states], Bavaria, Gross-Hessen, and Württemberg-Baden, occupied by American forces, marched in on Hoover this morning by scheduled appointment, accompanied by their agricultural and other experts. They gave him a complete picture of the food situation in the American Zone as they see it from the German viewpoint.

"Hoover explained at the outset that he was *not* here to allocate food or pass judgment on requests for assistance, but that he was on a purely fact-finding expedition which covered the food needs in all countries affected by World War II. He listened patiently to all that they had on their minds.

"Next the British deputy military commander, General Erskine, and the French commander, General L. Koeltz, successively visited the American Former President with expert aides at their sides to answer possible individual questions. According to men in Hoover's entourage they presented 'an impressive picture of the nutrition status in their respective zones.' . . .

"Immediately after a quiet lunch General William H. Draper of the OMGUS economic section appeared with a large staff of collaborators for a session of several hours.

"April 15. At the urgent request of his hosts Hoover did his first and only sight-seeing in Berlin this afternoon, but cut the planned tour in half in order to work for the rest of the day on coordinating the material on the food situation which he had until now assembled in Europe.

"During the tour he stopped only at the gaudy Reichs Chancellory and the bunker [airraid shelter] where Hitler reportedly committed suicide. 'Wanted to have a look at the *Ersatz* residence of a certain *Ersatz* German,' Hoover commented.

"The Former President also browsed among interesting captured manuscripts in the American Documents Center during the morning.

"As regards his Berlin stay, he expressed himself as well satisfied with the data received."

Of this round-the-world mission, a task quite separate from his later special economic mission to Germany and Austria in February, 1947, Mr. Hoover stated in a radio address delivered in Berlin, Germany, on November 27, 1954:

"In 1946, immediately after the Second World War, famine swept three-quarters of the globe. One-and-a-half million people suffered from hunger. In 1946, I was again charged by my Government to take up the struggle against this famine which affected no less than thirty-five nations. I will admit that I was frightfully concerned in those days that we would not succeed in preventing the death of from 300 to 500 million people. However, by carrying out extremely drastic measures in practically all these countries we succeeded in scraping together enough to get over the worst part of the crisis without suffering mass losses from hunger.

"Germany again played an important role in those days. But this time the situation was different in so far as the different zones were occupied and East Germany, the breadbasket of Germany, was under Soviet control. This breadbasket could have served to supply the East Zone if the Russians had only allowed it to do so. At first, we counted on this. . . . Although our plan also provided for aid to the Eastern part of Germany, this was made impossible by the measures which the Soviets had taken in completely sealing off their zone. . . .

"During the frightful famines of 1946 I addressed a direct appeal to the Soviet Government asking them to join us in a common fight against hunger. They categorically rejected this and even refused to receive me after I expressed the desire to initiate conferences in Moscow for this purpose, although the Soviets were in possession of substantial surpluses that could have aided in a common fight against hunger. . . . They refused, in any material way, to cooperate. . . .

"On the other hand, it was all the more necessary to carry through nutritional measures in West Germany, since the basis for an adequate diet was missing. . . . As we appeared on the scene [there], the ration had dropped to 1,000 calories—less than that which it should have been possible to provide through indigenous sources in the East Zone."

In his official report to President Truman, dated Washington, D.C., May 13, 1946, our past President wrote:

"We have completed your instructions to survey the principal nations affected by food shortages which have resulted, or may result, in widespread famine; to evaluate the minimum needs of these areas until the next harvest; and to discover such additional food resources as possible. In accordance with your instructions, we have also presented the American point of view on the food problem to these nations and the interest and understanding of our people in their plight. Finally, we have constantly advised American officials and the American public as to the situation as we found it.

"We have traveled some 35,000 miles, visited 22 countries which have a deficiency of food, and informed ourselves of the situation in several others. The only country of large reported deficiency we did not visit was the Union of South Africa. We visited five self-sufficient or surplus countries and informed ourselves of the situation in other consequential surplus nations.

"The dominant need of the world in this crisis is cereals, particularly wheat and rice. There is great need of fats and special food for children, but as cereals can furnish 85 percent of an emergency diet, we considered cereal requirements were the first concern, and the best indicator. If a foundation of bread can be assured, and as much fats and children's food as possible, mass starvation can be prevented. . . ."

A few days later, in a speech made in Chicago, Mr. Hoover further explained his mission:

"Of the Four Horsemen of the Apocalypse, the one named War has gone—at least for a while. But Famine, Pestilence, and Death are still charging over the earth. And the modern world has added four more to this evil brigade. Their names are Destruction, Drought, Fear, and Revolution. . . .

"Hunger hangs over the homes of more than 800,000,000 people —over one-third of the people of the earth. Hunger is a silent visitor who comes like a shadow. He sits beside every anxious mother three times each day. He brings not alone suffering and sorrow, but fear and terror. He carries disorder and the paralysis of government, and even its downfall. He is more destructive than armies, not only in human life, but in morals. All of the values of right living melt before his invasions, and every gain of civilization crumbles. But we can save these people from the worst, if we will. . . .

"And what of the children in Europe?

"This 1,500-calorie bottom level is dreadfully hard on children. It is hard because a larger portion of the average ration must go to heavy workers if essential services be kept going. While this diet, which is as much as 85 percent bread and the balance a little fat, sugar, and vegetables, will pull adults through, it is not adapted to children. Several nations give them priority in what little dairy supplies there are: extra food is given in some schools; and the charitable agencies are doing the best they can. But in all, they are touching only the fringe of the problem. The proof of this is an annual infant mortality rate as high as 200 per 1,000 among children under 1 year in many cities. The further proof is that there are somewhere from twenty to thirty million physically subnormal children on the Continent. After the war in 1919–20, we gave a good extra meal a day, of 500 or 600 calories of restorative food, to 10,000,000 children.

"I deplore that this special aid for children has had no counterpart through a widespread organization set-up after this war. Civilization marches forward upon the feet of healthy children. It is not too late to stop this most costly retreat and its debacle of endless evil."

Upon the victors over Hitler's Germany there rested an obligation which stemmed from the Potsdam Conference of July, 1945, between the chiefs of government of the United States, Great Britain, and Soviet Russia. The Potsdam Declaration of July 17 stated in Article III, Section B, Paragraph 14: "During the period of occupation Germany shall be treated as a single economic unit. To this end common policies shall be established."

The Soviets did nothing to implement the Declaration. In fact, they refused to cooperate in the attempt to bring about the economic unification to which they had pledged themselves. This meant that Germany's greatest indigenous source of food, especially grain—the Russia-occupied Eastern Zone—could not be counted upon to help alleviate the situation in the three Western Zones, occupied respectively by American, British, and French troops.

Additional food was provided Western Germany nevertheless

through the efforts of Mr. Hoover after his globe-encircling tour. United States Army supplies were made available in sufficient quantity to raise the average caloric content of German feeding from 1,000 calories to 1,350.

The situation in Western Germany, already bad when Mr. Hoover visited it during his round-the-world trip, kept worsening despite the fact that, with his energetic support, an appropriation of $425,000,000 for relief in the occupied areas of Europe, Japan, and Korea was obtained for the fiscal year 1947.

The War Department was keenly aware of the deteriorating food situation, and on November 7, 1946, directed Tracy S. Voorhees, Special Assistant to the Secretary of War, to coordinate within the Department all problems of "getting an adequate food supply to meet the requirements of Military Government in Germany, Austria, Japan, and Korea," and to secure "the cooperation of other agencies of the Government."

Howard C. Petersen, Assistant Secretary of War, with the approval of Secretary Patterson issued a directive to all interested staff divisions to "do everything possible to assist him [Mr. Voorhees] in order to expedite the program," and stated that "Mr. Voorhees has authority to act for me in all matters relating to the food program."

Mr. Voorhees brought about an appreciable amelioration of the German food situation by increasing the shipment for December to 300,000 tons.

In Mr. Voorhees' own words, contained in a private Memorandum: "During December [1946] I had seen General Clay and his food chief, Colonel (later Brigadier General) Hugh Hester. They had told me of the serious crisis in Germany, and Hester had estimated that minimum shipments continuing at the rate of 300,000 tons a month until the next summer would be required. The funds were not adequate to meet any such requirement.

"The job of explaining to the Congress that $425,000,000 was nowhere near sufficient to provide for feeding the peoples who had been shooting at us up to eighteeen months before looked almost impossible, particularly as the Administration had lost control of Congress to the Republican Party, and the Committee chairmen were certain to be firm on economy appropriations.

"At that time the public had not yet realized the necessity for large-scale foreign aid for any purpose. The post-war loan of some $3,750,000,000 to the British was still considered as an investment which would be repaid. There was no conception of the tremendous obligations which we had assumed in occupying Germany and Japan, and of the food problems which had arisen as a result of Russia's lowering of the Iron Curtain and the cutting off in large part of so much of the normal grain supply for West Germany.

"At the same time the population of the areas was being greatly increased. Some 6,000,000 Japanese were shipped back to the main islands. Hordes of refugees fleeing the Communist terror in Poland, the Sudetenland and East Germany were flowing into the American and British zones of Germany. It was apparent that a deficiency appropriation running into hundreds of million dollars would be necessary, together with an appropriation of well over a half billion dollars for the next fiscal year. The alternative was starvation for millions of persons under American Military Government in Germany and Japan.

"Faced with these problems, the idea occurred to me that we should ask Former President Hoover, as the world's recognized expert in mass relief feeding, to survey our needs. The thought was to ask him to go to Germany, and to designate persons to make a similar study concurrently in Japan and Korea. Mr. Petersen and Judge Patterson approved this. They authorized me to see Mr. Hoover. I found Mr. Hoover interested. . . ."

Mr. Hoover believed, however, that food relief alone would not meet the problem, and that Allied Occupation economic problems also needed examination concurrently if Germany, and therefore Western Europe as a whole, were again to become self-supporting.

President Truman formally invited his predecessor to undertake The President's Economic Mission to Germany and Austria, and the two statesmen conferred in the White House late in January of 1947. As a result of their meeting the Mission, originally conceived as solely one to survey food needs in the two occupied European countries, was broadened to include a survey of the economic situation in Germany and Austria.

The necessity for broadening the scope of the Mission's investigations was enhanced by the fact that the United States under the leadership of the American Military Governor, General Lucius D. Clay, and his economic adviser, General William H. Draper, had recently negotiated an economic "fusion" of the British and American Zones of Occupation, so that by January 1, 1947, much of the industrial heart of Germany was being brought together as an economic unit.

Mr. Hoover chose as his assistants Ambassador Hugh Gibson; Dr. Dennis FitzGerald, secretary-general of the International Emergency Food Council; Dr. William H. Sebrell, Jr., medical director of the United States Public Health Service; Frank E. Mason, public relations expert; Dr. Gustav Stolper, economist; and this writer, former chief of the Berlin Bureau of The Associated Press. Mr. Voorhees, who accompanied the Mission on Mr. Hoover's suggestion as the representative of Secretary of War Patterson, immediately became a much appreciated integral member of the team.

Before his departure Mr. Hoover conferred with Secretary of State George C. Marshall concerning his task. The Mission left New York on February 2, 1947, and visited Frankfurt-on-Main, Berlin, Hamburg, Stuttgart, and Vienna. In addition Mr. Hoover, accompanied by Ambassador Gibson, flew to Rome from Vienna to pay his respects to Pope Pius XII before rejoining his associates in Berlin. On the return flight to America a stopover was made in London to enable Mr. Hoover to inform Prime Minister Clement R. Attlee of his findings and the remedial measures he was about to propose.

Day after day and night after night throughout the stay of the Mission in Germany and Austria Herbert Hoover met with key men of the American and British Military Governments and with German officials as well as economic, financial, and nutritional experts.

Heated rooms for the sessions were a scarcity in this severest of winters in decades. We, his associates, marveled at the robust health of our then seventy-three-year-old Chief. We could not but be deeply impressed by the stamina evinced by his sitting for a whole day in an ice-cold room in Hamburg to preside over a meeting about which a United Press correspondent reported on February 10: "Former President Herbert Hoover, swathed in a blanket and wearing a heavy overcoat, today conferred with British regional commissioners on the critical German food problem." We envied him for the tireless energy displayed in not only listening patiently for hours to the testimony taken but also following full days of work with long nights devoted to the study of documents submitted. One night I heard him get up at four o'clock in the morning and turn page after page of the voluminous data submitted to him. The faint noise produced by the occasional breaking of a lead and the substitution of another pencil indicated that the Chief was taking notes as he read.

The members of his team were deployed to make special investigations of their own in the fields in which they were experts. Dr. Sebrell, for instance, spent much time visiting German hospitals to check up on cases of hunger edema and to confer with medical staffs on the general health situation. Messrs. Gibson, FitzGerald, and Voorhees on a mutually satisfactory basis adjusted the differences in estimates of food requirements between General Clay's staff and those of the Department of Agriculture. Frank Mason kept the press informed, while Dr. Stolper and I sought information from our many German friends and acquaintances.

It may interest the reader if at this point I quote from my *Always the Unexpected—A Book of Reminiscences* to illustrate how Mr. Hoover used us, his associates in The President's Economic Mission:

"With a twinkle the Chief (as everybody who has worked for him fondly calls him) said:

" 'I'm merely going to put "general assignment" after your name. That will keep everybody guessing and you will be able to move about as you deem best.'

"He then described what he wanted me to do. No matter how honest the men in American Military Government and the German and Austrian officials whom he would meet might be, he said, they would not be human if they did not slant their story, each according to his lights, in a somewhat biased manner. The truth, I understood the Chief to feel, would probably lie somewhere in the middle. To assist him in ascertaining it, he commissioned me to activate my European connections by visiting newspaper editors, trade-union leaders, employers' federation officials, social workers, clergymen, university professors, local government officials, and political leaders, as well as to talk to average people in various walks of life. I was also to get the view on the functioning of the instrumentality that was designed to 'democratize' Germany—American Military Government."

Even before touching America again, Mr. Hoover urged General Clay to release certain stocks of American food available in Germany to start the Children's Feeding Program immediately. Mr. Voorhees, armed with special powers from the Secretary of War, had ferreted out that $19,000,000 worth of stockpiled, highly nutritious food could be made available to begin at once a school lunch program which helped save a whole generation of German youngsters.

Mr. Voorhees' Memorandum on this point speaks for itself:

"One of the most appealing results of Mr. Hoover's trip was his Children's Feeding Program. Children up to six years were not in bad shape, but those from six to sixteen gave evidence of serious malnutrition. Mr. Hoover wanted to start a soup kitchen school-feeding program, at which the children would get one good meal a day, for 3,500,000 school children in the principal cities of the bizonal area.

"I had learned that there were large food supplies being held for Displaced Persons, most of whom were not Germans. This work was conducted by a division of the Army staff in Frankfurt, and was entirely separate from the relief feeding for the Germans. These Displaced Persons had, following the surrender, been put on a much higher calorie ration than the Germans. This was proper at the time as they were half-starved, and as they had been put in this condition by the Germans from whom they were now being liberated.

"I asked to have representatives of the staff division responsible for this feeding of refugees come to Berlin with their figures. This request was turned down, and I had to get orders issued to have them give me this information.

"We were to leave Berlin on a Thursday morning, and on Wednesday I had developed one of the worst colds I have ever had, and had completely lost my voice due to laryngitis. Through the day and during the evening until midnight, I probed the staff representatives as to the amounts of food reserves being held for the DPs [Displaced Persons]. The International Relief Organization was being organized, and was to take over responsibility for the DPs on July 1.

"After reserving enough food to maintain the ration for the DPs to July 1 and a three months' additional stock, I found that there was about $19,000,000 of additional food which could be used for the children's feeding. This included various Army surplus items containing fats and proteins, in which the children were most deficient. I remember one item of large quantities of chocolate.

"In the guest house in Berlin where the mission was quartered, I came up to bed pretty exhausted about midnight on that Wednesday, and happened to run into Louis Lochner, a member of the mission, who for twenty years had been the Associated Press correspondent in Berlin. I told him of my discovery of the food. The next day we told Mr. Hoover about the food."

My brief comment to Mr. Hoover, ventured when at his bidding I sat in on this fortuitous discovery, was that I had seen Tracy Voorhees the previous evening "registering simultaneously three distinct reactions: utter physical exhaustion; resentment that this food, which was so badly needed for immediate use, had been hidden; and happiness at the end result of his day's labors."

On the plane to London Messrs. Hoover and Voorhees went into a huddle to go over the figures carefully. Then and there a letter was written by Mr. Hoover to General Clay, informing him that this supply of food surplus for the DPs existed, and recommending that these foods be used immediately as the initial stock for the Children's Feeding Program. An executive order was issued by General Clay. The Program was begun.

Mr. Hoover's exacting Mission had a deplorable aftermath. Due to the unhealthy conditions under which our chief had to work, he had contracted a cold which bothered him considerably on our return flight. Because of bad weather and the presence of mountains not far from the airport at Stephenville, Newfoundland, where our plane refueled, the pilot maintained considerable altitude until he was almost directly over the airport, when he let down rather abruptly for some 8,000–10,000 feet.

Mr. Hoover's ear passages were partly blocked due to his cold, with the result that one of his eardrums was ruptured during the landing operation. This accident seriously affected his hearing, and it was not long before Mr. Hoover began using a hearing aid occasionally. He never spoke of this sacrifice which was an added contribution to that of his brains and experience, made to bring relief and hope to Germany and Austria.

Following his return to New York on February 23, Mr. Hoover gave his answer to the nutritional and economic problems of Western Germany in two detailed reports. One was entitled, *German Agriculture and Food Requirements,* the other, *The Necessary Steps for Promotion of German Exports, so as to Relieve American Taxpayers of the Burdens of Relief, and for the Economic Recovery of Europe.* A third report dealt with Austria and does not concern us here.

The reports on Germany were released to the press on February 28 and March 18, respectively, after their presentation to Mr. Truman in a heart-to-heart talk between President and former President.

A few quotations from the report on *German Agriculture and Food Requirements* will suffice to indicate its general tenor:

"The housing situation in the two zones [American and British] is the worst that modern civilization has ever seen. . . . Multitudes are living in rubble and basements. The average space among tens of millions is equivalent to between three and four people to a 12′ x 12′ room. . . . One consequence is the rapid spread of tuberculosis and other potentially communicable diseases. . . .

"The shortage of coal is, next to food, the most serious immediate bottleneck to both living and the revival of exports to pay for food. The Ruhr, which is now almost the sole coal supply of the Anglo-American Zones, is, due to lack of skilled men and physical vitality in labor, producing only 230,000 tons per day, as against a former 450,000 tons per day. Of the present production, a considerable amount must be exported to surrounding nations which are also suffering. The shortage leaves the two zones without sufficient coal for transport, household and other dominant services, with little upon which to start exports in the industry. . . .

"This terrible winter, with frozen canals and impeded railway traffic, has rendered it impossible to maintain even the present low basis of rationing in many localities. The coal shortage and the consequent lack of heat, even for cooking, has added a multitude of hardships. . . .

"Over half of the 6,595,000 children and adolescents, especially in the lower income groups, are in a deplorable condition. . . . In some areas famine edema (actual starvation) is appearing in the children. . . .

"A considerable part of the 'normal consumer' group of 17,910,000 is likewise in deplorable condition. . . . A large part of the group shows a steady loss of weight, vitality and ability to work. . . . Famine edema is showing in thousands of cases, stated to be 10,000 in Hamburg alone. The increased death roll among the aged is appalling. . . .

"While the workers' rations, due to supplements, are perhaps high enough in themselves, yet the universal tendency is for the worker to share his supplement with his wife and children, and therefore it does not have its full effect in supplying energy for the worker himself. . . .

"No one can say that in her utterly shattered state, Germany is a present economic menace to the world. . . ."

The concluding paragraphs read: "[Even] those who believe in vengeance and the punishment of a great mass of Germans not concerned in the Nazi conspiracy can now have no misgivings, for all of them—in food, warmth, and shelter—have sunk to the lowest level known in a hundred years of Western history.

"If Western civilization is to survive in Europe, it must also survive in Germany. And it must be built into a cooperative member of that civilization. That indeed is the hope of any lasting peace. After all, our flag flies over these people. That flag means something besides military power."

The second report, on *Necessary Steps for Promotion of German Exports,* observed in part:

"There is only one path to recovery in Europe. That is production. The whole economy of Europe is interlinked with German economy through the exchange of raw materials and manufactured goods. The productivity of Europe cannot be restored without the restoration of Germany as a contributor to that productivity. . . .

"I assume, in our own interest and that of Europe, that we wish to restore the productivity of the continent, that we wish to revive personal freedom, honest elections and generally to reconstruct the German people into a peace-loving nation cooperating in the recovery of Western civilization. . . .

"There is the illusion that the New Germany left after the annexations can be reduced to a 'pastoral state.' It cannot be done unless we exterminate or move 25,000,000 people out of it. This would approximately reduce Germany to the density of the population of France. . . .

"A still further illusion is that Europe as a whole can recover without the economic recovery of Germany. . . .

"Germany, under the 'level of industry' concept, unless she is to be allowed to starve, will be a drain on the taxpayers of other nations for years and years to come. . . . To persist in the present policies will create, sooner or later, a cesspool of unemployment or pauper labor in the center of Europe which is bound to infect her neighbors.

"We can keep Germany in these economic chains but it will also keep Europe in rags. . . ."

In his personal report to President Truman, Mr. Hoover added this solemn advice: "We can carry on the Military Government of Germany by the tenets of the Old Testament of 'a tooth for a tooth, and an eye for an eye,' or we can inaugurate the precepts of the New Testament. The difference in result will be the loss of millions of lives, the damage of all Europe, and the destruction of any hope of peace in the world. I recommend the New Testament method."

Mr. Truman accepted this recommendation immediately, as did also the people and the Congress of the United States in due time, albeit after a considerable struggle.

However, the followers of the so-called Henry Morgenthau school of thought, who believed Germany must be reduced to a vast agricultural pasture, fought Mr. Hoover's proposals passionately. They depicted him as an incorrigible friend of a Germany that could never be trusted. They championed the thesis that a third world war was indubitably in the offing in case German economic recovery were made possible.

Also, the Soviet-controlled radio station of East Berlin berated the Hoover Plan. "We do not want American assistance to become a means for strengthening the darkest reactionaries in numerous European countries in 1947, as was the case in 1919," the radio spokesman warned.

On the other hand, forty-eight leaders of American public opinion, men and women of varying political and social points of view, soon after publication of his tripartite report presented him with a letter warmly acknowledging his enlightened services to humanity as again exemplified in his most recent mission. The signers included statesmen, educators, churchmen, philanthropists, writers, publishers, and businessmen. Their names follow:

Charles C. Burlingham, Peter Grimm, George McAneny, Eugene Meyer, Oswald Garrison Villard, Dorothy Thompson, Henry R. Luce, Dorothy Canfield Fisher, Philip D. Reed, Winthrop W. Aldrich, Anne O'Hare McCormick, Lucius M. Boomer, Adolf A. Berle, Jr., the Rev. John Haynes Holmes, Shepard Morgan, Frank D. Fackenthal, Dr. James T. Shotwell, the Rev. Harry Emerson Fosdick, Dr. Nicholas Murray Butler, Roger N. Baldwin, Dr. Harry Woodburn Chase, Walter Damrosch, Norman Thomas, Dr. George N. Shuster, Ray Morris, Dr. Felix Morley, Walter Rosen, Christopher Emmet, Jr., George J. Gillespie, James Marshall, Charles F. Darlington, the Rev. Dr. George A. Buttrick, Dr. Oswald W. Knauth, Allen W. Dulles, Clare Boothe Luce, George Roosevelt, Eustace Seligman, Arthur Dean, Francis T. P. Plimpton, Jeremiah Milbank, William M. Chadbourne, Dr. Adriaan J. Barnouw, Carl W. Ackerman, Frederick G. Clark, Major General William J. Donovan, Vincent Sheean, and Thomas J. Watson.

The letter praised the Hoover Report as "a model in the complete detachment with which you wrote it, your refusal to yield to hate or bitterness or even to dwell upon the sins of those whose plight you studied in order to protect yourself from the charge of showing undue favoritism to the nation which plunged the world into its present desperate and desperately alarming misery. Instead, you stressed the indubitable fact that if Western civilization is to survive in Europe, it must survive in Germany. . . . In the finest historic American spirit of benevolence and justice, you ended with these words: 'After all, our flag flies over these people. That flag means something besides military power.'"

Mr. Hoover estimated that the food imports from America and Great Britain for the six months from January to July, 1947, would cost $384,000,000, and the food, fertilizer, and seed for the fiscal year beginning July 1, 1947, some $567,000,000. He also recommended that the low production ceilings be abolished to which German heavy industry was limited by agreement of the

Occupation Powers. Also, he urged that Mr. Voorhees be formally appointed what he was already in fact, viz., War Department Food Administrator for the Occupied Areas. Secretary Patterson on March 13 conferred the title as suggested.

Having made his estimates of what it would cost to keep Germany alive and enable her to get on her feet economically, thereby relieving the American taxpayer from a burden which might otherwise continue indefinitely, Mr. Hoover tackled his next, self-assigned job—that of seeing to it that his proposals were translated into action. As already indicated, there was violent opposition in some quarters.

Mr. Hoover did not spare himself. He gave radio addresses, wrote articles, appealed to the conscience of the nation, thereby building up a grass-roots movement to support him in his endeavor to influence Congress. He also pleaded personally with individual Senators and Congressmen to vote adequate funds for carrying out his recommendations. He accepted the invitations of Congressional committees to testify concerning his findings regarding Germany and Austria.

Take as one example his appearance on May 27, 1947, before the Subcommittee of the Committee on Appropriations, House of Representatives, in charge of deficiency appropriations, of which Congressman John Taber was chairman. He stoutly defended the allocation of $725,000,000 as "the very minimum that the people in Germany, Japan and Korea can get through with next year."

When a Representative asked whether any progress had been made by Germany as regards her export trade, as a result of which she might pay for some of the food and thus reduce the necessity for a $725,000,000 appropriation, Mr. Hoover replied forthrightly:

"There is very little progress. The British and American Military Governments have set up an import-export committee. So far, I do not think it has developed anything very great by way of exports because they are short of coal and otherwise completely paralyzed by the level-of-industry and removal-of-plant agreements. . . . The problem arises . . . that it is urgent that we throw those agreements overboard in order to get exports really started and a decrease of our burdens."

At the request of Chairman Taber, our Elder Statesman had prepared a memorandum for the committee, which served as a basis for discussion. It is a long, "meaty" statement, in which eleven specific recommendations are made and masterfully elucidated. A few salient passages are here reproduced. They throw into sharp relief Soviet Russia's failure to live up to her responsibilities undertaken at the Potsdam Conference of July, 1946. While France is also charged with certain shortcomings, her government could plead as an ameliorating circumstance that France was not represented at Potsdam.

Mr. Hoover wrote in part as follows:

"As matters stand this appropriation of $725,000,000 should be made. In addition to this proposed American appropriation, the British are also to contribute their share of bizonal relief in Germany. These enormous sums are inescapable for the next year unless millions of people under our flag are to die of starvation. They are about the same as during the present fiscal year and this year's experience demonstrates how near starvation is in these countries.

"Surely we must take steps to bring these burdens upon our taxpayers to an end.

"We are now providing relief for the third year after the war.

"The delay by Russia in making peace with Germany and Japan, together with the Allied policies of reparations and industrial demilitarization, have paralyzed the industrial productivity of these countries. They are unable to make substantial exports and are not contributing, as they otherwise could, to their own support.

"General Marshall in Moscow ably urged the immediate necessity for Russia and France to comply with the Potsdam Agreement, which provided for economic unification of the four zones; for the revision of the plant-transfers for reparations; and the revision of so-called levels of industry. Meanwhile, Russia and France are taking industrial exports from their zones, which under the Potsdam Agreement would contribute to paying the food bill in the American and British zones. Thus we are paying reparations. We are shipping fertilizers for relief which could be supplied from the French zone. We are supplying France with Ruhr coal which could be used for the manufacturing of exports in Germany with which to pay for food.

"In view of the Russian refusal of General Marshall's able presentation at Moscow, and the continued violation of the Potsdam Agreement to unify German economy in both Russia and France, we are surely no longer bound by that Agreement as to reparations and industrial policies. . . .

"We should at once abolish for good the destruction or removal of all industrial plants which can make peace-time goods or services. The heavy burden now borne by our taxpayers is ample proof of the folly of these policies. It is an illusion that there are any consequential reparations to be had by removal of peace-time industrial plants. The buildings, foundations, water, electrical and other connections in such plants have no value for removal. All that is removable of any use are machines, all second-hand and many obsolete. The cost of tearing them out, shipping them to some area where there is neither skilled labor nor skilled management, and of building new foundations, buildings, and connections, leaves even these values comparatively trivial."

Herbert Hoover's efforts were crowned with success despite the vociferous opposition. A deficiency appropriation of $300,000,000 for the fiscal year 1947 to cover needs for food, chemical fertilizer, and seed in the various occupied areas was passed by Congress, as was an appropriation of $600,000,000 for the fiscal year 1948. Also, many restrictions on German industry were lifted.

In the program for Germany during some three years of operation, a vast fleet of freighters thronged the Atlantic to bring relief. The shipments in wheat in one year alone amounted to 4,000,000 tons.

School lunches for the special Children's Feeding Program

reached 3,500,000 German children. Later more than 4,500,000 children and adolescents were provided this type of lunch.

Mr. Voorhees' Memorandum adds interesting details concerning the fate of The President's Mission to Germany and Austria:

"As part of the bizonal agreement the British were to pay for one-half of the imports of food [to Germany]. However, particularly as the food purchases were in dollars and the requirements proved to be very much larger than the British Treasury could stand, it soon became necessary for the United States to take over the bulk of the load in order to restore tolerable conditions in Germany. This was done. Throughout this time I was consulting at frequent intervals with Mr. Hoover and acting upon his advice in the above and similar matters. . . .

"In April [1947] I was away from the Pentagon for almost a month due to illness, and on returning I immediately checked up on the food figures. I could not make them add up. It soon became apparent that the actual stocks on hand in Germany were between 300,000 and 350,000 tons less than those which had been reported during the Hoover Mission to Germany. In other words, the collections of local food had failed much more than anticipated. A new and immediate food crisis was upon us. . . .

"There was by this time an acute shortage of wheat in the United States. There was still some corn. The corn was not desired by the Germans or Japanese, as they were not accustomed to eat corn and did not know how to prepare it. But corn was far better than nothing.

"I arranged for a meeting of the Cabinet Committee on World Food Programs and had Secretary Patterson present the facts of the German crisis. This resulted in a decision to give priority to shipments to Germany, and in the appointment of a sub-committee. . . .

"In May Secretary Patterson, at my instance, cabled General Clay and issued a public statement that we would ship 400,000 tons of food per month for the next three months to meet the crisis. This was done, and in fact very considerably exceeded. . . .

"For the time it seemed that, due to such actions, the crisis was over. However, in the late summer of 1947 Germany suffered one of its worst droughts. This was accompanied by a very unusual drought in America, which resulted in cutting the corn crop by 800,000,000 bushels. However, the American wheat crop was not affected, and was the largest ever harvested, being—as I now recall it—over 1,300,000,000 bushels."

One big problem was that the War Department had the responsibility for feeding the half-starved people in the occupied areas, but the Department of Agriculture controlled allocation of the food. Mr. Voorhees and his chief, Secretary of War Patterson, had urgently invited Secretary of Agriculture Clinton P. Anderson to go to Germany and see conditions for himself and had offered to provide a private plane for the trip.

After noting that Mr. Anderson accepted this invitation and during that drought summer went to Germany in July, 1947, Mr. Voorhees' Memorandum continues:

"Secretary Anderson, after going over the German food requirements, promised the Germans in a public statement that the Americans would ship 4,000,000 tons of food in the fiscal year just commencing. This was of great encouragement to the Germans. The promise was of course made before the drought in America and the resulting shrinkage of the corn crop. In spite of that, Secretary Anderson, with the utmost of good faith, maintained throughout that he was going to carry out his promise, and did so. In many ways that trip of Secretary Anderson and the promise went far to save Germany, for the next year's food crises proved bad enough anyway."

Summing up, it is no exaggeration to say that what was done under Mr. Hoover's continuing guidance to feed Germany averted Germany's going Communist. I use the phrase, "continuing guidance," deliberately. For Herbert Hoover's post-World War II activities on behalf of Germany were not limited to his 1946 worldwide mission as chairman of the Famine Emergency Commission, in which his concern for Germany played an important role; nor to his acceptance of the difficult and energy-consuming task of heading The President's Economic Mission to Germany and Austria in 1947 and persuading Congress to implement his recommendations. There was a third phase to his efforts, a phase about which little has become known: during fifteen months, from about April 1, 1947, to July 1, 1948, our Elder Statesman was virtually a famous coach who guided the play from the side lines as Tracy Voorhees, in his capacity of War Department Food Administrator for the Occupied Areas, was cast in the role of quarterback—able, but lacking the vast experience of the seasoned coach.

Mr. Voorhees reported frequently and fully to Mr. Hoover, with the approval, of course, of his superiors. The former President passed substantially on all of Mr. Voorhees' figures as to needs, and on major decisions. He gave the Food Administrator many an "assist" by telephoning or personally meeting Congressional leaders to discuss appropriations for the government and relief in occupied areas.

Fortunately the chairman of the House Appropriations Committee, Congressman Taber—*the* key figure in appropriations questions—was a devoted admirer of our past President and had complete confidence in his judgment. This fact was a deciding factor in providing the enormous funds that the situation then demanded.

But it was not only in funds, but also in policy matters that Herbert Hoover helped the War Department with wise guidance.

All during the German food crisis General Lucius D. Clay was the Military Governor for the American Sector of Germany. In an article published in Germany in November of 1954 he evaluated Herbert Hoover's work on behalf of Germany. The article was written in anticipation of Mr. Hoover's visit to Germany at the invitation of the German Government—an episode which will be described in the closing chapter of this book. A German translation of the article appeared in many German dailies.

A number of significant passages from General Clay's contribution follow:

"There is no parallel example of a victorious nation struggling so shortly after the defeat of an enemy nation to feed it and to restore economic opportunity. Fortunately, we realized that a people without food and without hope would become pawns in the hands of those who promised both.

"No individual recognized this any sooner than did Mr. Hoover. As he did not seek publicity from his two visits to Germany, neither Germans nor Americans fully realize what he did to revive hope in Germany and to make possible its eventual entry into the Atlantic group of nations. Mr. Hoover's first visit to Germany was made early in 1946 as a part of a tour of western Europe to determine the validity of the demands for food which were then reaching us from many places. Since these demands exceeded the available supply, priorities had to be established to prevent starvation. Mr. Hoover interviewed the responsible officials of Military Government as well as the German officials who had accepted responsible office under Military Government. He was convinced of the need for food in Germany and he did not question for an instant the responsibility of an occupying government to maintain life and health. Hence, even though the food supply was short, we were promised the necessary supplies to support an average ration of 1500 calories per day in western Germany.

"This limited ration which prevailed during most of 1946 seemed substantial indeed as we examined the food supplies available for the winter of 1946 and 1947. Production shortages in Germany and the short world supply made it necessary for the average ration during the winter of 1946 and 1947 to be reduced to 1100 calories per person. The fight against famine became the main occupation of military government and German government. To keep the German people alive and able to work at all was our principal concern. Those of us responsible for military government begged and argued for additional food, convinced that the American people would not want starvation and misery to take place where our flag was flying. Moreover, democracy could not grow in Germany on a foundation of hunger and a ruined economy. Lack of food and lack of work opportunity were creating the vacuum in which communist political exploitation could achieve success with its false promises. Desperate people do not reason.

"Our efforts to obtain food and economic assistance from the United States succeeded only because of the strong support which we received from former President Hoover. . . .

"When he arrived in Germany in 1947, little had been accomplished since his earlier visit to repair the damages of war. Conflicts between the western powers and Russia in the Allied Control Council had shown that it was impossible for Germany to be governed as a whole. Two-thirds of its principal cities still lay in ruins and industry was practically dormant. The German people needed coal, light, food, clothes and housing, and, above all, the restoration of their will to rebuild. . . .

"In view of these serious conditions, Secretary of War Robert P. Patterson had suggested that President Truman invite Mr. Hoover to undertake this mission in Germany. This request had the enthusiastic concurrence of United States Military Government in Germany. Mr. Hoover's first visit had convinced me of his real understanding of the German problem and I knew that he would appraise the problem objectively and accurately and that his report would carry great weight at home. He brought with him to Germany a team of experts in food requirements, public health, and economics. . . .

"After exhaustive hearings, Mr. Hoover and his team considered and evaluated Germany's needs. . . .

"President Truman accepted Mr. Hoover's report and gave it full support. However, the Republican Party had gained control of the Congress and had announced its determination to reduce government spending. Securing appropriations to buy food and other essentials for the German economy was not easy. Mr. Hoover did not rest on his report. He testified before the Congressional Committees and visited again and again leading Republican Senators and Congressmen to urge them to support aid for Germany. Because of his efforts, appropriations materialized promptly for food, chemicals, fertilizer, and seed, and we were able to increase the German ration in time to prevent real famine and sufficiently to restore their health and their will to work.

"An important phase of this program was the child feeding program . . . suggested by Mr. Hoover. . . . He proposed a special child feeding program to be supplied at the schools to reach approximately 3,500,000 children. [Army] Ten-in-one rations were shipped from the United States to form the principal basis for this program which was started almost as quickly as he had recommended it. It did more to convince the German people of our desire to re-create their nation than anything else could have done. The many expressions of gratitude from parents and children which came to us in Military Government were sincere and touching. Many of these expressions reached Mr. Hoover in America. . . .

"While Mr. Hoover's immediate and great concern in his survey of Germany was the food problem, his mission included a survey of the economic situation. The lowering of the Iron Curtain had cut Germany into two parts, and yet we were still discussing the further removal of German industry and substantial shipments of the removed equipment to the Soviet Union. While Military Government had refused to make further deliveries as long as Germany remained divided, American policy demanded a further reduction in Germany's ability to produce. We had not yet admitted that German production was essential to sound European economy. Moreover, we had not realized that Germany could live only if it exported enough industrial products to pay for the food which it could not produce in sufficient quantity to sustain its population. As Mr. Hoover said, certain 'economic illusions' still existed about Germany. . . .

"He advocated a new economic approach: the freeing of German industry except for a few safeguards against a revival of militarism and production for military purposes.

"It was still less than two years since we and our allies had defeated Germany in a bitter war. The strong emotions and hatreds which are an inevitable part of the aftermath of war were still intense in America and in those countries which had been allied with us in the war. Published disclosures of the war crimes of German leaders had added to the bitterness of the free world against Germany. It required courage and vision then to recognize the need to create a new Germany in which its people, with hope and faith in their economic future, might find the way to democracy. Only such a program could bring a lasting peace in Europe.

"Mr. Hoover did much to change thinking at home so that it would become possible for us to reform and stabilize German currency, to stop the dismantling of German industry, and to permit free competitive enterprise to begin the rebuilding of Germany to provide, among other products, coal from the Ruhr needed throughout western Europe."

Thousands of youngsters in Germany who profited by the Child Feeding Program did their own juvenile evaluation of it by writing letters, often accompanied by crude but expressive drawings and cartoons, to *Onkel Hoover.*

For instance, thirteen-year-old Friedrich Wilhelm Langguth of Coburg, Bavaria, wrote (grammatical mistakes, punctuation, and quaint turns of phrase have been left uncorrected) in laborious English:

"I want to thank you very much for your fine child feeding program. Our daily meals taste wonderful, especially because we became always hungry during school. We are three brothers and one sister, and all of us, except my eldest brother, who is already 18 years old, get the school-feeding. It is a great support for our dear mother, when we come from school after taking such a fine meal, because my mother apprehended very much, about our dear father, who is still a Prisoner of war in Moscow and whom the Soviets do not let home. . . . If every people will help the other, like you does, we should have a lasting peace soon."

From Esslingen, Wurttemberg, came a letter signed by the twenty-eight pupils of a class in the high school for girls. Its wording, too, is left unchanged:

"We German girls thank you very much for the school-meal, we get of your occasion. How glad we are about the good things, we are handed every day. Does it give soup, pap, or even chocolate, so the joy in the classe is very great. With the hope that the meal will last still very long,

"your grateful Classe IV-b,
"Highschool for girls,
"Esslingen/Neckar."

Much more natural, of course, were the letters written by German youngsters in their native tongue. Besides revealing deep gratitude, they indicated that children saw in Mr. Hoover not so much the man who once held the most powerful and responsible office in the world, but rather a kindly uncle who sends out dolls or shoes or food packages. Many of these letters stressed thanks not only to Mr. Hoover, but also to the American people.

For readers familiar with the German language, a typical letter is reproduced, first in its original version, and then in translation:

"Lieber Herr Hoover! Wir danken Ihnen für die gute Speisung, die Sie uns geben. Ich schicke Ihnen ein Bild. Die dicke Frau ist unsere Lehrerin, Sie heisst Frau Mayer und ist sehr streng, aber man lernt viel bei ihr.—Das Bild habe ich selber gemalt. Mein Name ist Waldtraut Hüpen und ich bin 10 Jahre alt. Ich habe noch 3 Schwestern und einen Bruder. Sie heissen Adelheid, Angela, Gabriele und mein Bruder heisst Michael. Lieber Herr Hoover wenn Sie einmal nach Deutschland kommen, besuchen Sie uns doch auch einmal. Wir wohnen in Vaihingen (das liegt bei Stuttgart) Silcherstrasse 113 am Wald.

"Viele Grüsse von
"Waldtraut Hüpen."

The translation:

"Dear Mr. Hoover! We thank you for the good food you are giving us. I am sending you a picture. The stout lady is our teacher. Her name is Frau Mayer. She is very strict, but one learns much with her.—I painted the picture myself. My name is Waldtraut Hüpen and I am ten years old. I have three sisters and one brother. Their names are Adelheid, Angela and Gabriele and my brother's name is Michael. Dear Mr. Hoover, if you should come to Germany sometime, do visit us, too. We live in Vaihingen (that's near Stuttgart), 113 Silcher Street, close to the woods.

"Kind regards from
"Waldtraut Hüpen."

Some youngsters went into detail to describe to Mr. Hoover just how his child feeding program was being administered. A typical letter in this category is one written by Liselotte Massholder of Heidelberg. Translated, her letter reads:

"Honored Mr. Hoover!

"Mr. Hoover, you have brought great joy to us with the school feeding program. We were very happy when our teacher told us to bring dishes along. We went home with beaming faces. The next day we returned with dishes in our hands. We were so excited that we were very restless, so that our teacher had often to warn us to be quiet. At 2.30 P.M. the janitor rapped at the door and said, 'Children, today you're going to get something good!'

"We then lined up in twos and proceeded in a body down into the cellar. Two nice Red Cross sisters handed out the food. We lined up again in the corridor and returned as a group to our classroom.

"The food was still very hot, wherefore we placed it on the window sills and continued to study intensely. During the big recess we ate the sweets with great relish. I have already gained four pounds in eight days. Dear Mr. Hoover, you are now feeding us hungry mouths every week with good food. You have helped German youth out of a great hunger disaster. That's why I thank you most sincerely!

"Kind regards from
"Liselotte Massholder,
"Age 12, Class VIc
"Girls' *Realgymnasium*
"Heidelberg."

Twelve years after these letters were written, Mrs. Lochner and I went to Europe on a three-and-one-half-months leisurely visit.

After some weeks spent in Germany, I felt impelled to write Mr. Hoover a letter dated Essen, September 30, 1959, from which the following is quoted:

"My wife and I have just returned from a series of visits which took us as far eastward as Hannover. Already upon our arrival two weeks ago in Essen we had been struck by something, the confirmation of which came so frequently during our trip that I feel justified to present it to you as a conclusion:

"There is so marked a difference in the stature of the young German women and men in their late teens or early twenties as compared with that of their parents that the fact is inescapable that there must be some connection between the towering figures of the youngsters and the food on which they were raised. In other words, the postwar Hoover Child Feeding Program of 1947 and the years following has paid off in a manner that perhaps even you—certainly we who were members of your team on The President's Economic Mission—could not envisage.

"At first, I confess, I was merely bewildered and could not figure things out. I merely *saw* what seemed like a miracle. I had sat at the feet of Dr. David Starr Jordan and heard him as a biologist state before audience after audience how the French population of his day was on an average two inches smaller than that of the days of Napoleon—all because the best and the bravest had become soldiers and were killed, leaving the procreation of the next generation to the weak, infirm, and unstable, with resulting deterioration of the race.

"Suddenly it dawned on me that there must be some cardinal difference between what happened to the youth of the post-Napoleonic period of France and the post-Nazi period of Germany. How come, I wondered, that a totally defeated nation, compelled by Hitler to produce 'cannons instead of butter,' could raise such strapping youngsters as we now see constantly? It dawned on me: Mr. Hoover came to prostrate Germany—and, for that matter, to all Europe—just in time to reverse the process and make 'butter instead of cannons' a reality.

"To reassure myself that I, who am by no means an expert on

nutritional and biological questions, am not totally wrong, I have asked husky, healthy teenagers and young people in their early twenties wherever I had an opportunity, whether they had been recipients in their early years of the 'Hoover-*Speisung*,' and all replied enthusiastically in the affirmative. I have asked their elders whether in their opinion the juvenile feeding program and the astounding height and apparent well-being of their offspring might be due to the 'Hoover-*Speisung*.' Again the reply was, 'most definitely so.' . . ."

On October 4, Mr. Hoover replied to this part of my letter:

"I have received your letter of September 30th.

"I have seldom had so thrilling an account of our good deeds—and it goes in my Echoes of the Past."

At the time of his 1947 Mission Germany's economic and nutritional situation was not the only cause for worry on the part of our Elder Statesman. The matter of German reunification weighed heavily on his mind. To him European peace is unthinkable so long as one large section of the former German Reich is under Soviet domination while the rest is a free democracy.

As early as 1942 Mr. Hoover observed in a book *The Problems of Lasting Peace,* written jointly with his intimate friend, Ambassador Hugh Gibson:

"GERMAN UNITY. A still larger question of nationalism will arise over Germany. Any survey of the history of Europe will show that, in its periodic defeats, this race has been dismembered into separate states. Then begins agitation for unity of this virile race under Prussian leadership. It moves into armament and explodes into wars. That was the case in 1866, 1870, and 1938.

"There can be no lasting peace in Europe with a dismembered Germany, any more than there could be a lasting peace in North America if other nations tried to separate the States or to put parts of them under Mexico. In the light of historical experience, the sound course is to give the Germans an incentive for abandoning their old ways and becoming a peaceful nation."

11

THE HOOVER MEMOIRS, GERMAN EDITION

Frequent mention has been made in this study of *The Memoirs of Herbert Hoover*. The three-volume autobiographical work appeared in the United States in 1951 and 1952, as a title in The Macmillan Company's list. The Matthias-Grünewald-Verlag of Mainz acquired the German language rights and secured the services of Werner von Grünau as translator. By 1954 the German public was able to read what our thirty-first President himself had to say about his times and his life.

The Hoover Archives at Stanford are in possession of fifty-eight reviews which appeared during 1954 and early 1955 in Germany. It is safe to say that many more were printed in the German press which did not chance to reach the Archives. The Stanford collection also includes the scripts of four radio broadcasts by competent critics.

How did German reviewers react? For one thing, all available reviews stress the "typically American" success story of a poor boy rising by his own efforts to become a world figure. Many place special emphasis upon Mr. Hoover's services to humanity and especially to Germany. Others welcome the *Memoirs* because they tell the German reader what was going on politically elsewhere in the world during the times when the involvement in two world wars had cut Germany off from enemy and many other foreign media of information. Still others draw lessons for the German people from hitherto—to them—unknown facts concerning international relations.

Even the captions (headlines) for the reviews are as revealing as they are varied. Here are some of them:

"Hoover: a Benefactor of Germany"
"A Man We Shall Never Forget"
"The Wonderful Life of a Self-Made Man"
"Memoirs of a Philanthropist"
"Errand Boy Became 'Mr. President' "
"A Combative Quaker"
"A Great Humanitarian"
"Personal Experiences During Years of Decision"
"A Late Justification"
"What Will History Say?"
"Statesman and Servant of Humanity"
"Consequences of an Economic Crisis"
"Herbert Hoover: Helper in Need"

In selecting the excerpts from German reviews which follow, repetitious material has been cut to the minimum. Instead, verbatim quotation is made in translation of passages that show the diversity of German approaches to an estimate of Herbert Hoover and his life and work.

First, the newspapers:

Die Welt, Hamburg: "In Hoover's *Memoirs* the life of a man is described which. . . in its multiplicity of experiences and in its colorfulness appears honestly and authoritatively to portray the best qualities of the American people.

"The German edition . . . is extremely timely and will remain so for long, especially as an important source for our analysis of America and Americans, yes, in general for an understanding of our time and its problems. For the only thing that has changed since World War II is the fact that the same problems have become even more urgent."

Süddeutsche Zeitung, Munich: These questions [concerning the Great Depression] will remain a subject for debate for a long time to come. Hoover himself will not cease to fight for his views, as doggedly and passionately as is permissible for a Quaker. And yet this obstinacy is not his most striking characteristic. The essence of his being is the readiness with which Hoover as an engineer, as organizer, as splendid Secretary of Commerce, and as unselfish adviser to many governments was always ready to serve when his country called him."

Osnabrücker Zeitung, Osnabrück: "The autobiography of Herbert Hoover is characterized by a talent for biography possessed by Anglo-Americans which is anchored in a flair for open-mindedness and fair play, in the art of not taking oneself excessively seriously, and in a nonetheless human warmth. . . .

"All characterizations of personalities whom he met are clear, precise, critical, but never sarcastic or sneering. All themes are discussed in the broad framework of discussion that transcends personal spheres of interest and the limitations of national considerations, and acknowledges its responsibilities to the world, yes, to humanity itself."

Westfälische Post, Soest: "Herbert Hoover, 31st President of the United States, is interesting to Germans not only because his forebear (Andreas Huber) hailed from the Palatinate. It was Hoover who at the conclusion of World War I organized the Quaker relief for Europe's hungry children on a grand style. No wonder that his *Memoirs,* written during 1951 and 1952, have been awaited here with eager curiosity. . . . Hoover's *Memoirs* are by no means of value only to the historian and the specialist on American affairs."

Vertriebenen-Anzeiger, Munich: "Hoover's *Memoirs* are extraordinarily worth while for a German reader, if for no other reason, because one sees the problems, which in part also concern Germany, in the perspective of an outsider and with the eyes of a contemporary who played an important part in the history of more recent times."

Industriekurier, Düsseldorf: "By virtue of his energy, his talent for organization, and his warm heart, Herbert Hoover has in all likelihood saved more human beings from death than any other living man. That sounds very American, but it is a sober fact. . . .

"It is indisputable that *timely* acceptance of the Hoover Moratorium (which was prevented by France) . . . might have constituted a last-minute strengthening of the Weimar Republic and in truth might even have meant deliverance from National Socialism [Nazism]."

Neue Zeitung, Frankfurt-am-Main: "In Hoover's *Memoirs* one will find remarkable material about the peace negotiations after the First World War and will be able to note the mistakes that later contributed essentially to the great crises in Central Europe. Hoover very early foresaw the later developments and did much to prevent them. . . .

"All this . . . can be read with interest, especially by politicians who must solve practical problems and cannot be content with rhetoric."

Neue Ruhrzeitung, Essen: "These three volumes with their pros and cons are a rich source for anyone who desires to study America's great Depression and learn from it.

"The greatness of this man is revealed in the mass of material which he has assembled concerning his world-embracing relief undertakings for combating disaster. One is impressed with the tremendous amount of painstaking labor that went into these books."

Der Mittag, Düsseldorf: "The period following 1925 was an epoch of irresponsible credits. At the same time that the U.S.A.

was seized with a speculators' fever which took possession of the entire population down to the waiter and hotel bellboy . . . Hoover demonstrates that he discerned the danger inherent in the credit and speculation excesses as early as 1925 and continuously opposed them."

Hamburger Echo, Hamburg: "One will not be able to accept all the political theses of Hoover the Liberal and Individualist, nor agree with his opinion that something like a return to the old course occurred in the U.S.A. during the last war. There is no such thing as a return in historical development; there is solely something new. These political thoughts have nothing to do, however, with the gratitude that we Germans—and not we alone—owe to the Man Hoover."

Hessische Nachrichten, Kassel: "This book is a document of human greatness. Above all, however, it is documentary evidence of the history of decisive years in a turbulent century."

Rhein-Neckar Zeitung, Heidelberg: "This great account of stewardship during an eventful and active life extending into advanced age . . . will constitute valuable source material for the future writing of history. Even if history should be of a different opinion from Hoover, it will have to listen to the forthright account of this man, whose picture was often distorted in such a petty and hateful manner. One is always conscious of the guiding line of Quakerism: one's own mistakes become better known as one sees the mistakes of others."

Der Kurier, Berlin: "Hoover with his sober realism has no feeling for imponderables, for conceptions and perceptions that are rooted in the historical development of Europe. . . . Nevertheless it is fascinating to read what experiences he encountered with narrow-minded, egocentric nationalism during the Paris Peace Conference which followed World War I. . . . Palpable parallels can be drawn from the statesmanlike 'wisdoms' which have dominated the years since 1945—a proof that obviously the ability to learn from history does not exist on this planet."

Der Pfälzer, Landau: Hoover . . . is a man of high ethical ideals . . . and he is a man of moderation, to whom all extremes are abhorrent. At the same time he is willing to act if the well-being of humanity or of his native land so demands. These attributes of character, which are not difficult to discern in his *Memoirs,* determine his path and his actions, in which the unswerving idealism of a humanitarian is united in a happy synthesis with the indispensable realism of a statesman."

Der Tagesspiegel, Berlin: "The climax of the entire work is to be found in Volume III, in which Hoover defends himself with great emphasis against [certain] propaganda lies . . . to the effect that the measures taken by Hoover brought about the great world economic crisis. He demonstrates that the big economic convulsions by no means originated in the United States, but began in Europe. The great crisis in Hoover's incontrovertible opinion stemmed from the political and economic confusion that ensued after the First World War, from the creation of new states with thousands of kilometers of new customs barriers, and last but not least from the foreign exchange muddle throughout Europe."

Next, a cross-section of German magazine reviews:

Bücherei und Bildung, Reutlingen: "Among the memoirs of statesmen and politicians of our time those of Hoover belong in the front rank, side by side with those of Churchill and Mannerheim. . . . Augmented and supported by numerous documents, [they] are a fertile and important source of historical research, especially as regards the First World War and the peace conferences which followed. . . .

"Many nuggets of gold stemming from the ripe wisdom of a life of experience are strewn among the seemingly dry reports and projects, as for instance the observations concerning research in the realm of pure and applied sciences."

Geschichte in Wissenschaft und Unterricht, Stuttgart: "For the German reader, no doubt, [the *Memoirs*] will first and foremost awaken memories of the humane helper in the First World War and the postwar period. For, comprised in the Hoover relief work for Europe, which began with an action on behalf of occupied

Belgium, was also the feeding of uncounted children of school age as well as the supplying of medicines and textiles."

Welt und Wort, Tübingen: "Today it has already become a tradition of taking for granted that in time of need of every kind an appeal is made to America, and that one can be almost certain that relief was already under way from the moment that a catastrophe occurred anywhere. This trait, which deserves more gratitude and reflection than often is extended, in no mean degree goes back to the example set by Hoover and the success which his will-to-do achieved."

Westermanns Monatshefte, Braunschweig: [The third volume] draws an excellent picture of the forces at work that hurled the peoples of the earth in 1939 into a Second World War."

Der Büchermarkt, Munich: "An extremely important and instructive book which should be read by everyone who desires to become acquainted with the history of the American democracy and the foundations of the Age of the Masses."

Finally, excerpts from radio scripts:

Hessischer Rundfunk, Frankfurt-am-Main, script by Dr. Gabriele Strecker: "The careful reader will learn more about the America of the last third of the nineteenth century, also about success in the engineering profession, than in many other books. . . .

"European history covering the twenties and thirties, the history of the League of Nations, of the Weimar Republic, the complicated interrelationships existing indissolubly between Europe and the United States—all this becomes clearer upon reading the Hoover *Memoirs.* . . .

"In a chapter entitled, 'Building the Trojan Horse of Emergency,' Hoover sketches a portrait of the demagogues of all times, who paint the devil on the wall and transform the country into a place of collective hysteria in order to seize power—whether democratically and legally or by the use of brute force is in the final analysis immaterial."

Süddeutscher Rundfunk, Stuttgart: "The Hoover *Memoirs* with their detailed description of the conditions and the human beings with whom Hoover had to deal—Wilson, Clemenceau, Lloyd George—give brilliant testimony not only regarding the personality of Mr. Hoover. Inasmuch as they were written from personal experience, they are an exemplary exposition of the entire period which Hoover helped to shape and which continues to have its effect even today."

Südwestfunk, Baden-Baden, script by Carl Dryssen: "It is a part of Herbert Hoover's nature not to make much of a fuss about himself even in the most important situations and events. Perhaps this fact in the last analysis explains why this ever modest, objectively sober-minded man received more honors than any other living man in the public eye, including Churchill. . . .

"After having received an overpowering impression of his life's work I should like to describe him as a sort of 'Albert Schweitzer in Politics,' in other words, as a man who in as prosy and callous an epoch as ours dared to embark upon the adventure of the heart and bring it to a successful conclusion."

12

GERMANY RENDERS THANKS

On November 22, 1954, most newspapers of importance in Germany published a feature story which began with these words: "When Dr. Adenauer arrived for his first visit in the U.S.A. in the spring of 1953, he went directly from the ship to the Waldorf-Astoria Hotel in New York. Before meeting any representative of official America, he stood face to face with a man with whom he considered it his first duty as guest of the American people to shake hands in gratitude. That man was Herbert Hoover."

The story was accompanied by the news that Mr. Hoover would arrive in Bonn that same day in response to an invitation by the German Government. It paid tribute to the honor guest's humanitarianism in the following words: "For millions the name of Hoover recalls to memory the relief work which rescued countless compatriots from hunger's merciless onslaught during Germany's hard times after the first and second world wars. Twice in his life of eighty years the white-haired former President of the United States has mobilized the hearts of his contemporaries for his campaigns against the nutritional catastrophes of the world."

There followed a thumbnail sketch of Mr. Hoover's life.

Typical headlines calling attention to the story were:

"America's 'Grand Old Man' in Bonn"

"Friend of German People Visits Federal Republic"

"Herbert Hoover—a Great American"

"A Big Heart Behind Figures"

"A Great Humanitarian"

The official invitation to come to Germany as guest of the nation had been presented to Mr. Hoover during Dr. Adenauer's second visit to America, on October 30, 1954. President Eisenhower had given evidence of his hearty approval by placing his plane, the *Columbine,* at Mr. Hoover's disposal for the journey.

Meticulous preparations preceded the arrival of America's past-President. Tracy S. Voorhees had been invited by Mr. Hoover to be a member of his party, the other being John B. Hollister, his long-time co-worker in international relief work, Dr. Fordyce B. St. John, his physician for the journey, and Hugo Meyer, his secretary on his foreign missions. Instead, Mr. Voorhees with the former Chief Executive's approval preceded him to Germany as his personal representative in making arrangements for his visit and his speeches, and joined the party only after its arrival in the Federal Republic.

In clearing matters with the German authorities Mr. Voorhees, of course, acted through U.S. Ambassador James B. Conant and his staff. In preparing visits of this nature there enter questions of protocol, of timing, of coordination with the media of mass communications, of acquainting the parties concerned with the honor guest's wishes regarding topics for his public addresses, of acceptances of invitations to entertain the distinguished foreign visitor —details concerning which the public has little or no inkling.

The German Chancellor, accompanied by a retinue of high dignitaries, welcomed Mr. Hoover at the Cologne-Bonn Airport as "a man whose constant aim was to serve humanity." From the brief ceremony the guest of honor was driven to the ambassadorial residence of Dr. Conant in near-by Bad Godesberg, where Mr. Hoover resided while in the Bonn area, as he also did later in the Ambassador's official home in Berlin which our Government maintained because of the city's occupation status.

The first round of official receptions began the following forenoon with a visit to Professor Theodor Heuss, President of the Federal Republic of Germany, in the German "White House," the Villa Hammerschmidt. After an hour's confidential chat between the two statesmen, during which my son Robert of the U.S.I.A. staff at Bonn, who acted as interpreter, was the only "outsider" present, Professor Heuss gave a luncheon in his American colleague's honor. It was attended by top level American and German personalities of note.

In a prepared speech, from which excerpts are here quoted, President Heuss proposed a toast to the guest of honor: ". . . Almost four decades have passed since we first came across your name. . . . What we heard was that there was an American citizen who had undertaken the task of fighting threatening hunger on the part of the civilian population of Belgium which had been forced into the stresses of war—a task which in a precarious situation demanded formal tactfulness and personal backbone, circumspection, imagination, and tenacity.

"What to begin with had been merely a name to us, gradually developed into an image of a great humanitarian. This conception assumed a more definite, strong profile when, after 1918, the German people themselves became the object and goal of that readiness and desire of yours to lead the good impulses of the American people into deeds of relief and succor.

"In those years—1919–1920—the German people learned to pronounce the name of Hoover with gratitude, and a quarter century later, in 1944–1945, to listen prayerfully for his possible advent as the hope of a confused world. This hope was not disappointed. Your name was intertwined with the quiet and firm conviction that love can overcome hatred and revenge. . . .

"As statesman you saved a world threatened by confusion and conflict, when in 1931 you virtually compelled acceptance of the Moratorium on German war debts. Unfortunately disaster could not be prevented after all. But when this disaster reached its culmination in the form of World War II, your attitude, which paired politico-economic insight with the ability to suffer with others, always was one of moderation.

"There resulted the Hoover Child Feeding Program. To my great relief I learned at the time that you, Mr. Hoover, were not always the model of a well behaved boy. My wife, who had undertaken the beautiful task of administering the program in Württemberg, delivered a speech about you before children and adults who have remained children, including Americans who like to remain children. . . .

"In a few days you will accept an honorary doctor's degree from Tübingen University. I was very happy to learn this. . . . This university in 1817 was the first in Germany to create an autonomous faculty of Political Science. I hope I won't spoil the dean's speech by telling you this: the man who created this faculty was Friedrich List. An ardent democrat, he was harassed so much by the authorities of the day that he emigrated to America in 1825, where he remained until homesickness brought him back to Europe, to Germany, and into new tragedies.

"While in America, List had not only organized the first American railway, but also, in 1827, had written America's future industrial program under the title of *Outlines of a New System of Political Economy*. He was thus the theoretical founder of the independence of a then not yet existing American industrialism. For me, a compatriot of List, this connection adds spice to your visit. . . ."

The speech by Elly Heuss-Knapp, to which her husband referred, was delivered in Stuttgart during the observance of Mr. Hoover's seventy-fifth birthday anniversary. As an illustration of the fact that the boy Hoover was as mischievous as any other youngster, Frau Heuss had cited his secret absorption of Daniel Defoe's *Robinson Crusoe* in a garret with some of his buddies. Quaker ethics forbade the reading of such worldly books of adventure.

The later First Lady of Germany at that time was a member, as was also her husband, of the Württemberg-Baden Diet, or state legislature. Always an independent personality, she, a Democrat, occasionally voted with the Social Democrats although her husband was chairman of the Democratic Party. Albert Schweitzer, whom she had known since her childhood in Alsace, was one of her and her husband's closest friends. She died July 2, 1952.

A few excerpts from her address in commemoration of Herbert Hoover's seventy-fifth birthday follow: "Dear Children and Dear Big Folk! Nowadays the children are the chief personalities. We want to celebrate a birthday—and our birthday child is already completely grown up; he will be seventy-five years old today! . . . His name is Herbert Hoover, former President of the United States, a great friend of children. Let's talk about him for a few moments. . . .

"The Quakers always settled together. They had strict rules of conduct—no smoking, no drinking, no cursing, no military service. The Sermon on the Mount was their law. . . . [Mr. Hoover] had lost his father early, when he was only six years old. He then had to lead a very restricted life; even the reading of worldly books was sternly forbidden. But he had playmates and lived out in Nature, so that he never lacked opportunity for recreation. Only, it was not permitted to scuffle and fight; that was considered a serious sin. . . . In our exhibit you can see pictures of many an episode of the time, such as his reading *Robinson Crusoe* secretly. . . .

"Then came the Second World War. We won't say much about it; most of you remember it and we are still right in [the] midst [of] the postwar period. Two years ago last February, in the year 1947, the present President Truman had the good idea of sending Mr.

Hoover into all the distressed areas. Mr. Hoover found that not 50 million Europeans were threatened with hunger as in 1919, but 150 million, not to mention Asia. And now, dear children, comes the part that you must remember, even though you forget everything else that I have told you:

"Just think how many people would in such a case have thought and said: the distress is too great; we can't help everybody. But Hoover said something quite different. He said, true, we can't help everybody, but we do want first and foremost to help the children, and that . . . immediately. That's how the Hoover Feeding Program started which benefits many, many children and youths and is a great help to their families. It is easy to prove that Mr. Hoover intervened with great success, for in the schools all pupils are weighed and practically all have gained weight. The moment the Hoover Feeding is interrupted, the weight recedes.

"You all know how the Hoover Feeding is handled. And I believe you also know that the Americans are donating all food as a present from one people to another. Please stop to think that this is not self-evident. It may well be that it is unexampled in history. Therefore, let us today render thanks from honest hearts. The fact that we are celebrating this birthday together is in itself an evidence of our gratitude. . . .

"I've been wondering whether Mr. Hoover this morning thought of the fact that within our area in Germany many thousands of children even in their vacation camps and hostelries are starting out with their little pots and pans in happy anticipation of a decent, warm Hoover lunch. It must be a beautiful thought for him. . . . I believe he saved more lives than any other man of our times. You all should know that. That's why I told you something about the life of Herbert Hoover and that's why we shall now all rise and say with a loud voice: 'Hoover *hoch, hoch, hoch!*'"

But to return to President Heuss's luncheon in honor of Mr. Hoover: a beautiful pewter bowl, designed by the Rhenish Professor Ewald Mataré, was the German Chief Executive's parting gift to his American guest of honor.

Innumerable German cities and towns have a Golden Book in which distinguished visitors are requested to write their names. The burgomasters of Bonn, the temporary German capital, and near-by Bad Godesberg, where the American Settlement for the employees of the American Embassy is located, saw to it in ceremonies long hallowed by custom and tradition that Herbert Hoover's name was personally penned by him as a cherished addition to their Golden Books.

The ceremony in Bonn took place in the City Hall which with its lofty steps dates back to 1782. The burgomaster, Peter Busen, welcomed his guest, saying: "I should like at this time to thank you on behalf of the many plain people who profited by your readiness to help during the darkest hour of need of our nation. I beg leave to do it with an unpretentious word which, however, comes from the heart of our people: *Vergelt's Gott!* (God's reward to you!)"

Mayor Busen then presented his guest with a hand-carved wooden platter. Outside, a large, cheering crowd had meanwhile assembled to pay homage to the nation's guest.

The ceremony in Bad Godesberg had a musical note: Burgomaster Heinrich Hopmann received Mr. Hoover in the Redoute, a festival concert hall made famous by Ludwig van Beethoven, who played there for his much older colleague, Joseph Haydn of Austria. (Beethoven was born in near-by Bonn.)

Herr Hopmann, who continued as teacher besides heading the city administration, stressed the fact that the German children, no less than the grownups, had a deep affection for Mr. Hoover. The latter replied that Beethoven and his music had won the hearts of the American people. As to the Golden Book, he observed: "As I enter my name in the Golden Book I am certain that I shall take golden memories back with me."

Mayor Hopmann on behalf of his city presented his guest with an artistic etching of the Redoute.

In the evening a state dinner was tendered by Dr. Adenauer in his official residence, Palais Schaumburg. The Chancellor expressed his feelings regarding the guest of honor in an address of welcome ending in a toast, "I raise my glass to your health and to the friendship between our peoples." Excerpts from his after-dinner speech follow:

". . . We consider it a high honor for you to have faced the hardship of a long journey, all the more so since great tasks in your own country are occupying you fully at present. [This refers to Mr. Hoover's exacting labor as chairman of the Committee on Organization of the Executive Branch of Government.]

"Mr. President, for us Germans your name is the epitome of the most striking qualities of the American people. It personifies for us the pluck of the pioneers who opened up the great wide spaces of your country, the faith in the creative powers of the free human personality, the respect for the rights of every individual, and the truly Christian love of fellowman. . . .

"We are under an obligation of deepest gratitude to you and the American people for the efficacious neighborly love which prompted you twice to come to the aid of the German people, who only shortly before had been your adversaries, at a time of direst need. . . .

"We also owe it to your political farsightedness, to your comprehensive knowledge of economic life, that we could again build up our country and our economy after the ravages of the Second World War. . . . The limitations upon our economy were relaxed and, thanks to the magnanimous aid of the American people, we could begin the reconstruction of our native land. During your travels through our countryside and our cities you will see that great changes have taken place since your last visit. . . .

"Scarcely ten years after the conclusion of the war the Federal Republic will stand beside the United States and in the Atlantic Community as a free, democratic partner in the service of peace. . . . As to ourselves, we shall do our part to strengthen the peoples united in freedom and thereby also relieve your people of part of the burden which it has hitherto carried for the common cause."

Mr. Hoover thanked the Chancellor briefly and gave expression to his satisfaction that Germany was again respected throughout the world.

On the following day Mr. Hoover was the guest of the German parliament, the Bundestag. Dr. Eugen Gerstenmaier, its presiding officer, had been summoned to the bedside of his gravely ill father. In his place, Professor Carlo Schmidt, the first vice-president and a Social Democratic deputy, welcomed the American statesman with these words: "Every member of the Bundestag knows what thanks are due Mr. Hoover. Almost without exception those who are here assembled have children who owe it to Mr. Hoover that they could survive the evil times that followed the war.

"After the Second World War you, Sir, were one of the small number of individuals who spoke about the German people in a manner that enabled them to have faith again in themselves. You are proving by example that one can be a great statesman and at the same time a truly good person."

Mr. Hoover responded to the effect that too much personal honor was being showered upon him; that he had merely been an instrument of his people and his country. The enormous comeback of Germany, he continued, was an indication of the great vitality of her people. This was true not only of the will to work but also of the spiritual and democratic potentialities of the German people.

As a memento of his visit Vice-President Schmidt presented him with an illustrated volume, *Germany Today,* printed in English.

A luncheon at the German Press Club of Bonn, to which all accredited foreign correspondents were also invited, furnished the platform for Mr. Hoover's first formal pronouncement while on German soil. His address was entitled, "Some Hopes for Peace."

A somewhat abbreviated text follows:

". . . When I learned that you wished me to make some sort of an address, I inquired as to what subject within my province might be of interest to you. Your officials suggested that I appraise the Hopes of Peace as seen through some American eyes.

"There never was a time when the Western world was more

anxious for peace. All our peoples have had their fill of war. The daily prayer of all free men is for a lasting peace.

"In these nine-and-a-half years since the guns were silenced the disordered world with all its aftermaths has made some progress toward stability and peace. And from this progress there is hope.

"You will remember the Biblical legend of the Four Horsemen of the Apocalypse, the names of which were War, Death, Famine, and Pestilence. Fighting, War and Death have abated. Through aroused compassion, Famine and Pestilence were overcome at that time.

"But out of these gigantic tumults has come another Horseman to ravish the world with Fear, Hate and a passion to destroy Western civilization. The ancient prophet was unacquainted with him, but his name is Communism.

"The tensions of military conflict with Russia seem to have abated in these recent months and from this abatement, I believe, we can have at least a gleam of hope. Moscow has made many declarations of peace-loving intent. They speak of 'peaceful co-existence.'

"It may be that they want more time to consolidate their gains. They may want more time to promote their infiltration of conspiracies in free nations. It may be that the growth of our deterrents against military aggression has influenced their minds.

"It may be that internal forces are working within to restrain them. Every deep-seated social or political revolution has generated within itself a dynamism of military aggression or a crusading spirit to spread their new ideas. That was the case of the Mohammedan Revolution, the French Revolution, the American Revolution, as well as the Russian Revolution. Incidentally, in the American case, we had a vacant continent to invade, but we have been nonetheless crusaders to spread our concepts of freedom.

"With time, the original leaders of these revolutions die off and some revolutions have the bad habit of devouring their young. At least their successors are less violent. They become more concerned with their dangers and improvements at home. From all this it may be that the Communist protestations are genuine. All of which possibly warrants a faint hope.

"But from our many years' experience with the Communists, we should learn more about what peaceful co-existence means—and we must await works rather than words. The Western world has many times enumerated some of these works to which the Communists might contribute. They could join in the completely free unification of Germany; they could sign the peace with Austria. They could cease their germ warfare of conspiracies directed to overthrowing free governments.

"With such steps, we might at least advance out of the thunder and lightning of this cold war into the dawn of a cold peace.

"But all this is too much to expect, and we should not be lulled into the abandonment of our means of defense. The only hope for our safety is the building up of arms and a united front among free nations which *will deter* Communist aggression against us. . . .

"In this role of deterrents, the present proposed agreements looking to the arming of Germany and Europe have a very large part. Without the consummation of those agreements, the security of Western civilization in Europe becomes dependent on the malevolent will of the Communists.

"The coming of the fission bomb and guided missiles has contributed to the deterrents. But one of its discouraging effects has been that, for fear of its use upon them by the Communists, some nations engage in the futile hope to escape its ravages by neutrality in a great conflict.

"Neutralism is no answer to the security of free nations in case of a major conflict. And moreover, it gives comfort only to the spirit of aggression from the Communists. . . .

"Our American people have joined in the defense of Western Europe. It is an illusion of some European statesmen that we have joined and spent huge efforts for the selfish purpose of defending ourselves. I and most of my countrymen have held that this is untrue. We can defend ourselves at much less cost in manpower and money, and build effective deterrents against Communist attack upon us. The fundamental reason for our participation is to preserve Western civilization in Europe and the freedom of nations in the world.

"The strength of the West in effective defense is not a goal in itself but only a pre-condition and guarantee of freedom for unlimited development of our cultural and spiritual life.

"Nor is there an atom of truth in the assertion that American action is animated by imperialistic ambitions. The world should know from our many actions in the past there is no imperialism in our blood.

"Our people have met many discouragements and frustrations in these efforts. We have greatly reduced our resources with which we could increase the comfort and living of our own people. Europe must realize that many of my countrymen had lost confidence in these projects of European defense.

"But the statesmanship of Chancellor Adenauer and your Parliament, through joining Germany in the effective defense of Europe, has done much to restore confidence and hope in the American people. We await similar action by other nations, but our patience is not inexhaustible.

"At one time we builded great hopes on the organization of the United Nations.

"When that temple was built to guard the flame of peace, the world concerned itself with the architecture of the super-structure, but neglected its foundation. When Communists were taken into that structure, the foundation of its major purpose, which was to stop military aggression, was destroyed.

"But it has some values as a forum whereby with electronic equipment we can denounce the ways of the Communists in five languages all at once. It does perform useful services in mediating minor conflicts, in public health, in some economic and philanthropic fields. It might also be a place where free nations can promote their unity. But the inability of the United Nations to prevent military aggression has given rise to defensive alliances intended for the protection of the free world.

"One of the real foundations of peace is the rise of what is sometimes derisively called 'Nationalism.' There are those who with the organization of the United Nations had further dreams of some sort of World Government where the independence of nations would be curtailed or abolished. They denounce nationalism as a sin against peace and progress and as a wicked force.

"But the spirit of nationalism in its true sense springs from the deepest of human emotions. It springs from a thousand rills of inspiring national history, its heroes, its common language, its culture and its national achievements. It rises from the yearning of men to be free of foreign domination, to govern themselves. . . .

"And equally do these emotions flow wide and deep in all free nations. Within them and their religious faith is their spiritual strength. It sustains their resolution to defend themselves against aggression and domination.

"Nationalism does not mean isolation from unity of action among nations. Rather does internal spiritual strength make common action for defense more secure and more potent. . . .

"I have rejoiced at the rise of a peaceful and constructive spirit in Germany. It has brought great steps in her independence and her strength. From her full freedom alone can come the common defense and her full contribution to all mankind.

"I can well claim that advocacy of German unification is no afterthought of mine for this occasion.

"Twelve years ago, just after America entered the war, some of our leaders in a spirit of revenge and as a necessity of peace began to demand dismemberment of Germany. At that time, I said:

" 'The Germans like all virile races are cohesive. The history of Europe's wars might be written around her dismemberments and the explosions from her movements to unity. . . . There can be no lasting peace . . . with a dismembered Germany. Nations cannot be held in chains.'

"In my country we hold that unification must be the purpose

of free nations. We hold that the work of unification must have their full cooperation. . . .

"The German peoples have before now been the bastion of Western civilization which deterred its destruction by the Asiatic hordes. My prayer is that Germany may be given the unity and full freedom which will restore her to that mission in the world."

The scene now shifted to Southern Germany where, at the end of the Second World War, three southwestern states had been set up: Württemberg-Baden, South Baden, and Württemberg-Hohenzollern. (They are now amalgamated in the new state of Baden-Württemberg). Upon his arrival at the Stuttgart-Echterdingen Airport in the late afternoon of November 24, Mr. Hoover was greeted by the Premier of the Baden-Württemberg State Government, Dr. Gebhard Müller, and taken to a private dinner to meet the Premier's cabinet associates.

Hundreds of children from the schools of Echterdingen who had been recipients of the Hoover Child Feeding Program were on hand at the airport to give him a vociferous and enthusiastic reception. A girl pupil presented him with an attractive bouquet of flowers.

The following day was a rainy one. Nevertheless hundreds upon hundreds of children again lined the streets and stood, dripping wet, along a stretch of over one mile to cheer and wave as Mr. Hoover drove to Tübingen University. It was a spontaneous manifestation of gratitude which gave him more joy than the most generous words of praise by great statesmen.

At venerable Tübingen University Germany's honor guest received further reinforcement of the claim in learned circles that Mr. Hoover holds more honorary degrees than any other living man. To his collection of then eighty, now almost one hundred such degrees, Tübingen added that of *Dr. rer. pol. h.c.* (Honorary Doctor of Political Science).

The *Stuttgarter Zeitung,* leading newspaper of Baden-Württemberg, described the picturesque ceremony in detail:

"The auditorium of Tübingen University presented a festive

picture when at 11 o'clock the former American President, Herbert Hoover, escorted by the *Rektor* [President] of the university, Professor Dr. [Franz Xaver] Arnold, entered, followed by the entire faculty. Besides many personalities from political life, industry, and administration, numerous foreign consuls as well as Bishop [Martin] Haug, D.D., and Vicar-General Dr. [August] Hagen were in attendance. Every seat of the auditorium was occupied. The gallery was crowded with students who had failed to find seats.

"The *Rektor* of the university paid tribute to the venerable former president as a man of action who was a friend and helper, and extended a heartfelt welcome to him on behalf of Tübingen University.

"The people of Germany, he said, looked upon Hoover with veneration because he had proven himself a genius of the heart and a herald of Christian brotherly love during the darkest hours of humanity. In earliest childhood Herbert Hoover's heart had already become compassionate for human suffering. To this compassion had been added the ability to organize in a large way. The relief work for Europe has saved many human beings from death. During the worst period which the German people ever experienced, viz., after the end of the Second World War, when, atoning for the crimes of National Socialism, they were considered outlaws and forsaken by the entire world, Hoover again set the table for millions of German school children and students at universities. The students of Tübingen were eager in this hour to wish the great helper and humanitarian a hearty '*Vergelt's Gott*' ('God's reward to you') on behalf of all German youth.

"Stormy applause lasting for minutes interrupted the proceedings before a representative of the student body could transmit the thanks of the students. During the period following World War II [he pointed out] the name of Herbert Hoover had been transmuted into a verb: whenever the students went to a Hoover Feeding, they were said to have 'hooverized.' The youth of Germany felt a deep sense of gratitude for this American statesman.

"The dean of the Economic Section of the Legal-and-Economic

Sciences Faculty, Professor Dr. Hero Möller, announced that the university had conferred the honorary degree of Doctor of Political Science upon the venerated guest. He then gave a review in English of the eight decades of Herbert Hoover's life and work and a short biographical sketch of the former president. Herbert Hoover, he said, had never tried to advance human progress by words alone. He had arranged his entire life so as to enable himself to advance progress by deeds.

"The conferment of the honorary diploma upon Herbert Hoover was almost lost amidst the bulb flashes of the numerous local and foreign photographers; tremendous searchlights illuminated the scene for the representatives of newsreels. The ceremony was broadcast over many networks.

"When Hoover stepped before the lectern to deliver his address of thanks, and again after he finished, he was swamped with applause. After an organ selection he left the auditorium, again followed by the professors of Tübingen University. Before the university building many citizens of Tübingen had meanwhile assembled. They brought the distinguished guest heart-warming ovations."

In accepting his degree, *Doktor honoris causa,* Herbert Hoover spoke in part as follows:

"On this occasion I can not fail to acknowledge the obligations which our much younger universities of America owe to their older German brothers. The structure of our faculties and our methods of instruction were established almost wholly on the pattern of German universities. You will realize that more than 25 per cent of the races which have poured into the melting pot of America are of Germanic origin. The very names of many American leaders in every branch of our national life are witness to the value of this inheritance.

"There is no better example of this fruitful interchange of intellectual life than the case of Friedrich List. His name especially comes to my mind because I have received the distinguished honor of being made an honorary citizen of Reutlingen, the city of his birth. List was indeed one of the great economists during the first half of the nineteenth century. As a member of your faculty, his pioneering ideas on economic freedom brought him trouble and exile. He naturally migrated to America where he took part in molding American life. After becoming an American citizen he was appointed American Consul at Stuttgart. . . .

"I have been in Germany many times, but one occasion was on a scholastic adventure. Some years before the First World War, together with Mrs. Hoover, we undertook to translate from the Latin the first comprehensive book published on my branch of the engineering profession. That was a work entitled *De Re Metallica* by Georgius Agricola—being a huge folio of 600 pages with many intelligent illustrations. It was published almost 400 years ago. . . . Agricola had a tendril of memory with this university. Although he was a staunch Catholic, he was a lifelong friend of Melanchthon, a lecturer here, who aided in securing the publication of his book. . . .

"It might interest you to know that this book by a long since forgotten German scholar had some responsibilities for the torrent of gold and silver with which the Spanish Conquistadors of Peru and Mexico flooded the world in the fifteenth and sixteenth centuries. It seems highly probable that the processes used in working the mines were taken from Agricola's book. No other text existed at that time, and the particular processes which they needed were not used in Spain. And as a further tribute to this scholar, he was the first to illuminate correctly the principles of many metallurgical processes which we still use today. However, we have improved the machinery.

"I have been interested in your library and its ancient setting. Again I can establish a certain comity of action. I began during the First World War to make use of my many opportunities to collect what has become millions of items about this forty years' tumult of wars, peace and revolutions. In this library at my university we have certain collections of German history of the First World War that were given to me by the [Friedrich] Ebert regime which I do not believe are available in Germany.

"Again, after the Second World War with the aid of our American officials and certain Nazis who wanted to be rid of their documents, we formed an extensive collection on the rise and fall of the Hitler regime, which might otherwise have been lost.

"Some of the First World War documents we agreed would not be disclosed for a term of years not yet expired. Sometime this Library may be of use to your students of your own history.

"An added burden has fallen upon our universities. The Communists, by infiltration, propaganda and conspiracy are seeking to corrupt the truth, the morals, the religion and in fact to destroy the freedoms of Western civilization. They use our freedoms to destroy freedom itself, but they do not comprehend the spiritual, moral and educational force which will defeat them. . . .

"One of the greatest contributions of the universities is to keep open the channels of free exchange of knowledge between all the universities in the world. It is one of the pillars of freedom today.

"It is by the free shuttle of ideas between our universities that we weave the great tapestries of knowledge. Our academic traditions have developed a system that is peculiarly effective in spotting outstanding intellects and putting them to work in a climate that fosters creative, original thinking.

"From the mutual building by our university faculties and laboratories devoted to abstract science have come most of the great discoveries of natural law. The application of these discoveries through invention and production has been the task of the engineers and technicians whom we train. Applied science dries up quickly unless we maintain the sources of discovery in pure science. From these dual activities of the scientists and the technicians, a great stream of blessings in health, comfort and good living has flowed to all our peoples.

"It may be that at one time scientific discovery and invention were the product of a poverty-driven genius in a garret. Even if that were so, it is no longer the case. The discovery of natural law does not come as a sudden concept. It comes mostly slowly—step by step—through the action and reaction among our university scientific faculties and their laboratories.

"For instance, the parents of our radio communications of today were not the broadcasters. Its parents were Maxwell from one university, who by mathematics formulated the hypothesis of electrical wave motion. It was Hertz of another university who experimentally confirmed Maxwell's deductions and carried them further to the demonstration that these waves could traverse the atmosphere. Then university-trained technicians from a score of institutions gave the world mounting inventions which finally handed this great tool to the broadcasters.

"We have another mutual duty. For it is our universities which must train the men for leadership in our professions and as executives of great economic institutions. It is they who must guide them away from incompetence and in their social responsibilities. It becomes the mutual obligation of our universities to inculcate in these future administrators morals, rectitude and their responsibilities to the public.

"But our universities have a still greater purpose. From them must come the expansion of the human spirit; with its ever-widening penetration into the unknown; and finally, as Huxley says, 'the inculcation of veracity of thought.'

"But again I return to the fundamental of all—that is freedom itself. The discoveries of natural law can flourish only in an atmosphere of free minds and free spirits. And inventions and production flourish only in a climate of reward for effort.

"And finally, as a tribute to the influence of German universities, I may mention that my own university bears on its seal the words *Die Luft der Freiheit weht.*

"It has been indeed the universities of the world which have molded and defended the freedoms of mankind. That has been your greatest mission over 400 years and it is our greatest mutual mission today. . . ."

The third focal point of Mr. Hoover's visit to Germany was Berlin, still occupied by four former enemy powers as an anomalous oasis in a Russia-dominated Communist desert. His coming had been heralded for days by the Berlin press of every political shade except the Communist.

On his arrival at Berlin-Tempelhof Airport, the acting burgomaster, Dr. Walther Schreiber, welcomed him with these words: "We see in you not only the statesman, but above all the man who helped us by alleviating suffering and misery. We are grateful to you. No one in Berlin will ever forget what you did for us."

The former President replied that, when he last visited Germany, the country had been in a state of total despair. Today, however, it had recovered almost completely and was showing remarkable vitality.

On the following forenoon, Mr. Hoover inspected the temporary barracks for refugees from Communist East Germany in the Borough of Marienfelde. According to the *Tagesspiegel* of Berlin, "He was especially happy to visit with the children in their shelter. A little girl presented him with flowers on behalf of the group."

Mr. Hoover also called at the American Headquarters, where he was greeted by a salute of twenty-one guns fired by American tanks. In the afternoon he inspected the American Memorial Library.

The climax of the stay in Berlin came in the evening, when the government and city parliament of West Berlin gave a reception and banquet in his honor. It was held in the city hall of the Borough of Schöneberg, the largest of Greater Berlin's boroughs and presently the seat of the city government for all the western boroughs. It is here that the World Freedom Bell is located, which was donated to West Berlin in October, 1950, by the Crusade for Freedom, a privately sponsored American campaign organization for broadcasting the truth about democracy to the peoples behind the Iron Curtain.

As usual, Mr. Hoover entered his name in the city's Golden Book and became the recipient of a present—this time a replica of the World Freedom Bell and an antique engraving depicting Berlin in the year 1688.

Pleased though he was at these gifts, for Mr. Hoover the highlight of the evening was the singing, by the Schöneberg Boys' Choir, of an American folk song. He beamed all over, applauded demonstratively and asked whether he might not hear the boys once more before the banquet was over. The request was readily granted. In the course of the evening's festivities the boys appeared once again, this time to offer several Berlin songs. Mr. Hoover insisted upon shaking hands with every young songster.

During the *Festbankett* (festival dinner) Professor Otto Suhr, President (Speaker) of the Berlin House of Deputies, paid tribute to the guest of honor, saying that President Hoover, beside Fridtjof Nansen, was proof and example that matter-of-fact politics and selfless love of one's neighbor can be found in one and the same person. He proposed a toast to "Mr. Hoover, the man of good deeds."

Herbert Hoover then delivered his third and last formal address, entitled, "Resistance to Communism." Excerpts follow:

"Outstanding in my eyes is that you have devoted your energies to the rebuilding of homes for the people rather than the repair of ancient monuments. And I have witnessed the tender care with which you attend the children and the refugees who seek sanctuary from the oppression which haunts you next door.

"It is a great work, of which you may well be proud.

"This city of Berlin is on the front line of the cold war. You are combat soldiers in that war. Should it, which God forbid, ever become a hot war, you would be the first to face the enemy. Thus you more than others have the right to feel a sense of relief that the tensions of imminent war have sensibly decreased during these recent months. We can only speculate upon the outcome of this change in Moscow's protestations.

"Whatever the outcome we must remember that the Communists still confront us with three problems.

"The first is their declared basis of immoral relations between nations. That must cause us to hesitate to accept their assurances of good will toward men without more particulars. St. James said: 'Even so faith, if it hath not works, is dead.'

"The second of our problems is that ever since the war the Communists have held to increasing armament. And that even in the period when other nations had demobilized. That does not seem to spell simple defense measures. We have been compelled to resume arming to the teeth in order to deter any possible aggression from them.

"The third is their militant promotion of the Communist faith. They incessantly seek by propaganda, infiltration and conspiracy within all the free nations to destroy the very foundations of civilization.

"For 6,000 years, since recorded time, every civilized race has believed in a Supreme Being. They have realized that the laws which control the orderly movement of the stars were not economic materialism. For the first time in this long corridor of human history, a group of men with the resources of a powerful nation and all the modern techniques of communication are seeking to inflict Red atheism on the whole world.

"Let there be no mistake about it. Lenin repeated over and over again that 'religion is the opiate of a people.' And his malign announcements have been ratified before his tomb every year with fanatic zeal. And their agents at work every day in every free country provide ample confirmation of this wickedness. Their crusade would destroy men's belief in God. It would destroy the moral foundations of mankind. It rots the souls of men.

"And the dreadful degenerations of thirty years of war have fertilized the soil of even free nations for the growth of these malign ideas.

"Those dangers cannot be met by suppressing our own freedoms. Our governments can take care of definite conspiracies to overthrow them by violence. But the organized infiltration of Communist ideas into disturbed and weak minds can be met only by moral and spiritual resistance. . . .

"One of the greatest resistances to Communism has been the increase in productivity in the Western world. And among the many discouraging events in the world, it is a heartening encouragement. . . .

"Without this increase in productivity my country would have been unable to carry the burden of aid to other countries. And in Germany these improvements in productivity and the invigoration of private initiative under economic freedom have enabled you to carry the almost overwhelming burdens of the refugees and ruined industry.

"Nor have you neglected the solution of stupendous social problems and the building of moral and spiritual bulwarks of resistance to Communist corruption.

"With all this promise of increasing productivity, if the world could have peace, we would find a new Golden Age.

"But meanwhile you, the leaders of Berlin, have a great responsibility towards the free world. And may I add the nations of Western Europe have a great responsibility towards you. You face an enemy who lives just across the street. You have seen your duty and have performed it well. Thanks to the spirit and courage of men under the leadership of two great Mayors, you can, like the men of ancient Athens, hold your heads high and say: 'I am a Berliner.'"

Before departing for New York after the Berlin ceremony, Mr. Hoover addressed a telegram of thanks to Chancellor Adenauer, in which he referred to the time spent in Germany as "one of the most stimulating weeks in my life."

On February 6, 1956, an *Oberschule technischer Zweig* (school for boys specializing in the applied sciences) which hitherto bore merely a number, was renamed *Herbert Hoover Schule.* It is located in the Borough of Wedding, a working-class district named after Gustav Friedrich Hermann Wedding, one of the outstanding metallurgists of his time. Wedding lived from 1824 to 1908 and was Professor of the Science of Iron Industry at the Mining Academy of Berlin.

The former President's older son, Herbert Hoover, Jr., then Undersecretary of State, was invited to attend the dedication ceremony and deliver an address. He began by reading a message from his father:

"There is no greater honor that can come to a man than to have a school named for him; there is no part of our life with which I would rather be associated than the education of our young people, for within it lies the basis for our future.

"I am particularly pleased that education is playing such an important role in this embattled city, and feel certain that the students of this school hold firmly to the maintenance of freedom and justice, even under the most trying of circumstances.

"I am deeply honored by your action in naming this school in Wedding after me. I send you all my best wishes."

The Undersecretary of State then spoke on his own behalf, saying in part:

"This school symbolizes the spirit of the people of Berlin. It will carry forward your heritage of a thorough technical education that has been the basic foundation of the great industrial economy of your country for so many years.

"Both my father and I were trained as engineers. From my own experience, I know the close relationship between the practical background of the engineer and the problems that face us in government. The reconstruction of your city, physically and politically, is evidence of the productive combination of professional skills and political progress in your free, modern and competitive economy. . . ."

On June 20, 1956, Herbert Hoover received an unusual surprise when a message (in German), sent by the *Präsidium* of the *Bundesverband der Deutschen Industrie* (National Federation of German Industries), reached him. A somewhat abbreviated English translation follows:

"Esteemed President Hoover:

"During your presidency the United States of America on June 20, 1931, proclaimed the 'Hoover Moratorium,' which postponed for one year the reparations demanded of Germany after the First World War. The Moratorium became effective on July 1, 1931. The twenty-fifth anniversary of this day will come on July 1, 1956.

"German industry seizes upon this opportunity to renew the

feelings of sincere gratitude which it has always had for your courageous step, for it is conscious of the fact that your action back in 1931 opened the way for our economic recovery. . . .

"With your correct view of an impending crisis in the situation you then were years ahead of world public opinion. The entire weight of your personality and of your exalted office had to be exerted to achieve the support of your step by the other states. That step was all the bolder inasmuch as it actually meant the beginning of the end of reparations and thereby led the way toward the final solution of the most serious postwar problem.

"German industry feels even more strongly today, as it looks back upon the past twenty-five years with their fateful vicissitudes, how beneficent your decision at that time was. German industry received further proof of your penetrating intellect when, after the Second World War, you turned emphatically and successfully against the dismantling policy imposed upon Germany, . . . thereby laying the cornerstone for the development of a European economy.

"In a most beautiful manner you permitted your truly compassionate heart to lead you to come to Germany's assistance after both world wars. . . . With all this you have elicited unending, grateful veneration in Germany for your name.

"The *Präsidium* of the *Bundesverband der Deutschen Industrie* unanimously instructed us to express the warmest thanks of German industry for all these steps, and to wish you further happy years made joyous by the retrospective realization that your endeavors have brought untold blessings.

"We should like to underscore the sincerity of this wish and of our gratitude by a gift which accompanies this message. We hope it will give pleasure to you who have so strong a feeling for all that is good and beautiful and truthful.

"Yours in gratitude and deep respect,
"Fritz Berg, Dr. Beutler, Gustav Stein."

The gift referred to was a complete *de luxe* edition of the works of Johann Wolfgang von Goethe. It was presented to Mr. Hoover by the German Ambassador to the United States, Dr. Heinz Krekeler.

Once again an important and powerful organization of Germany thus gave evidence that, as far as the Federal Republic is concerned, Herbert Hoover to its teeming millions is the American statesman whom Germany will never forget.

EPILOGUE

As this manuscript was about to be submitted to my publisher, Herbert Hoover celebrated his eighty-fifth birthday anniversary in splendid health, undiminished zest for work, continued passionate love of our country, and an ever-readiness to give counsel requested by an astonishing number of men in high positions of government and in leading civilian undertakings.

Once again Germany is of necessity in his thoughts, for he is in the midst of writing a three-volume work to be called *An American Epic*. This latest work from one of the most fertile book-producing chiefs of state in history is to convey the facts about American compassion lavished generously upon foreign peoples and nations, both foes and friends irrespective of race, color, religion, and political belief during the years beginning in the autumn of 1914 and lasting for forty-five years into our very day.

To use his own words spoken during his annual birthday interview with the press:

"I shall attempt to show that the American people, by their

longer hours of labor on our farms and their self-denial—without any financial repayment—have provided the margin of food, medical aid and supplies and clothing that have in the last forty-five years saved the lives of 1,400,000,000 people who otherwise would have perished."

To tell this story with the same penchant for accuracy that has been a characteristic of all his written or spoken utterances, our thirty-first President is putting in a fifteen-hour day. With the aid of his staff he must cull and personally evaluate facts contained in many hundreds of reports as well as books by authoritative writers, and from some two million newspaper clippings.

It is a task that few men in our nervous age would have the patience to tackle. In taking it upon his shoulders, Mr. Hoover is true to his philosophy of "retirement," expressed in the birthday interview in these words:

"Those who retire without some occupation can spend their time only in talking about their ills and pills. And the other fellow wants only to talk about his."

It is safe to say that no other country in the world besides the United States owes a greater debt of gratitude to Mr. Hoover than Germany and her people. The United States has twice within one generation been engaged in a war with this Teuton Power.

Both times it was the acceptance of the teachings of the Sermon on the Mount as his rule of life, the dogged determination that women and children as well as the superannuated must be exempted from the status of belligerents as far as feeding was concerned, and the idealistic approach of helping the prostrate enemy onto his feet again evinced by one man—Herbert Hoover—that saved Germany from the cataclysmic fate that seemed twice to be inevitable.

As he writes his three-volume *American Epic,* the question and problem of Germany must inescapably once again occupy the mind of the man whose deeds are the inspiration for *Herbert Hoover and Germany.*

INDEX